Cambridge English

Complete IELTS

Bands 5–6.5

Student's Book *without Answers*

Guy Brook-Hart and Vanessa Jakeman

CAMBRIDGE UNIVERSITY PRESS
Cambridge, New York, Melbourne, Madrid, Cape Town,
Singapore, São Paulo, Delhi, Tokyo, Mexico City

Cambridge University Press
The Edinburgh Building, Cambridge CB2 8RU, UK

www.cambridge.org
Information on this title: www.cambridge.org/9780521179492

© Cambridge University Press 2012

This publication is in copyright. Subject to statutory exception
and to the provisions of relevant collective licensing agreements,
no reproduction of any part may take place without the written
permission of Cambridge University Press.

First published 2012

Printed in China by Golden Cup Printing Co. Ltd

A catalogue record for this publication is available from the British Library

ISBN 978-0-521-17948-5 Student's Book with Answers with CD-ROM
ISBN 978-0-521-17949-2 Student's Book without Answers with CD-ROM
ISBN 978-0-521-18516-5 Teacher's Book
ISBN 978-0521-17950-8 Class Audio CDs (2)
ISBN 978-0521-17953-9 Student's Book Pack (Student's Book with Answers with CD-ROM and Class Audio CDs (2))
ISBN 978-1107-40197-6 Workbook with Answers with Audio CD
ISBN 978-1107-40196-9 Workbook without Answers with Audio CD

Cambridge University Press has no responsibility for the persistence or
accuracy of URLs for external or third-party internet websites referred to in
this publication, and does not guarantee that any content on such websites is,
or will remain, accurate or appropriate. Information regarding prices, travel
timetables and other factual information given in this work is correct at
the time of first printing but Cambridge University Press does not guarantee
the accuracy of such information thereafter.

Contents

	Map of the units	4
	Introduction	6
	IELTS Academic Module: content and overview	7
1	**Starting somewhere new**	8
2	**It's good for you!**	17
	Vocabulary and grammar review Units 1 and 2	26
3	**Getting the message across**	28
4	**New media**	37
	Vocabulary and grammar review Units 3 and 4	46
5	**The world in our hands**	48
6	**Making money, spending money**	57
	Vocabulary and grammar review Units 5 and 6	66
7	**Relationships**	68
8	**Fashion and design**	77
	Vocabulary and grammar review Units 7 and 8	86
	Speaking reference	88
	Writing reference	92
	Language reference	100
	Word list	108
	IELTS practice test	116
	Recording script	133
	Acknowledgements	149

Map of the units

Unit title	Reading	Listening	Speaking
1 Starting somewhere new	Reading Section 1: *Australian culture and culture shock* • True / False / Not Given • Table completion	Listening Section 1: Joining an international social club • Form completion • Multiple choice	Speaking Part 1 • Answering questions about yourself • Giving reasons and extra details
2 It's good for you!	Reading Section 2: *Organic food: why?* • Matching headings • Pick from a list	Listening Section 2: A welcome talk • Multiple choice • Labelling a map or plan	Speaking Part 2 • Giving a talk • Introducing the points • Beginning and ending the talk
Vocabulary and grammar review Units 1 and 2				
3 Getting the message across	Reading Section 3: *Why don't babies talk like adults?* • Yes / No / Not Given • Summary completion with a box • Multiple choice	Listening Section 3: A student tutorial • Pick from a list • Matching • Short-answer questions	Speaking Part 2 • Using discourse markers
4 New media	Reading Section 1: *The World Wide Web from its origins* • True / False / Not Given • Note completion • Short-answer questions	Listening Section 4: A lecture on journalism • Sentence completion • Flow-chart completion	Speaking Parts 2 and 3 • Using relevant vocabulary • Giving a full answer • Giving reasons and examples
Vocabulary and grammar review Units 3 and 4				
5 The world in our hands	Reading Section 2: *Out of Africa: solar energy from the Sahara* • Matching information • Matching features • Summary completion	Listening Section 1: Booking an eco-holiday • Note completion • Table completion	Speaking Parts 2 and 3 • Preparing notes • Using adjectives • Talking in general about a topic
6 Making money, spending money	Reading Section 1: *The way the brain buys* • Labelling a diagram • True / False / Not Given • Flow-chart completion	Listening Section 2: A talk about banks and credit cards • Matching • Labelling a diagram	Speaking Parts 2 and 3 • Using reasons and examples • Strategies for self-correction and expressing oneself more clearly
Vocabulary and grammar review Units 5 and 6				
7 Relationships	Reading Section 2: *The truth about lying* • Matching headings • Matching features • Sentence completion	Listening Section 3: A student discussion about a project • Multiple choice • Flow-chart completion	Speaking Part 1 • Using openers • Paraphrasing
8 Fashion and design	Reading Section 3: Passage about restoring a dress • Multiple choice • Yes / No / Not Given • Matching sentence endings	Listening Section 4: A lecture on Japanese stitching • Sentence completion	Speaking Parts 2 and 3 • Making comparisons • Providing a list of points • Supporting a view with reasons • Structuring a Part 3 answer
Vocabulary and grammar review Units 7 and 8				

Writing	Vocabulary	Pronunciation	Key grammar
Writing Task 1 • Introduction to graphs and charts • Writing an introduction • Selecting important information • Planning an answer	• *Problem* or *trouble*? • *Affect* or *effect*? • *Percent* or *percentage*?	Sentence stress 1: stressing the words which answer the question	Making comparisons
Writing Task 2: A task with two questions • Analysing the task • Brainstorming ideas • Organising ideas into paragraphs	Word formation	Intonation 1: using intonation to indicate new information and to finish what you are saying	Countable and uncountable nouns
Writing Task 1 • Summarising trends in graphs and tables	• *Teach*, *learn* or *study*? • *Find out* or *know*? • Study-related vocabulary	Confused consonant sounds	• Tenses: past simple, present perfect simple and present perfect continuous • Prepositions in time phrases and phrases describing trends
Writing Task 2: To what extent do you agree or disagree? • Answering the question • Writing an introductory paragraph • Analysing paragraphs • Using linkers	• *Cause*, *factor* and *reason* • Internet-related vocabulary	Chunking: pausing between word groups	Articles
Writing Task 1 • Summarising a diagram • Analysing the task • Writing in paragraphs • Ordering information • Using sequencers	• *Nature*, *the environment* or *the countryside*? • *Tourist* or *tourism*? • Descriptive adjectives	Sentence stress 2: emphasis	The passive
Writing Task 2: Discussing advantages and disadvantages • Introducing and linking ideas in paragraphs • Constructing the middle paragraphs of an essay	• Verb + *to do* / verb + *doing* • Words connected with shops and shopping • Words connected with finance	Word stress	Relative pronouns and relative clauses
Writing Task 1 • Analysing similarities and differences in charts / graphs • Writing an introductory paragraph • Using reference devices	• *Age(s)* / *aged* / *age group* • Words related to feelings and attitudes	Sentence stress 3: emphasis and contrast	Zero, first and second conditionals
Writing Task 2: Discussing two opinions • Including your own opinion • Introducing other people's opinions • Concluding paragraphs	*Dress* (uncountable) / *dress(es)* (countable) / *clothes* / *cloth*	Linking and pausing	Time conjunctions: *until* / *before* / *when* / *after*

Introduction

Who this book is for

Complete IELTS Bands 5–6.5 is a short preparation course of 50–60 classroom hours for students who wish to take the Academic module of the International English Language Testing System (IELTS). It teaches you the reading, writing, listening and speaking skills that you need for the exam. It covers all the exam question types, as well as key grammar and vocabulary which, from research into the Cambridge Learner Corpus, are known to be useful to candidates doing the test. If you are not planning to take the exam in the near future, the book teaches you the skills and language you need to reach an upper–intermediate level of English (Common European Framework (CEF) level B2).

What the book contains

In the **Student's Book** there are:

- **eight units for classroom study**, each containing:
  - one section on each of the four papers in the IELTS exam. The units provide language input and skills practice to help you to deal successfully with the tasks in each section.
  - a range of enjoyable and stimulating speaking activities designed to enable you to perform to the best of your ability in each part of the Speaking test and to increase your fluency and your ability to express yourself.
  - a step-by-step approach to doing IELTS Writing tasks.
  - key grammar activities and exercises relevant to the exam. When you are doing grammar exercises, you will sometimes see this symbol: ⊙. These exercises are based on research from the Cambridge Learner Corpus and they deal with the areas which cause problems for students in the exam.
  - vocabulary related to IELTS topics. When you see this symbol ⊙ by a vocabulary exercise, the exercise focuses on words which IELTS candidates confuse or use wrongly in the exam.
  - a unit review. These contain exercises which revise the vocabulary and grammar that you have studied in each unit.
- **Speaking and Writing reference sections** which explain the tasks you will have to do in the Speaking and Writing papers. They give you examples, together with additional exercises and advice on how best to approach these two IELTS papers.

- a **Language reference section** which clearly explains all the areas of grammar and vocabulary covered in the book and which will help you in the IELTS exam.
- a complete **IELTS practice test**.
- eight photocopiable **word lists** (one for each unit) containing topic-based vocabulary found in the units, accompanied by a definition supplied by a corpus-informed Cambridge dictionary.
- complete **recording scripts** for all the listening material.
- complete **answer keys**.
- a **CD-ROM** which provides you with many interactive exercises, including further listening practice exclusive to the CD-ROM. All these extra exercises are linked to the topics in the Student's Book.

Also available are:

- two **audio CDs** containing listening material for the eight units of the Student's Book plus the Listening Test in the IELTS practice test. The listening material is indicated by different coloured icons in the Student's Book as follows: 🎧 CD1, 🎧 CD2.
- a **Teacher's Book** containing:
  - **step-by-step guidance** for handling all the activities in the Student's Book.
  - a large number of suggestions for **alternative treatments** of activities in the Student's Book and suggestions for **extension activities**.
  - advice on the test and task types for teachers to pass on to students.
  - **extra photocopiable materials** for each unit of the Student's Book, to practise and extend language.
  - complete **answer keys**, including sample answers to writing tasks.
  - four **photocopiable progress tests**, one for every two units of the book.
  - eight **photocopiable word lists** (one for each unit) taken from the International Corpus which extend the vocabulary taught in the units. Each item in the word list is accompanied by a definition supplied by a corpus-informed Cambridge dictionary.
- a **Workbook** containing:
  - **eight units for homework and self-study**. Each unit contains **full exam practice** in one part of the IELTS Reading and Listening papers.
  - **further practice** in analysing the tasks from the Writing paper and writing answers.
  - further practice in the **grammar and vocabulary** taught in the Student's Book.
  - an **audio CD** containing all the listening material for the Workbook.

6 Introduction

IELTS Academic Module: content and overview

part/timing	content	test focus
LISTENING approximately 30 minutes	- four sections - 40 questions - a range of question types - **Section 1:** a conversation on a social topic, e.g. someone making a booking - **Section 2:** a monologue about a social topic, e.g. a radio report - **Section 3:** a conversation on a study-based topic, e.g. a discussion between students - **Section 4:** a monologue on a study-based topic, e.g. a lecture Students have ten minutes at the end of the test to transfer their answers onto an answer sheet. The recording is heard ONCE.	- Candidates are expected to listen for specific information, main ideas and opinions. - There is a range of task types which include completion, matching, labelling and multiple choice. - Each question scores 1 mark; candidates receive a band score from 1 to 9.
READING 1 hour	- three sections - 40 questions - a range of question types - **Section 1:** a passage with 13 questions - **Section 2:** a passage divided into paragraphs with 13 questions - **Section 3:** a passage with 14 questions At least one passage contains arguments and/or views. This is usually Section 3.	- Candidates are expected to read for / understand specific information, main ideas, gist and opinions. - Each section contains more than one task type. They include completion, matching, paragraph headings, True / False / Not Given and multiple choice. - Each question scores 1 mark; candidates receive a band score from 1 to 9.
WRITING 1 hour	- two compulsory tasks - **Task 1:** a 150-word summary of information presented in graphic or diagrammatic form - **Task 2:** a 250-word essay presenting an argument on a given topic Candidates are advised to spend 20 minutes on Task 1 and 40 minutes on Task 2, which is worth twice as many marks as Task 1.	- Candidates are expected to write a factual summary and a discursive essay. - Candidates are assessed on a nine-band scale for content, coherence, vocabulary and grammar.
SPEAKING 11–14 minutes	- three parts - one examiner + one candidate - **Part 1:** The examiner asks a number of questions about familiar topics such as the candidate's studies/work, hobbies, interests, etc. *4–5 minutes* - **Part 2:** After a minute's preparation, the candidate speaks for two minutes on a familiar topic provided by the examiner. *3–4 minutes* - **Part 3:** The examiner and the candidate discuss some general questions based on the theme of the Part 2 topic. *4–5 minutes*	- Candidates are expected to be able to respond to questions on familiar and unfamiliar topics and to speak at length. - Candidates are assessed on a nine-band scale for fluency, vocabulary, grammar and pronunciation.
All candidates who take the test receive an **Overall Band Score** between 1 and 9 that is an average of the four scores for each part of the test. For information on courses, required band scores and interpreting band scores, see www.ielts.org.		

Unit 1 Starting somewhere new

Starting off

1 Work in small groups. Match the reasons for studying in a different country (a–d) with the photos (1–4).

- a to get internationally recognised qualifications
- b to learn a foreign language
- c to experience living in a different culture
- d to make friends with people from other countries

2 Now discuss these questions.

- Which reason for studying abroad would be the most important for you?
- What other reasons do people have for studying abroad?

Listening Section 1

Exam information

- You hear a conversation between two people on a social or practical topic.
- In this section only, you are given an example at the beginning.
- You write your answers on the question paper while you listen.

1 Work in pairs. You are going to hear a conversation with a woman who wants to join an international social club. Before you listen, look at the advert below.

1 What is an international social club?
2 Would you enjoy being a member? Why? / Why not?

International Social Club

Meet people from around the world at the International Social Club!

We organise events for people from different countries to meet and share ideas and experiences.
If you want to widen your horizons by meeting people of different nationalities in a social atmosphere, click here to join.

8 Unit 1

❷ Work in pairs. Read Questions 1–5 in this Listening task. Decide what information you will need for each gap; for example, which answers might need numbers? Which might need the name of an activity?

Questions 1–5

Complete the form below.

Write ONE WORD AND/OR A NUMBER for each answer.

International Social Club	Application form
Name:	Jenny Foo
Age:	21
Nationality:	1 ....
Address:	2 .... Road, Bondi
Mobile phone:	3 ....
Occupation:	4 ....
Free-time interests:	Singing and 5 ....

❸ 🔊 Now listen and answer Questions 1–5.

Exam advice   Form completion

- While you read the questions, think what type of information you need for each gap.
- You will often hear someone spell a name or say a number. Make sure you know how to say letters and numbers in English.
- Write numbers as figures, not words.

❹ Read Questions 6–10. <u>Underline</u> the key idea in each question.

Questions 6–10

Choose the correct letter, A, B or C.

6 According to Don, what might be a problem for Jenny?
   A her accent
   B talking to her colleagues
   C understanding local people

7 How many members does the club have now?
   A 30
   B 50
   C 80

8 How often does the club meet?
   A once a week
   B once every two weeks
   C once a month

9 What is the club's most frequent type of activity?
   A a talk
   B a visit
   C a meal

10 The main purpose of the club is to help members to
   A meet Australians.
   B learn about life in Australia.
   C enjoy themselves together.

❺ 🔊 Now listen and answer Questions 6–10.

Exam advice   Multiple choice

- Before you listen, <u>underline</u> the key idea in each question.
- The correct answer is often expressed using different words from the words in the question.

❻ Work in pairs. Imagine that you want to join the International Social Club. Take turns to interview each other to complete the form in Exercise 2.

Starting somewhere new

Reading Section 1

Exam information

- Reading Passage 1 is usually a factual text.
- You need to find specific information.
- It is usually easier than the other parts, so it's a good idea to do it first.

1 Work in small groups. Look at the list of things people do when they live or study in a different country. Which do you think are quite easy and which are more difficult? Why?

- eating different food
- understanding people
- getting to know local people
- using public transport
- missing family and friends
- obtaining the correct papers

2 You are going to read a passage about culture shock. Read the title of the passage and the subheading in *italics*. What do you think *culture shock* is?

3 Read the whole passage quickly. Which stage of culture shock seems to be the most uncomfortable?

Australian culture and culture shock
by Anna Jones and Xuan Quach

Sometimes work, study or a sense of adventure take us out of our familiar surroundings to go and live in a different culture. The experience can be difficult, even shocking.

Almost everyone who studies, lives or works abroad has problems adjusting to a new culture. This response is commonly referred to as 'culture shock'. Culture shock can be defined as 'the physical and emotional discomfort a person experiences when entering a culture different from their own' (Weaver, 1993).

For people moving to Australia, Price (2001) has identified certain values which may give rise to culture shock. Firstly, he argues that Australians place a high value on independence and personal choice. This means that a teacher or course tutor will not tell students what to do, but will give them a number of options and suggest they work out which one is the best in their circumstances. It also means that they are expected to take action if something goes wrong and seek out resources and support for themselves.

Australians are also prepared to accept a range of opinions rather than believing there is one truth. This means that in an educational setting, students will be expected to form their own opinions and defend the reasons for that point of view and the evidence for it.

Price also comments that Australians are uncomfortable with differences in status and hence idealise the idea of treating everyone equally. An illustration of this is that most adult Australians call each other by their first names. This concern with equality means that Australians are uncomfortable taking anything too seriously and are even ready to joke about themselves.

Australians believe that life should have a balance between work and leisure time. As a consequence, some students may be critical of others who they perceive as doing nothing but study.

Australian notions of privacy mean that areas such as financial matters, appearance and relationships are only discussed with close friends. While people may volunteer such information, they may resent someone actually asking them unless the friendship is firmly established. Even then, it is considered very impolite to ask someone what they earn. With older people, it is also rude

10 Unit 1

to ask how old they are, why they are not married or why they do not have children. It is also impolite to ask people how much they have paid for something, unless there is a very good reason for asking.

Kohls (1996) describes culture shock as a process of change marked by four basic stages. During the first stage, the new arrival is excited to be in a new place, so this is often referred to as the "honeymoon" stage. Like a tourist, they are intrigued by all the new sights and sounds, new smells and tastes of their surroundings. They may have some problems, but usually they accept them as just part of the novelty. At this point, it is the similarities that stand out, and it seems to the newcomer that people everywhere and their way of life are very much alike. This period of euphoria may last from a couple of weeks to a month, but the letdown is inevitable.

During the second stage, known as the 'rejection' stage, the newcomer starts to experience difficulties due to the differences between the new culture and the way they were accustomed to living. The initial enthusiasm turns into irritation, frustration, anger and depression, and these feelings may have the effect of people rejecting the new culture so that they notice only the things that cause them trouble, which they then complain about. In addition, they may feel homesick, bored, withdrawn and irritable during this period as well.

Fortunately, most people gradually learn to adapt to the new culture and move on to the third stage, known as 'adjustment and reorientation'. During this stage a transition occurs to a new optimistic attitude. As the newcomer begins to understand more of the new culture, they are able to interpret some of the subtle cultural clues which passed by unnoticed earlier. Now things make more sense and the culture seems more familiar. As a result, they begin to develop problem-solving skills, and feelings of disorientation and anxiety no longer affect them.

In Kohls's model, in the fourth stage, newcomers undergo a process of adaptation. They have settled into the new culture, and this results in a feeling of direction and self-confidence. They have accepted the new food, drinks, habits and customs and may even find themselves enjoying some of the very customs that bothered them so much previously. In addition, they realise that the new culture has good and bad things to offer and that no way is really better than another, just different.

adapted from *Intercultural Communication for Students in the Faculty of Economics and Commerce*, University of Melbourne

4 Read the paragraph in blue in the passage and say which of these statements is TRUE, which is FALSE and which is NOT GIVEN.

1 Culture shock affects most people who spend time living in another country.
2 Culture shock affects certain types of people more quickly than others.
3 Culture shock only affects how people feel.

5 Use the underlined words in Questions 1–6 below to find the relevant part of the passage. Then read those parts of the passage carefully to answer the questions.

Questions 1–6

Do the following statements agree with the information given in the reading passage?

Write

TRUE *if the statement agrees with the information*

FALSE *if the statement contradicts the information*

NOT GIVEN *if there is no information on this*

1 Australian teachers will suggest alternatives to students rather than offer one solution.
2 In Australia, teachers will show interest in students' personal circumstances.
3 Australians use people's first names so that everyone feels their status is similar.
4 Students who study all the time may receive positive comments from their colleagues.
5 It is acceptable to discuss financial issues with people you do not know well.
6 Younger Australians tend to be friendlier than older Australians.

Exam advice True / False / Not Given

- If the passage expresses the same information, write TRUE.
- If the passage expresses the opposite information, write FALSE.
- If the passage does not include the information expressed in the question, write NOT GIVEN.

6 Work in pairs. Look at Questions 7–13 below.

1 Will you need to read the whole passage again to answer the questions?
2 What type of word(s) (noun, adjective, verb) do you need for each gap?
3 What type of information do you need for each gap?

Questions 7–13

Complete the table below.

Choose **NO MORE THAN TWO WORDS** from the passage for each answer.

THE STAGES OF CULTURE SHOCK

	name	newcomers' reaction to problems
Stage 1	7	They notice the **8** .... between different nationalities and cultures. They may experience this stage for up to **9** ....
Stage 2	Rejection	They reject the new culture and lose the **10** .... they had at the beginning.
Stage 3	Adjustment and reorientation	They can understand some **11** .... which they had not previously observed. They learn **12** .... for dealing with difficulties.
Stage 4	**13**	They enjoy some of the customs that annoyed them before.

7 Now read the relevant sections of the passage and answer Questions 7–13.

8 Work in small groups.

- Have you ever lived or travelled abroad? If so, how did you feel about the different culture? Did you suffer from culture shock to start with?
- How is your culture similar to or different from Australian culture as described in the passage?

Exam advice Table completion

- Check how many words you are allowed to use.
- Use words exactly as they are spelled in the passage.
- Check that your answers are grammatically correct.

Vocabulary
Problem or trouble? Affect or effect?

1 IELTS candidates often confuse *problem/trouble* and *affect/effect*. Read these extracts from the *Cambridge Advanced Learner's Dictionary* (**CALD**) and the *Cambridge Learner's Dictionary* (**CLD**). Then circle the correct word in sentences 1–4.

trouble or **problem**?
Problem means 'a situation that causes difficulties and that needs to be dealt with'. You can talk about **a problem** or **problems**.
  *Tell me what the **problem** is.*
  *He's having a few **problems** at work.*

Trouble means 'problems, difficulties or worries' and is used to talk about problems in a more general way. **Trouble** is almost always uncountable, so do not use the determiner **a** before it.
  *We had some **trouble** while we were on holiday.*

affect or **effect**?
Affect is a verb which means 'to cause a change'.
  *Pollution seriously **affects** the environment.*
Use the noun **effect** to talk about the change, reaction or result caused by something.
  *Global warming is one of the **effects** of pollution.*

1 They may have some (problems) / troubles, but usually they accept them.
2 They notice only the things that cause them a *problem / trouble*.
3 Feelings of disorientation and anxiety no longer *affect / effect* them.
4 These feelings may have the *affect / effect* of people rejecting the new culture.

2 ⊙ Five of these sentences contain a mistake made by IELTS candidates. Find and correct the mistakes.

1 Many students' studies are ~~effected~~ by difficulties with language. *affected*
2 Overseas students have accommodation problems.
3 Modern lifestyles have an affect on our health.
4 Other countries effect our customs.
5 Immigrants have an affect on the local economy.
6 Most children can deal with their own troubles.

12 Unit 1

Speaking Part 1

Exam information

- The examiner asks you about yourself, your home, work, studies and other topics.
- This part lasts between four and five minutes.

1 ⓘ **Listen to four IELTS candidates – Svetlana, Huan, Reva and Mateusz – each answering one of the questions below. Which question does each candidate answer?**

a Svetlana ...3...

c Reva ....

b Huan ....

d Mateusz ....

1 Can you tell me a little bit about your home town / where you are from?
2 How long have you been living here/there?
3 What do you like about living here/there?
4 Is there anything you find difficult about living here/there?
5 How do you get to school/college/work?
6 Tell me a little bit about what you study.
7 What do you like about your studies? Is there anything you dislike?
8 Have you travelled to another country? (Which one?)
9 Do you enjoy travelling? Why? / Why not?
10 What's your favourite form of travel? Why?

2 Work in pairs. Which of these statements are good things to do in Speaking Part 1? Tick (✓) the boxes.

1 Answer each question as briefly as possible in two or three words. ☐
2 Give reasons for your answers. ☐
3 Offer extra details. ☐
4 Sound interested in what you are saying. ☐
5 Repeat the exact words of the question. ☐
6 Speak clearly so that the examiner can hear you easily. ☐

3 ⓘ **Listen to the four candidates again. Which of the things in Exercise 2 do they all do?**

▶ Pronunciation: *Sentence stress 1*

4 Think about how you would answer questions 1–10 in Exercise 1 and write notes.

Example: *Moscow, large city, western Russia*

5 Work in pairs. Take turns to interview each other using the questions in Exercise 1.

Exam advice Speaking Part 1

- Give reasons for your answers.
- Offer extra details.
- Use your own words when possible.

Pronunciation
Sentence stress 1

You should put the stress on the words you think give the most important information. When you answer a question, you normally stress the words which give the answer.

1 ⓘ **Read and listen to these extracts from the four candidates' answers in Speaking Part 1. Underline the stressed words in each extract.**

1 Well, I think the <u>people</u> here are very <u>friendly</u> and I've made a <u>lot</u> of <u>new friends</u>.
2 Well, I'm not too keen on flying because you spend too long at airports.
3 I find it hard being away from my family and not seeing my friends.
4 I've been here since I came to university, so for about two years.

2 Work in pairs. Take turns to read the candidates' answers in Exercise 1.

Starting somewhere new

Writing Task 1

Exam information

- You write a summary of information from one or more graphs, tables, charts or diagrams.
- You must also compare some of the information and write an overview.
- You must write at least 150 words in about 20 minutes.

1 Work in pairs. Look at the different ways of showing information (A–E) and match them with their names (1–5).

1 pie chart B   2 diagram   3 bar chart
4 line graph   5 table

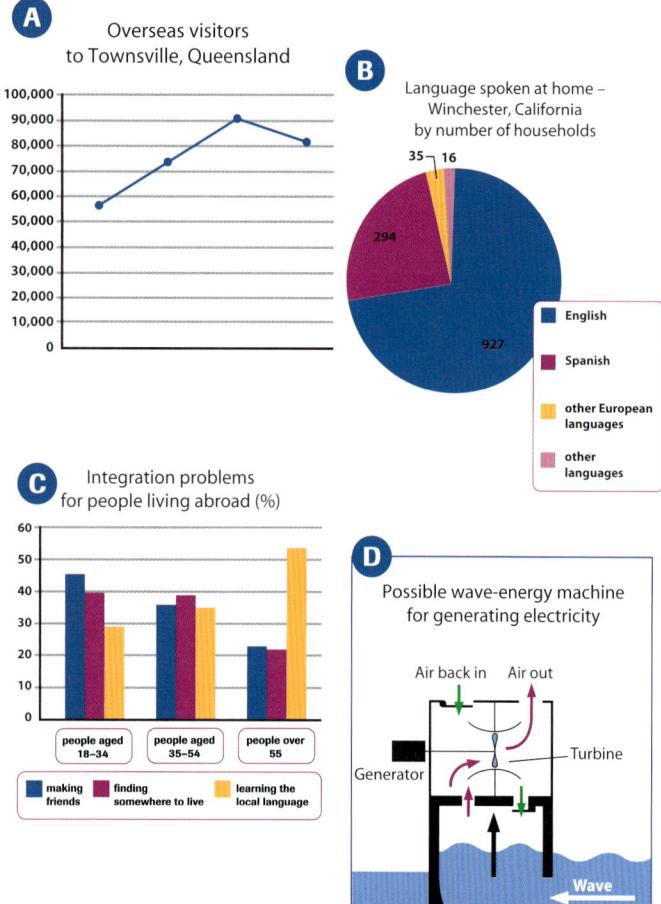

2 Work in pairs. Look at this introductory sentence to a summary of the information in the line graph (A) in Exercise 1 and answer the questions below.

The graph shows the changes in the number of people from abroad who visited Townsville, Queensland, over a four-year period.

Which word(s) …
1 say how the information is shown?
2 explain the purpose of the graph using the writer's own words?
3 express the time period the information covers?

3 Write introductory sentences for the pie chart (B) and the bar chart (C) by putting these phrases in the correct order.

B and the languages / in Winchester, California, / The chart shows / the number of households / which people speak there

C according to age / how the problems vary / into a new country and / The chart shows / the difficulties people have / when they integrate

4 Work in pairs. Write your own introductory sentences for the diagram (D) and the table (E).

5 Work in pairs. Look at this Writing task and answer questions 1–3 on the opposite page.

The chart below shows information about the problems people have when they go to live in other countries.

Summarise the information by selecting and reporting the main features, and make comparisons where relevant.

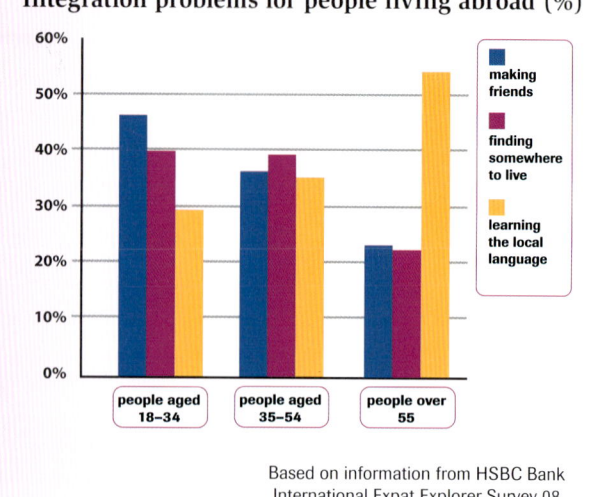

Based on information from HSBC Bank International Expat Explorer Survey 08

14 Unit 1

1 What is the greatest problem for 18–34-year-olds? How many of them experience this problem? How does this compare with the other age groups?
2 What is most problematic for people in the oldest age group? How does this compare with the youngest age group?
3 What thing does the oldest age group have the least difficulty with? How does this compare with the other age groups?

6 Read the sample answer below to the Writing task.
1 Which paragraphs answer questions 1–3 in Exercise 5?
2 What is the purpose of the last paragraph?

> The chart shows the difficulties people have when they move to a new country and how the problems vary according to people's ages.
>
> The greatest problem for young people aged 18 to 34 is forming friendships, <u>a problem experienced by 46 percent of the people in this age group</u>. However, only 36 percent of 35- to 54-year-olds find it hard to make friends, while even fewer people over 55 (23 percent) have this problem.
>
> Fifty-four percent of the older age group find learning to speak the local language the most problematic. In comparison, the youngest age group finds this easier, and <u>the percentage who have problems learning the language is much lower, at 29 percent</u>.
>
> In contrast to their language-learning difficulties, only 22 percent of people in the oldest age group have trouble finding accommodation. However, this is the second most significant problem for the other two age groups with 39 to 40 percent of the people in each group finding it hard.
>
> In general, all age groups experience the same problems to some extent, but the percentage of older people who find language learning difficult is much higher than the others.

▶ page 16 *Key grammar: Making comparisons*

7 You will get higher marks in the exam if you use your own words, not the words in the Writing task.
1 What words does the writer use in the sample answer for these words?
   a problems   *difficulties*
   b go to live
   c other countries
2 What other information does the writer add in the introductory paragraph?

8 ⊙ IELTS candidates often make mistakes when they use *percent* and *percentage*. Look at the two <u>underlined</u> sentences in the sample answer in Exercise 6.
1 Which word – *percent* or *percentage* – is used after a number?
2 Which word is not used with the exact number given?
3 Do we use *a* before *percent*?
4 Which word do we use before *percentage*?
5 Can we make *percent* plural?

9 ⊙ Each of these sentences contains a mistake made by IELTS candidates. Find and correct the mistakes.
1 The graph shows the increase in the ~~percent~~ of people who used rail transport between 1976 and 1999. *percentage*
2 The graph shows the percentage of people with a criminal record according to their age and percentage of people in prison according to their gender.
3 By 1995, the numbers had fallen to a two percent.
4 In 2004, the number rose to approximately 58 percents.
5 It is surprising that percentage of people watching television remained the same.
6 On the other hand, socialising with friends rose sharply to 25 percentage in comparison with 1981.

Exam advice   Chart summary

- Write a short introductory paragraph saying what the chart shows.
- Compare the important information.
- Include figures from the chart in your summary.
- Don't suggest reasons for the data which are not included in the information you are given.

10 Work in pairs. Look at the Writing task below.

1 What does the chart show?
2 What information would you put in your introductory sentence?
3 What is the biggest problem for the middle age group? What percentage of them experience this problem? How does this compare with the other age groups?
4 Which age group seems to have the most problems related to money? How does this compare with the other age groups?
5 Which group has the most problems finding a school for their children? And which has the least?
6 In general, which group has to deal with the most problems?

The chart below shows information about the problems people have when they go to live in other countries.

Summarise the information by selecting and reporting the main features, and make comparisons where relevant.

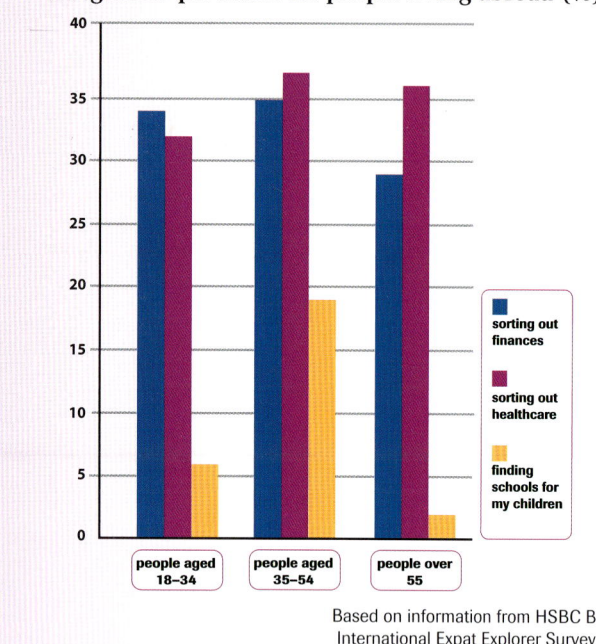

Based on information from HSBC Bank International Expat Explorer Survey 08

11 Write a brief plan for your summary.

- How many paragraphs will you need?
- What information will you include in each paragraph?

Write your answer to the task in at least 150 words. Use the sample summary in Exercise 6 to help you.

Key grammar
Making comparisons

1 Match the rules for making comparisons (1–4) with the examples from the sample summary from Exercise 6 (a–d).

a *easier* — 3
b *higher*
c *the greatest*
d *the most problematic*

1 Form comparatives of adjectives with one syllable by adding *–er*.
2 Form superlatives of adjectives with one syllable by adding *the –est*.
3 Form comparisons and superlatives of adjectives with two syllables ending in *–y* by changing *y* to *i* and adding *–er* and *–est*.
4 Form comparisons and superlatives of adjectives with more than one syllable by adding *more* and *the most*.

▶ page 100 *Making comparisons*

2 Complete these sentences by putting the adjective in brackets into the correct form.

1 Learning the language is the *most important* (important) thing for people going to live in a new country.
2 Many people find making friends .... (hard) than finding a job.
3 Local people are often .... (friendly) than you expect.
4 If the climate is .... (warm) or .... (cold) than at home, it affects the way people feel about their new country.
5 .... (old) people are often .... (good) at making friends than younger people.

3 IELTS candidates often make mistakes with comparisons of adjectives and adverbs. Find and correct the mistakes in each of these sentences.

1 I can read English ~~easyier~~ than before.
  more easily
2 Living in the country is the better way to learn the language.
3 Travelling is becoming more clean and safe.
4 The most highest percentage appeared in 1991.
5 Workers' salaries got worser in the year 2001.
6 I want to study abroad so that I can get a more well job in the future.

Unit 2 It's good for you!

Starting off

1 Work in pairs. Match the photos (1–6) with the phrases in the box.

| pesticide use | outdoor farming | genetic engineering |
| battery farming | crop rotation | natural fertiliser |

2 Work in small groups.

1 What is 'organic' food?
2 Do you eat organic food? Why? / Why not?
3 Which of the photos in Exercise 1 relate to organic food?
4 How important are these points when you choose food to eat?
   a price
   b taste
   c freshness
   d appearance
   e packaging
   f country of origin
   g contents
   h farming methods

It's good for you! 17

Reading Section 2

Exam information

- Reading Passage 2 is divided into paragraphs or sections: A, B, C, etc.
- The paragraph headings task comes before the passage.

❶ Work in pairs. You are going to read a magazine article about organic food. First, read the title and the subheading, then discuss what you expect to read about in the rest of the article.

❷ Quickly read the article. Are the writers for or against organic food?

❸ Read headings i–ix below and underline the key ideas. An example (viii) has been done for you.

Questions 1–7

The reading passage has seven paragraphs, **A–G**. Choose the correct heading for paragraphs **B–G** from the list of headings below.

List of Headings
i   Research into whether organic food is better for us
ii   Adding up the cost of organic food
iii The factors that can affect food quality
iv   The rich and poor see things differently
v   A description of organic farming
vi   Testing the taste of organic food
vii Fear of science has created the organic trend
viii The main reason for the popularity of organic food
ix   The need to remove hidden dangers from food

1 Paragraph **A** ....viii....
2 Paragraph **B** ....
3 Paragraph **C** ....
4 Paragraph **D** ....
5 Paragraph **E** ....
6 Paragraph **F** ....
7 Paragraph **G** ....

❹ Now read the article and choose the correct heading for each paragraph.

Exam advice   Matching headings

- Read the headings, underlining the key ideas.
- Read each paragraph carefully, one by one, to choose the best heading.

Organic food: why?

by Rob Lyons and Jan Bowman

Today, many governments are promoting organic or natural farming methods that avoid the use of pesticides and other artifical products. The aim is to show that they care about the environment and about people's health. But is this the right approach?

A   Europe is now the biggest market for organic food in the world, expanding by 25 percent a year over the past 10 years. So what *is* the attraction of organic food for some people? The really important thing is that organic sounds more 'natural'. Eating organic is a way of defining oneself as natural, good, caring, different from the junk-food-scoffing masses. As one journalist puts it: 'It feels closer to the source, the beginning, the start of things.' The real desire is to be somehow close to the soil, to Mother Nature.

B   Unlike conventional farming, the organic approach means farming with natural, rather than man-made, fertilisers and pesticides. Techniques such as crop rotation improve soil quality and help organic farmers compensate for the absence of man-made chemicals. As a method of food production, organic is, however, inefficient in its use of labour and land; there are severe limits to how much food can be produced. Also, the environmental benefits of not using artificial fertiliser are tiny compared with the amount of carbon dioxide emitted by transporting food (a great deal of Britain's organic produce is shipped in from other countries and transported from shop to home by car).

C   Organic farming is often claimed to be safer than conventional farming – for the environment and for consumers. Yet studies into organic farming worldwide continue to reject this claim. An extensive review by the UK Food Standards Agency found that there was no statistically significant difference between organic and conventional crops. Even where results indicated there was evidence of a difference, the reviewers found no sign that these differences would have any noticeable effect on health.

D   The simplistic claim that organic food is more nutritious than conventional food was always likely to be misleading. Food is a natural product, and the health value of different foods will vary for a number of reasons, including freshness, the way the food is cooked, the type of soil it

18   Unit 2

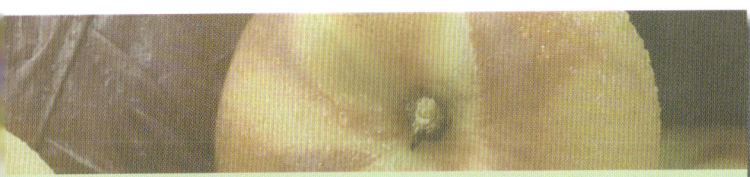

is grown in, the amount of sunlight and rain crops have received, and so on. Likewise, the flavour of a carrot has less to do with whether it was fertilised with manure or something out of a plastic sack than with the variety of carrot and how long ago it was dug up. The differences created by these things are likely to be greater than any differences brought about by using an organic or non-organic system of production. Indeed, even some 'organic' farms are quite different from one another.

E   The notion that organic food is safer than 'normal' food is also contradicted by the fact that many of our most common foods are full of natural toxins. Parsnips cause blisters on the skin of agricultural workers. Toasting bread creates carcinogens. As one research expert says: 'People think that the more natural something is, the better it is for them. That is simply not the case. In fact, it is the opposite that is true: the closer a plant is to its natural state, the more likely it is that it will poison you. Naturally, many plants do not want to be eaten, so we have spent 10,000 years developing agriculture and breeding out harmful traits from crops.'

F   Yet educated Europeans are more scared of eating traces of a few, strictly regulated, man-made chemicals than they are of eating the ones that nature created directly. Surrounded by plentiful food, it's not nature they worry about, but technology. Our obsessions with the ethics and safety of what we eat – concerns about antibiotics in animals, additives in food, GM crops and so on – are symptomatic of a highly technological society that has little faith in its ability to use this technology wisely. In this context, the less something is touched by the human hand, the healthier people assume it must be.

G   Ultimately, the organic farming movement is an expensive luxury for shoppers in well-manicured Europe. For developing parts of the world, it is irrelevant. To European environmentalists, the fact that organic methods require more labour and land than conventional ones to get the same yields is a good thing; to a farmer in rural Africa, it is a disaster. Here, land tends to be so starved and crop yields so low that there simply is not enough organic matter to put back into the soil. Perhaps the focus should be on helping these countries to gain access to the most advanced farming techniques, rather than going back to basics.

adapted from articles in *Spiked*

5 Look at Questions 8–13 below and underline the key ideas in the questions and the options (A–E).

6 Now scan the passage to find where the key ideas are mentioned. Read those parts carefully and choose the correct options.

Questions 8–13

*Choose **TWO** letters, A–E*

Questions 8–9

*Which **TWO** of the following points does the writer mention in connection with organic farming?*

A   the occasional use of pesticides
B   using the same field for different crops
C   testing soil quality
D   reducing the number of farm workers
E   the production of greenhouse gases

Questions 10–11

*According to the writer, which **TWO** factors affect the nutritional content of food?*

A   who prepares the food
B   the weather conditions during growth
C   where the food has been stored
D   when the plants were removed from the earth
E   the type of farm the food was grown on

Questions 12–13

*Which **TWO** negative aspects of organic farming does the writer mention?*

A   Consumers complain about the extra cost.
B   Organic food may make people ill.
C   Farm workers have to be specially trained.
D   It requires too much technological expertise.
E   It is not possible in some countries.

Exam advice   Pick from a list

- Use the key ideas in the questions to help you find the right place in the passage.
- Underline the answers in the passage and match them to the options.
- The answers may come from one section of the passage or from several paragraphs.

7 Work in pairs.

- How popular is organic food in your country?
- Do you think people should be encouraged to eat organic food? Why? / Why not?

It's good for you!   19

Listening Section 2

Exam information
- You hear one speaker talking about a social topic.

1 Work in pairs. You are going to hear a supervisor talking to a group of new nurses at a large hospital. Ask and answer questions based on the pictures below. Who do you think has the healthier lifestyle – you or your partner?

- When did you last ...?
- What's your favourite ...?
- How often do you ...?

2 Look at Questions 1–5 below and underline the key ideas in the questions.

3 (05) Listen to the first part of the talk and choose the correct answers for Questions 1–5.

Questions 1–5

Choose the correct letter, A, B or C.

1 According to Debbie, why do some people fail to eat a balanced diet?
   A They don't know how to cook.
   B They don't have enough time to cook.
   C They don't feel hungry enough to cook.

2 Debbie recommends that staff should keep fit by
   A using a gym.
   B taking up a new sport.
   C changing some daily activities.

3 Which benefit of exercise does Debbie think is most important?
   A It helps you sleep.
   B It keeps your heart healthy.
   C It improves mental skills.

4 What advice does Debbie give the nurses about health and safety?
   A to avoid drinking coffee
   B to use the canteen at night
   C to take regular breaks

5 When she talks about hygiene, Debbie asks the nurses to
   A wash their hands regularly.
   B keep away from germs.
   C help with the cleaning.

Exam advice   Multiple choice
- Listen for the correct idea or information – don't just match words.
- Make sure you answer all the questions.

20 Unit 2

4 Work in pairs. Look at the places A–H on the map below. Pick a place and tell your partner how to get there from the main building. Use the words and expressions in the box to help you.

| next to   traffic lights   west/east (of) |
| turn (east/west/right/left)   behind   turning |
| right/left (of)   go straight on   opposite |
| roundabout   go past/beyond   beyond   corner |

> You go out of the front of the main building, turn left and it's directly opposite you.

> It's G.

5 🔊 06 Now listen and choose the correct answer for Questions 6–10.

Questions 6–10

Label the map below.

*Write the correct letter, **A–H**, next to questions 6–10.*

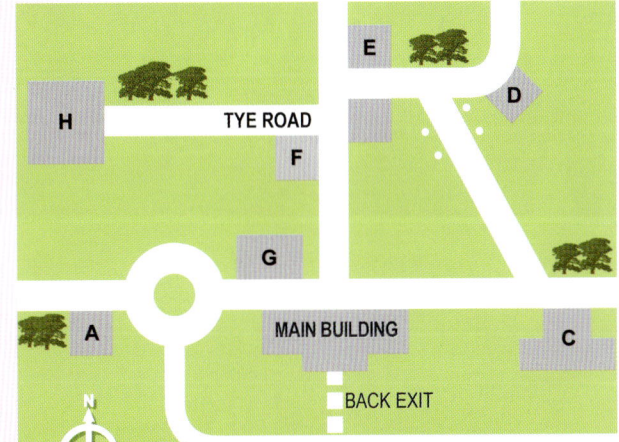

6 recreation centre ....
7 health centre ....
8 swimming pool and sauna ....
9 health-food store ....
10 Jenny's Restaurant ....

Exam advice   Labelling a map or plan

- Look at the location of each option on the map.
- The answers will come in the same order as the questions.
- Listen for each place name and follow the speaker's directions.

Vocabulary
Word formation

1 Complete each of the sentences below with a word in the box.

| ~~health~~   healthy   unhealthy   healthier |
| healthiest   healthily |

1 The key to good *health* is eating a balanced diet.
2 Cooking at home can help people eat more ....
3 Hospitals can become .... if they are not very clean.
4 People need exercise as well as a .... diet.
5 Being generally active is much .... than doing lots of exercise just occasionally.
6 Employees should be the .... people in the hospital.

▶ page 100 *Word formation*

2 Which of the words in the box in Exercise 1 …

1 is a noun? *health*
2 is an adverb?
3 are adjectives?

3 Work in pairs. Which of the suffixes or prefixes underlined in the words below …

1 forms a noun? *–ness*
2 forms an adverb?
3 form an adjective?
4 give a word an opposite or negative meaning?

| fit<u>ness</u>   stress<u>ful</u>   reason<u>able</u>   <u>in</u>active   <u>ir</u>regular |
| ris<u>ky</u>   general<u>ly</u>   care<u>less</u>   <u>un</u>usual |

4 🅘 IELTS candidates often use the wrong form of words or misspell words because of changes in form. Correct the mistake in each sentence.

1 In general, people should eat more ~~healthy~~ and do some exercise. *healthily*
2 Pesticides may be harmy to our health.
3 Some farmers feel that using natural fertiliser is too unconvenient.
4 The media often give usefull advice about food.
5 There has been a slightly drop in the popularity of fast food in my country.
6 I don't think that wealth people should get the best food.
7 Most people can easy do some exercise.
8 The number of people who live to 100 has increased dramatically.

It's good for you!   21

Speaking Part 2

Exam information

- You must speak alone for between one and two minutes on a topic the examiner gives you.
- You have one minute to write some notes before you speak.
- The examiner tells you when to stop speaking.

1 Work in pairs. Read this Speaking task and discuss what you could say.

> Describe somewhere you like to shop for food.
> You should say:
>   where this place is
>   what this place is like
>   what you buy there
> and explain why you like buying food at this place.

2 Listen to Eva doing the task in Exercise 1. Which of the places in the photos does she talk about?

3 Eva uses the points in the task to guide her talk. Complete this chart showing her key points.

place where I shop	Students – shop frequently Local 1 .... Organic – very 2 ....
where this place is	Near my 3 .... Pedestrian, busy Opposite 4 ....
what this place is like	Crowded, busy, popular Lots of 5 ....
what I buy there	Fruit, veg, meat, cheese, 6 .... Favourite – old 7 ....
why I like buying food at this place	Food good 8 .... place Colourful

▶ Pronunciation: *Intonation 1*

4 Listen again to Eva's talk. Complete this chart showing the phrases she uses to start her talk, introduce her points and end her talk.

starting a talk	I'm going to 1 .... Like most people, …
introducing points	I really like 2 .... So let me 3 .... where it is. And 4 .... ? I usually 5 .... As I've 6 ....
ending a talk	Yeah, all 7 ....

22 **Unit 2**

5 Look at this Part 2 task and make some notes in the table below about what you want to say for each point.

> Describe a meal that you enjoyed eating in a restaurant.
>
> You should say:
>   where the restaurant was
>   what you ate
>   who ate the meal with you
> and explain why you enjoyed eating the meal so much.

meal I enjoyed	
where the restaurant was	*in the town centre*
what I ate	
who ate with me	
why I enjoyed the meal	

6 Work in pairs. Listen to each other doing the task in Exercise 5.

Exam advice Speaking Part 2

- Note down some key ideas for each bullet to prompt you.
- Use your notes and the points on the card to guide your talk.
- Use phrases to introduce your points and to help you keep going.
- Use intonation to highlight key information and help your examiner follow your talk.

Pronunciation
Intonation 1

When we speak, the tone of our voice rises and falls. A rise helps your listener understand that you haven't finished what you are saying or that the information is new or exciting; a fall indicates the end of a sentence or utterance.

1 (08) Work in pairs. Look at this extract from Eva's talk and listen to how her voice changes on the words with arrows. Take turns to repeat what she says.

> Er, she weighs everything very quickly → … and you can't bargain →
>
> with her … but the price is always reasonable. →

2 Work in pairs. Look at some of Eva's sentences. Discuss where her voice might rise or fall.

1 … we're students, so we can't afford to eat in restaurants very often.

2 I really like going to the local market …

3 … everything you get there's fantastic – it's so fresh.

4 … it's a pedestrian street … you know, there are no cars.

5 There's a large number of stalls that sell food – and some shops, too.

6 I've got a favourite stall, it's run by a little old lady …

7 As I've mentioned, I like it because the food tastes good, but also it's a very sociable place.

8 All in all, I like it because it's a great place to go … it's a colourful experience.

3 (09) Listen to the sentences and check your answers.

4 Take turns to read the extracts to each other, using the same intonation.

It's good for you!

Writing Task 2

Exam information

- Task 2 is a discursive essay.
- The question may contain more than one part to discuss.
- You must write at least 250 words in about 40 minutes.

1 Work in pairs. Read this Writing task and say whether the statements below are true (T) or false (F). Correct the false ones.

> Write about the following topic.
>
> Most people are not interested in how their food has been produced. They only care about how much it costs.
>
> How true is this statement? What influences people when they buy food?
>
> Give reasons for your answer and include any relevant examples from your own knowledge or experience.

1. This essay is about consumers and food. T
2. There is one part to the question.
3. It is only necessary to discuss food production and cost.
4. I do not have to agree with the first statement.
5. Some personal experience and examples have to be included.

2 Work in small groups. Make some notes on these questions relating to the task in Exercise 1. Discuss your opinions and ideas.

1. How much do people care about a) how their food has been produced, and b) the cost of their food?
2. What other things do people care about when they buy food?

3 IELTS candidates often make mistakes with linking words and phrases. Read the sample answer on the right and circle the best option from each pair of expressions in *italics* (1–10).

4 Read the sample answer again. Which of your ideas in Exercise 2 does the writer discuss?

1 Nowadays / Over time, a wide range of food products has become available in shops and there are plenty of ways that it can be produced, packaged and sold. *2 As a result / Therefore*, there are many different attitudes towards food, and not everyone makes the same decisions when they go shopping.

Most people shop to suit their lifestyle. *3 In particular / Especially*, single people who work long hours may buy frozen or pre-cooked food, because they worry about how much time they have. Some parents with large families may *4 as well / also* worry about time, but are likely to think about their finances too. If they only have a little money, they will be interested in special offers, such as two for the price of one.

5 On one hand / On the other hand, people who have plenty of time to prepare food themselves may choose what they buy more carefully and consider a range of aspects that include quality and taste. *6 In addition / Besides*, a few of these people will be concerned about how animals are treated and whether the food has been organically produced.

7 Another / The other factor affecting choice is where you live. In my country, a great deal of importance is placed on the freshness of food. We eat a lot of fish and vegetables, and most of this is caught or produced locally. So cost is not an issue. *8 In fact / So*, very few consumers talk about it.

9 Concluding / In conclusion, it seems that cost is only one of a number of factors that people take into consideration when they purchase food. *10 Although / Even* some people look at price before quality, others have little interest in these things and will spend a considerable amount of money on food in order to satisfy their needs and beliefs.

5 Work in pairs.

1. How many paragraphs are there?
2. What does the writer include in the first paragraph?
3. Where is the writer's opinion about the statements in the task?
4. Does the writer include any personal experience? Where?
5. Underline the writer's two main ideas.
6. Which ideas and examples in the sample answer were also mentioned during your discussion?
7. Do you agree with the writer's conclusions? Why? / Why not?

24 Unit 2

6 Use your answers to Exercise 5 to write the plan for the sample essay on page 24.

▶ Key grammar: *Countable and uncountable nouns*

7 Work in pairs. Say whether these statements about the Writing task are true (T) or false (F).
1 You shouldn't copy from the question paper.
2 The answer can be in bullet points.
3 It is important to plan the answer.
4 Paragraphing is important.
5 Spelling does not have to be correct.

8 Work in small groups. Read this Writing task and answer the questions below.

> Write about the following topic.
>
> *Many children these days have an unhealthy lifestyle. Both schools and parents are responsible for solving this problem.*
>
> *To what extent do you agree with this statement?*
>
> Give reasons for your answer and include any relevant examples from your own knowledge or experience.

1 Is it true that many children have an unhealthy lifestyle? Why?
2 Are parents responsible? Why? What should they do?
3 Are schools responsible? Why? What should they do?
4 Is anyone else responsible? Who?

9 Write a plan for the task. Decide how many paragraphs to write and which ideas will go in each paragraph. Also plan your introduction and conclusion.

> *Exam advice* Writing Task 2
> - Analyse the question carefully first. You will lose marks if you don't deal with all parts of the task.
> - Brainstorm your ideas and write a quick plan.
> - Write your answer in paragraphs following your plan.

10 Now write your answer in about 40 minutes and check your word count. You should write at least 250 words.

Key grammar
Countable and uncountable nouns

1 Look at this extract from the sample answer on page 24. Which underlined noun is countable and which one is uncountable?

> ... there are many different <u>attitudes</u> towards <u>food</u> ...

▶ page 102 *Countable and uncountable nouns*

2 Look at the highlighted words in the sample answer. Which are countable and which are uncountable?

3 Look at these words/phrases that are often used with countable/uncountable nouns. Put them in the correct column of the table below.

> a (wide) range of   a little   (very) few   plenty of
> a lot of   a (large) number of   many   a few   little
> most   a great deal of   a considerable amount of
> much   a/an   any   some

countable nouns	uncountable nouns	countable or uncountable nouns
a (wide) range of		

4 🎧 IELTS students often make mistakes with countable and uncountable nouns. Choose the correct expression to complete each sentence.
1 Recently, the *number* / *amount* of fast food that is eaten has increased.
2 For example, *few* / *a few* years ago there were not many microwave ovens in our country.
3 Technology brings *much* / *many* advantages to our lives.
4 I think *many* / *a lot of* research must be done on organic farming.
5 You can't get *many* / *much* information about your health these days without using the Internet.
6 Unfortunately, I have *little* / *a little* time to cook when I get home.
7 I think the *amount* / *number* of fast-food stores should be reduced.
8 Some children eat *much* / *a lot of* oily and fatty foods.

It's good for you! 25

Vocabulary and grammar review Unit 1

Vocabulary

1 Complete these sentences with the correct form of *problem, trouble, affect* or *effect*.

1 I hope my visit won't cause you too much *trouble*.
2 Studying at a foreign university will greatly .... the way you see the world.
3 If you are not careful about money, you can get into a lot of .... financially.
4 Investigators are carrying out research into the .... of culture shock on overseas students.
5 Some students have had many .... adapting to our very different lifestyle.
6 New technologies have had an enormous .... on the way we interact.

2 Study the graph below and complete these sentences with *percent* or *percentage*. Then decide if the sentences are true (T) or false (F) according to the graph. Correct the false ones.

1 Sixty-five *percent* of overseas workers in Germany learn to speak German.
False: 75%
2 The .... of workers from abroad who learn to speak English is lowest in the United States.
3 Workers from other countries who learn to speak English in the UK and the USA are 18 and 15 .... respectively.
4 Belgium has the third highest .... of overseas workers learning to speak the language, with the figure standing at 70 ....

Grammar

3 Complete these sentences with the correct form of the adjective or adverb in brackets.

1 People who are ready to change their views often find it *easier* (*easy*) to adapt to a new culture.
2 You will learn the language much .... (*quickly*) if you share accommodation with people from the country – in other words, it will save you a lot of time.
3 Many students are attracted to this university because it has the reputation of being the one with the .... (*good*) teachers.
4 I think this is the .... (*complicated*) language I have ever tried to study; I really don't know if I'm making progress.
5 You'll find the film much .... (*funny*) if you watch it in the original version.
6 Many overseas students find understanding other students a .... (*big*) problem than understanding their teachers.
7 The .... (*successful*) students are not always the ones with the best brains.
8 Many people prefer travelling by train because they think it is .... (*safe*) than travelling by plane.

Workers from abroad who learn local languages by country (%)

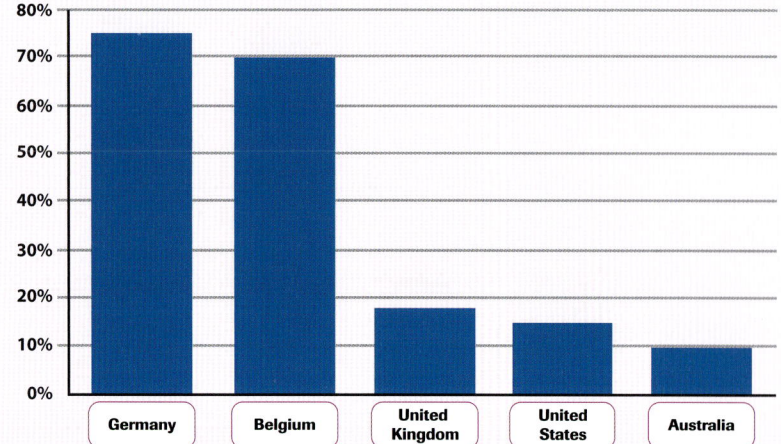

(figures from HSBC Bank International Expat Explorer Survey 08, Report Three: Expat Experience)

26 Vocabulary and grammar review Unit 1

Vocabulary and grammar review Unit 2

Vocabulary

1 Complete these sentences using the correct form of the word in brackets.

1 It must be very hard work being a *farmer* (farm).
2 Although pesticides protect plants, they can be .... (harm) to humans.
3 Our .... (enjoy) of the meal was spoilt by the loud music in the restaurant.
4 I've done so much exercise at the gym that I'm .... (total) exhausted.
5 Someone told me this soup was very .... (taste), but I don't like the flavour.
6 The vegetables in our local shop have been .... (organic) produced.
7 My brother has a really .... (health) diet – he eats nothing but fried food!
8 Some people .... (critic) conventional farming methods, but they do produce high yields.

2 Write nouns for each of these adjectives. Three adjectives have two possible noun forms.

adjective	noun
developing	1 *development*
active	2
dangerous	3
fit	4
happy	5
independent	6
toxic	7
nutritious	8
reliable	9
accurate	10

Grammar

3 Circle the correct option in each of these sentences.

1 Can you give me some *(advice)* / *advices* on how to stay fit?
2 Children need clear *information* / *informations* about the food they eat.
3 *A balanced diet* / *Balanced diet* consists of plenty of fruit and vegetables.
4 Organic farming causes less *pollutions* / *pollution* than traditional farming.
5 Some people say that a little *knowledges* / *knowledge* can be a dangerous thing.
6 I go to *fast-food shop* / *fast-food shops* as little as possible.
7 A shift worker can have *very stressful lifestyle* / *a very stressful lifestyle*.
8 More *research* / *researches* is needed to make genetic engineering safe.

4 Complete the sentences below with the expressions in the box. Use each expression only once. There are two extra expressions that you do not need.

a/an	a few	amount of	deal of	few	little
many	much	~~number of~~	plenty of		

1 Only a small *number of* consumers buy organic food.
2 I can't stand cooking in .... dirty kitchen.
3 Everyone needs to spend a .... time relaxing.
4 At the end of the week, I don't have .... money left to buy food.
5 You need to put a large .... fertiliser on young plants.
6 You need .... free time in order to do your own cooking.
7 It's a pity that so .... people are interested in reading the labels on food.
8 Obviously someone has put a great .... work into this meal – it's delicious!

Unit 3 Getting the message across

Starting off

❶ Work in pairs. Look at these photos. Who is …

1 attending a lecture?
2 making a presentation?
3 writing a term paper?
4 taking part in a tutorial?

❷ Now discuss these questions.

1 What links these situations?
2 Have you had experience of any of these situations?
3 Which situation do you think is the most/least enjoyable? Why?

Listening Section 3

Exam information

- You hear a conversation between two or more speakers on a study-based topic.
- Some questions may be on the speaker's opinions.

❶ Work in pairs. You are going to hear a student talking to her course tutor about an assignment. Before you listen, match the words (1–9) with their definitions (a–i).

1 assignment
2 self-assessment
3 weaknesses
4 peer evaluation
5 extract
6 authentic
7 feature
8 structure
9 finding

a particular parts or qualities of someone that are not good
b a judgement which you make about the quality of something you have done
c a particular part of a book, poem, etc. that is chosen so that it can be used in a discussion, article, etc.
d a piece of work or job that you are given to do
e a typical quality or important part of something
f a piece of information that has been discovered as a result of an official study
g carefully considering or studying something done by a colleague/classmate/friend and judging how good or bad it is
h the way that parts of something are arranged or put together
i real or true

28 Unit 3

2 Work in pairs. Read Questions 1–4 and underline the key ideas in the questions (not the options).

Questions 1–4

Choose TWO letters, A–E.

Questions 1–2

Which TWO activities will students do as part of Amanda's assignment?

A analyse their own speech
B record other students' speech
C read something from a book
D repeat part of a lecture
E remember part of a lecture

Questions 3–4

Which TWO features must Amanda check when she chooses the extract?

A the time it takes to read
B the overall organisation
C the number of words
D the number of sentences
E the inclusion of key ideas

3 🎧 **Now listen to the first part of the recording and answer Questions 1–4.**

Exam advice **Pick from a list**

- Underline the key ideas in the question(s).
- Read through the options and remember that only two of them are correct.
- As you listen, tick the options you hear. The correct answers may not come in the same order in the recording as they do in the question.

4 Work in pairs. Read all the information for Questions 5–8.

1 What are Questions 5–8?
2 Underline the key ideas in A–F. How many extra options are there?
3 What should you write as your answer for each question?

Exam advice **Matching**

- Underline key ideas in the question and options.
- You will hear the answers to the questions in the same order as the questions appear on the paper.

Questions 5–8

Which comments do the speakers make about each lecture?

Choose FOUR answers from the box and write the correct letter, A–F, next to Questions 5–8.

Lectures

5 History of English
  ....
6 Gestures and signs
  ....
7 Intonation patterns
  ....
8 Language and rhythm
  ....

Comments
A The content is repetitive.
B It took a long time to write.
C It was shorter than the others.
D It was well structured.
E The content is relevant.
F The topic was popular.

5 Read Questions 9–10 and underline the key ideas in the question.

Questions 9–10

Answer the questions below.

Write NO MORE THAN TWO WORDS for each answer.

Which TWO pieces of equipment will the students use in the study?

9 ....
10 ....

Exam advice **Short-answer questions**

- Underline the key ideas in the question.
- Make sure you don't use more words than you are allowed.
- Check that you have spelled your answers correctly.

6 🎧 **Now listen to the second part of the recording and answer Questions 5–10.**

Getting the message across 29

Reading Section 3

Exam information

- Reading Passage 3 usually contains arguments and opinions as well as information.
- There are 14 questions.

1 Work in small groups. You are going to read an article about different theories on how babies learn to talk. Before you read, look at the speech bubbles below.

1. How would you express each of these utterances?
2. Why do you think babies talk like this?
3. How do you think babies learn language?

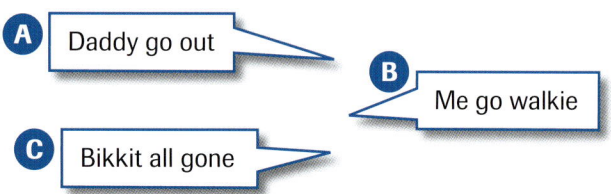

A Daddy go out
B Me go walkie
C Bikkit all gone

2 Work in pairs. Read the title and subheading of the passage quickly. What do you expect to read about in the article?

3 Now read the whole passage. When do children start talking in longer sentences?

Why don't babies talk like adults?

Kids go from 'goo-goo' to talkative one step at a time

by Joshua Hartshorne

A recent e-trade advertisement shows a baby speaking directly to the camera: 'Look at this,' he says, 'I'm a free man. I go anywhere I want now.' He describes his stock-buying activities, and then his phone rings. This advertisement proves what comedians have known for years: few things are as funny as a baby who talks like an adult. But it also raises an important question: Why don't young children express themselves clearly like adults?

Many people assume children learn to talk by copying what they hear. In other words, they listen to the words adults use and the situations in which they use them and imitate accordingly. Behaviourism, the scientific approach that dominated American cognitive science for the first half of the 20th century, made exactly this argument.

However, this 'copycat' theory can't explain why toddlers aren't as conversational as adults. After all, you never hear literate adults express themselves in one-word sentences like 'bottle' or 'doggie'. In fact, it's easy for scientists to show that a copycat theory of language acquisition can't explain children's first words. What is hard for them to do is to explain these first words, and how they fit into the language acquisition pattern.

Over the past half-century, scientists have settled on two reasonable possibilities. The first of these is called the 'mental-developmental hypothesis'. It states that one-year-olds speak in baby talk because their immature brains can't handle adult speech. Children don't learn to walk until their bodies are ready. Likewise, they don't speak multi-word sentences or use word endings and function words ('Mummy opened the boxes') before their brains are ready.

The second is called the 'stages-of-language hypothesis', which states that the stages of progress in child speech are necessary stages in language development. A basketball player can't perfect his or her jump shot before learning to (1) jump and (2) shoot. Similarly, children learn to multiply after they have learned to add. This is the order in which children are taught – not the reverse. There's evidence, for instance, that children don't usually begin speaking in two-word sentences until they've learned a certain number of single words. In other words, until they've crossed that linguistic threshold, the word-combination process doesn't get going.

The difference between these theories is this: under the mental-development hypothesis, language learning should depend on the child's age and level of mental development when he or she starts learning a language. Under the stages-of-language hypothesis, however,

Unit 3

it shouldn't depend on such patterns, but only on the completion of previous stages.

In 2007, researchers at Harvard University, who were studying the two theories, found a clever way to test them. More than 20,000 internationally adopted children enter the US each year. Many of them no longer hear their birth language after they arrive, and they must learn English more or less the same way infants do – that is, by listening and by trial and error. International adoptees don't take classes or use a dictionary when they are learning their new tongue and most of them don't have a well-developed first language. All of these factors make them an ideal population in which to test these competing hypotheses about how language is learned.

Neuroscientists Jesse Snedeker, Joy Geren and Carissa Shafto studied the language development of 27 children adopted from China between the ages of two and five years. These children began learning English at an older age than US natives and had more mature brains with which to tackle the task. Even so, just as with American-born infants, their first English sentences consisted of single words and were largely bereft of function words, word endings and verbs. The adoptees then went through the same stages as typical American-born children, albeit at a faster clip. The adoptees and native children started combining words in sentences when their vocabulary reached the same sizes, further suggesting that what matters is not how old you are or how mature your brain is, but the number of words you know.

This finding – that having more mature brains did not help the adoptees avoid the toddler-talk stage – suggests that babies speak in babytalk not because they have baby brains, but because they have only just started learning and need time to gain enough vocabulary to be able to expand their conversations. Before long, the one-word stage will give way to the two-word stage and so on. Learning how to chat like an adult is a gradual process.

But this potential answer also raises an even older and more difficult question. Adult immigrants who learn a second language rarely achieve the same proficiency in a foreign language as the average child raised as a native speaker. Researchers have long suspected there is a 'critical period' for language development, after which it cannot proceed with full success to fluency. Yet we still do not understand this critical period or know why it ends.

adapted from *Scientific American: Mind Matters*

4 Work in pairs. Look at the underlining in Question 1 below, then read the first paragraph of the passage. What is the answer?

Questions 1–4

Do the following statements agree with the claims of the writer in the reading passage?

Write

YES if the statement agrees with the claims of the writer

NO if the statement contradicts the claims of the writer

NOT GIVEN if it is impossible to say what the writer thinks about this

> This is a paraphrase of *few things are as funny* in the first paragraph of the passage.

1 People are extremely amused when they see a baby talk like an adult.
2 Behaviourists of the early 20th century argued that children learn to speak by copying adults.
3 Children have more conversations with adults than with other children.
4 Scientists have found it easy to work out why babies use one-word sentences.

> These words are similar to words in the passage, so they help find the right place.

5 Now underline the words in Questions 2–4 that help you find the right place in the passage. Then answer Questions 2–4.

Exam advice   Yes / No / Not Given

- You should use the same approach for *True / False / Not Given* and *Yes / No / Not Given* questions (see page 11).
- Write your answer clearly. If the examiner is not sure what you have written, it will be marked wrong.

Getting the message across

6 Work in pairs. Read the title of the summary below and use this to find the right part of the passage. Look at Question 5. Why is 'C' correct?

Questions 5–9

Complete the summary using the list of words and phrases, A–H, below.

Two theories about babytalk

According to the writer, there are <u>two main theories</u> related to babytalk. <u>One</u> states that a <u>young child's</u> brain needs **5** ..C.. to <u>master language</u>, in the same way that it does to master other abilities such as **6** ....

The second theory states that a child's **7** .... is the key factor. According to this theory, some key steps have to occur in a logical sequence before **8** .... occurs. Children's **9** .... develops in the same way.

A	vocabulary level	E	mathematical knowledge
B	physical movement	F	sentence formation
C	time	G	learning
D	attention	H	teaching

Exam advice **Summary completion with a box**

- Read through the summary and decide what type of word or phrase you need for each gap.
- <u>Underline</u> words and phrases around the gaps to help you find the right place in the passage.
- <u>Underline</u> the words in the passage that provide the missing information.
- Choose the option that means the same.

7 Answer Questions 6–9 on your own. Then check your answers with your partner.

8 Look at Questions 10–14 in the next column.
1 <u>Underline</u> the key ideas in Questions 10–14, then quickly find the right place in the passage.
2 Read that part of the passage carefully, then choose the correct options.

Exam advice **Multiple choice**

- Use key ideas in the question to find the right place in the passage.
- Read that part of the passage and <u>underline</u> the words which answer the question.

Questions 10–14

Choose the correct letter, A, B, C or D.

10 What is the writer's main purpose in the seventh paragraph?
   A to give reasons why adopted children were used in the study
   B to reject the view that adopted children need two languages
   C to argue that culture affects the way children learn a language
   D to justify a particular approach to language learning

11 Snedeker, Geren and Shafto based their study on children who
   A were finding it difficult to learn English.
   B had come from a number of language backgrounds.
   C were learning English at a later age than US children.
   D had taken English lessons in China.

12 What aspect of the adopted children's language development differed from that of US-born children?
   A their first words
   B the way they learnt English
   C the rate at which they acquired language
   D the point at which they started producing sentences

13 What did the Harvard finding show?
   A Not all toddlers use babytalk.
   B Language learning takes place in ordered steps.
   C Some children need more conversation than others.
   D Not all brains work in the same way.

14 When the writer says 'critical period', he means a period when
   A studies produce useful results.
   B adults need to be taught like children.
   C immigrants want to learn another language.
   D language learning takes place effectively.

9 Work in small groups.
- Do you agree that there is a critical period for learning language? When do you think this might end?
- What do you think is the best way for an adult to learn another language?

Unit 3

Speaking Part 2

1 Work in pairs. Read this task and match the phrases (1–8) below with the points in the task.

> Describe a situation you remember when you had to use a foreign language to communicate.
>
> You should say:
>   what you were doing
>   what happened
>   how well you communicated in the language
> and explain why you remember this situation or experience.

1 on holiday
2 what have I learned
3 difficult situation
4 took a trip
5 summer break
6 the emergency services
7 didn't know how to say
8 hired a car

2 🎧12 Listen to Abi doing the task in Exercise 1 and make brief notes about the following.

1 Where was Abi?
2 What happened?
3 How well did he communicate?
4 Why does he remember the situation?

3 🎧12 Abi uses phrases to mark the stages in his story. Listen again and complete the chart below with these phrases.

> ~~A couple of years ago~~   Eventually
> So the next thing we did   This was because
> Before we went   At the time   The reason why
> As soon as   However, one morning

introducing a stage in the story	giving reasons / explanations
A couple of years ago	

- Pronunciation: *Consonant sounds*
- page 34 Key grammar: *Present perfect and past simple*

4 Write some brief notes that you could use in a two-minute talk on the topic in Exercise 1.

5 Work in pairs. Take turns to give your talks.

> **Exam advice** Speaking Part 2
> - Structure your talk by using your notes and introducing your points clearly to the examiner.
> - Use appropriate phrases to mark the stages in your talk.

6 Read this Speaking task and prepare notes for each point. Think about how you will link your ideas.

> Describe an English lesson that you really enjoyed.
>
> You should say:
>   where and when it took place
>   who the teacher was
>   what you did in the lesson
> and explain why you enjoyed it so much.

7 Work in pairs. Take turns to give your talks. After listening to your partner, give feedback.

Pronunciation
Consonant sounds

> IELTS candidates often confuse consonant sounds, and this can change a word or meaning.

1 🎧13 Listen to and read these examples.

similar sounds	examples
/ʃ/ and /dʒ/	sheep / jeep
/l/ and /r/	climb / crime
/v/ and /w/	vent / went

2 🎧14 Work in pairs. Listen again to the first part of Abi's talk and write the missing words.

> A couple of years ago, I **1** ...went.... on holiday with a friend to Windsor. Um, the **2** .... why we chose Windsor is that I've got an aunt who **3** .... there. She's been living there for 20 years now. And, well, I've always enjoyed travelling ... I've always wanted to go to the UK. At the time, my friend and I had **4** .... finished our exams at school and we were **5** .... to go to university. It was the summer break, and **6** .... invited us to visit her, so we decided to go.

3 Work in pairs. Take turns to read the paragraph to each other. Which sounds are most difficult for you to pronounce?

4 Work in pairs. Read the audioscript of the talk on page 136. Mark six sounds that you find difficult. Read the script extracts to your partner.

Getting the message across 33

Vocabulary
Teach, learn or study? Find out or know?

1 IELTS candidates often confuse *teach/learn/study* and *find out/know*. Circle the correct words in these extracts from the Reading passage.

1 This advertisement proves what comedians have (known) / *found out* for years.
2 Over the past half-century, scientists have *known / found out* much about babytalk.
3 Children don't *study / learn* to walk until their bodies are ready.
4 *Knowing / Learning* how to chat like an adult is a gradual process.
5 Yet we still do not understand this critical period or *know / find out* why it ends.

2 Read these extracts from *CLD* to check your answers.

learn, teach or **study**?
To **learn** is to get new knowledge or skills
  *I want to **learn** how to drive.*
When you **teach** someone, you give them new knowledge or skills.
  *My dad **taught** me how to drive. My dad learnt me how to drive.*
When you **study**, you go to classes, read books, etc. to try to understand new ideas and facts.
  *He is **studying** biology at university.*

---

know or **find out**?
To **know** something means to already have information about something.
  *Kelly **knows** what time the train leaves.*
To **find out** something means to learn new information for the first time.
  *Can you **find out** what time the train leaves?*

3 Work in pairs. Complete these questions with *teach, learn, study, know* or *find out*.

1 How many English words do you ...know... ?
2 Do you prefer to .... a language by talking to people or reading books?
3 If you worked in a school, which subject would you prefer to .... ?
4 How would you .... where the best language schools are in your home town?
5 Did you .... hard for your school exams?

4 Work in pairs. Ask and answer the questions in Exercise 3.

Key grammar
Present perfect and past simple

1 Match the underlined verbs in these sentences from Abi's talk (1–3) with the tenses (a–c).

1 I've always enjoyed travelling.
2 It was a summer break.
3 She's been living there for 20 years now.

a past simple
b present perfect simple
c present perfect continuous

2 Which sentence from Exercise 1 describes:

a something in the past that is now ended?
b a situation that started in the past and is still going on?
c a feeling from the past that is still present?

3 Underline the verb forms in these sentences from Abi's talk and say what tense they are.

4 Before we went, we hired a car, which we picked up when we reached the airport.
5 I didn't know the word for tyre.
6 Twenty minutes later, a recovery van arrived.
7 So, what have I learned from this experience?

4 Match the sentences (1–7) in Exercises 1 and 3 with the uses of the past simple, present perfect and present perfect continuous tenses (a–d).

a a past action or state that is clearly now over (often with a time expression) 2, ...
b a situation or state that started in the past and continues into the present (often with a time reference)
c a series of events that took place in the past
d an action or activity that started in the past and is still continuing

▶ page 103 *Tenses*

5 ⊙ IELTS candidates often make mistakes using tenses. Circle the correct verb form in these sentences.

1 In the last few decades, *there was* / (*has been*) a rapid development in computer technology.
2 The most popular country that UK residents *have visited / visited* in 1999 was France.
3 I *was / have been* responsible for taking care of myself since I was eight years old.
4 Obesity *became / has become* a global problem.
5 Sometimes people who have been on a diet eat even more afterwards than they *have eaten / ate* before.
6 One day, the company *has been / was* shut down.

Writing Task 1

1 Work in pairs. Look at the graph below.

1 What does the graph show?
2 What is the main difference between the two lines on the graph?
3 Are there any significant similarities or differences between the two language trends?
4 What are the main features of each trend?
5 How could you divide the information into paragraphs?

The graph below shows information about the languages that 13-year-old students in one school chose to study.

Summarise the information by selecting and reporting the main features, and make comparisons where relevant.

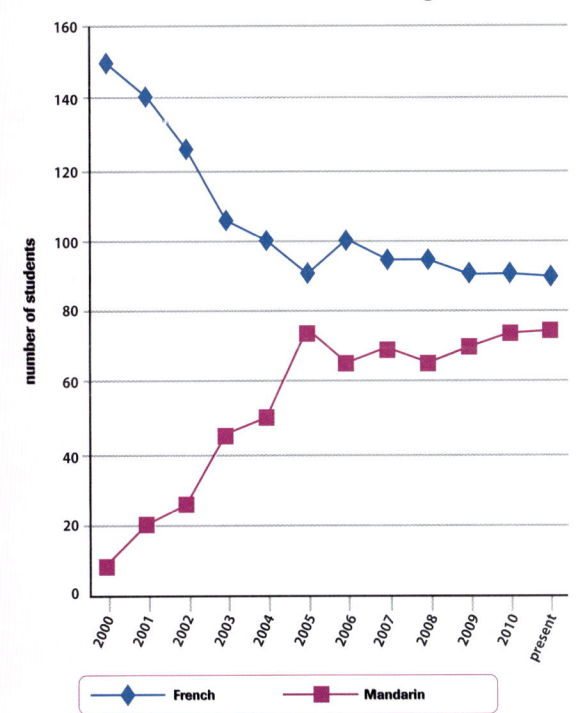

2 Put these sentences in the correct order.

a Overall, it can be seen that more students have been choosing to study Mandarin, but French is still the most popular language option. ☐
b Over the next five years, the figure fell considerably for French, but rose dramatically for Mandarin and reached a peak at 75 students. ☐
c In 2000, the number of students who took French was 150, compared to just under 10 students who chose Mandarin. ☐
d French gained some popularity in 2006, but has remained fairly stable since then at about 90 students. ☐
e The graph shows how many 13-year-old students studied French and Mandarin between 2000 and the present day in a school in England. ☐ 1
f On the other hand, the trend for French is the opposite. ☐
g So there was a significant difference in numbers at this time. ☐
h According to the data, Mandarin has increased in popularity during this time. ☐
i In contrast, the number of students taking Mandarin dipped in 2006 and then fluctuated, before it returned to 75. ☐
j Since 2005, the trends have not changed as much. ☐

3 Work in pairs. Look at the text in Exercise 2 again and find verb phrases which mean the following.

1 went down (two phrases)
2 hit a high point
3 has stayed the same
4 went up a lot
5 went up and down

4 Work in pairs. Look at this table and discuss what it shows. Which column:

1 increases significantly?
2 fluctuates?
3 peaks then falls slightly?

Global statistics: Shore Hotel
Staff: 1975–2010

	with language qualification %	speaking two or more languages %	previous work experience %
1975	5	10	75
1980	10	12	70
1985	12	14	78
1990	17	23	55
1995	21	48	65
2000	22	50	50
2005	21	65	45
2010	20	79	67

5 Complete the gaps in this summary with the correct percentages.

> The table provides some background information on the staff working in a global hotel chain. The information goes back to 1975 and covers languages spoken and qualifications, as well as previous work experience.
>
> Between 1975 and 2000, there was a significant rise in the percentage of employees who held a qualification in a foreign language, from **1** .... to **2** .... After this, there was a slight fall of **3** .... over the next ten years.
>
> **4** .... of staff were able to speak at least two languages in 1975. At first, this figure rose by 13 percent to **5** .... in 1990. However, from 1990 to 2010, it rocketed to **6** ....
>
> Finally, the percentage of staff with experience in the hotel industry fluctuated between 1975 and 2010. In 1985, there was a peak at **7** ...., and this was followed by a sudden fall to **8** .... five years later. Figures then went up and down over the next 15 years.

6 Underline the expressions that describe trends in the summary in Exercise 5.

7 Write an overview of the information in the summary in one or two sentences.

▶ page 102 *Prepositions*

8 Using the rules in the Language reference, complete these sentences with the correct prepositions.

1 Car sales rose by five percent ...*in*... August.
2 The chart shows the number of people finding jobs .... 2003 and 2007.
3 The number of new employees fell .... 12 percent last year.
4 Yesterday, there was a fall .... ten degrees in city temperatures.
5 There will be an increase .... taxi fares next month.
6 Customer complaints have gone down .... below 100.
7 The percentage of people needing medical treatment peaked .... 35 in 2009.

9 ⊙ Find and correct the mistakes made by IELTS students in these sentences.

1 The oldest underground railway was built in London ~~on~~ 1863. *in*
2 In general, all the figures gradually increased over 1911 to 2001.
3 There is no evidence that a rise of petrol prices leads to less traffic.
4 The number of people peaked to 5,523 in 2001.
5 Spending on teachers' salaries fell on 5%.
6 The temperature decreased until a low of three degrees in December.
7 During the period of 1986 and 1999 there was a gradual increase.
8 The profits experienced an increase by $2m.

10 Work in pairs. Look at the Writing task below and decide:

- what the graph shows
- how you will organise your report – what each paragraph will contain
- what your overview will include.

Work alone and write your summary. You should write at least 150 words.

The graph below shows information about the recruitment of teachers in Ontario between 2001 and 2007.

Summarise the information by selecting and reporting the main features, and make comparisons where relevant.

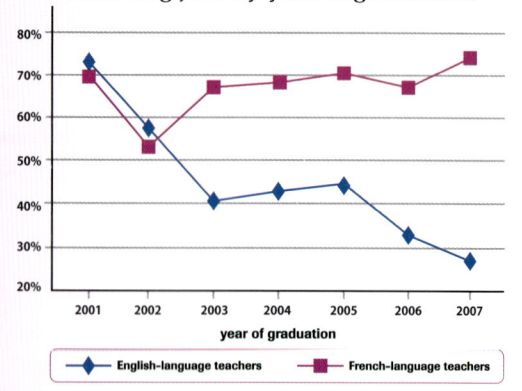

Percentage of first-year teachers with regular teaching jobs by year of graduation

Exam advice **Describing trends**

When you have to describe trends:
- look at the similarities and differences.
- use appropriate language to describe them.

Unit 4 New media

Starting off

1 Work in pairs. Look at the photos of different media. Which do you normally use to do the following?

- keep up to date with the news
- do research for your work or studies
- relax when you're alone
- keep up with the latest ideas and fashions
- enjoy yourself with friends

Reading Section 1

1 Work in small groups. You are going to read a passage about the World Wide Web. Before you read, discuss these questions.

1 How is the World Wide Web different from the Internet?
2 How do you personally use the Web?

2 Now read the passage on page 38 quite quickly. How many uses of the Web are mentioned?

New media 37

The World Wide Web from its origins

Science inspired the World Wide Web, and the Web has responded by changing science.

'Information Management: A Proposal'. That was the bland title of a document written in March 1989 by a then little-known computer scientist called Tim Berners-Lee, who was working at CERN, Europe's particle physics laboratory, near Geneva. His proposal, modestly called the World Wide Web, has achieved far more than anyone expected at the time.

In fact, the Web was invented to deal with a specific problem. In the late 1980s, CERN was planning one of the most ambitious scientific projects ever, the Large Hadron Collider*, or LHC. As the first few lines of the original proposal put it, 'Many of the discussions of the future at CERN and the LHC end with the question "Yes, but how will we ever keep track of such a large project?" This proposal provides an answer to such questions.'

The Web, as everyone now knows, has many more uses than the original idea of linking electronic documents about particle physics in laboratories around the world. But among all the changes it has brought about, from personal social networks to political campaigning, it has also transformed the business of doing science itself, as the man who invented it hoped it would.

It allows journals to be published online and links to be made from one paper to another. It also permits professional scientists to recruit thousands of amateurs to give them a hand. One project of this type, called GalaxyZoo, used these unpaid workers to classify one million images of galaxies into various types (spiral, elliptical and irregular). This project, which was intended to help astronomers understand how galaxies evolve, was so successful that a successor has now been launched, to classify the brightest quarter of a million of them in finer detail. People working for a more modest project called Herbaria@home examine scanned images of handwritten notes about old plants stored in British museums. This will allow them to track the changes in the distribution of species in response to climate change.

Another new scientific application of the Web is to use it as an experimental laboratory. It is allowing social scientists, in particular, to do things that were previously impossible. In one project, scientists made observations about the sizes of human social networks using data from Facebook. A second investigation of these networks, produced by Bernardo Huberman of HP Labs, Hewlett-Packard's research arm in Palo Alto, California, looked at Twitter, a social networking website that allows people to post short messages to long lists of friends.

A proud father

At first glance, the networks seemed enormous – the 300,000 Twitterers sampled had 80 friends each, on average (those on Facebook had 120), but some listed up to 1,000. Closer statistical inspection, however, revealed that the majority of the messages were directed at a few specific friends. This showed that an individual's active social network is far smaller than his 'clan'. Dr Huberman has also helped uncover several laws of web surfing, including the number of times an average person will go from web page to web page on a given site before giving up, and the details of the 'winner takes all' phenomenon, whereby a few sites on a given subject attract most of the attention, and the rest get very little.

Scientists have been good at using the Web to carry out research. However, they have not been so effective at employing the latest web-based social-networking tools to open up scientific discussion and encourage more effective collaboration.

Journalists are now used to having their articles commented on by dozens of readers. Indeed, many bloggers develop and refine their essays as a result of these comments. Yet although people have tried to have scientific research reviewed in the same way, most researchers only accept reviews from a few anonymous experts. When *Nature*, one of the world's most respected scientific journals, experimented with open peer review in 2006, the results were disappointing. Only 5% of the authors it spoke to agreed to have their article posted for review on the Web – and their instinct turned out to be right, because almost half of the papers attracted no comments. Michael Nielsen, an expert on quantum computers, belongs to a new wave of scientist bloggers who want to change this. He thinks the reason for the lack of comments is that potential reviewers lack incentive.

adapted from **The Economist**

* The Large Hadron Collider (LHC) is the world's largest particle accelerator and collides particle beams. It provides information on fundamental questions of physics.

❸ Read Questions 1–6 below, underline the key words in the statements, then use these to find the right place in the passage.

❹ Now read those sections of the passage carefully to decide if the statements are true, false or not given.

Questions 1–6

Do the following statements agree with the information given in the reading passage?

Write

TRUE if the statement agrees with the information

FALSE if the statement contradicts the information

NOT GIVEN if there is no information on this

1 Tim Berners-Lee was famous for his research in physics before he invented the World Wide Web.
2 The original intention of the Web was to help manage one extremely complex project.
3 Tim Berners-Lee has also been active in politics.
4 The Web has allowed professional and amateur scientists to work together.
5 The second galaxy project aims to examine more galaxies than the first.
6 Herbaria@home's work will help to reduce the effects of climate change.

Exam advice True / False / Not Given

- Find words in the passage that are the same as or similar to words in the statement.
- Quickly find the part of the passage that deals with each statement; you will be able to find this, even when an answer is Not Given.

❺ Work in pairs. Look at Questions 7–10 in the next column.

1 Read the title of the notes and find the section of the passage which deals with this.
2 Read Questions 7–10 and decide what type of information you need for each gap.
3 Read the relevant section of the passage carefully and answer Questions 7–10.

Questions 7–10

Complete the notes below.

*Choose **NO MORE THAN TWO WORDS** from the passage for each answer.*

Social networks and internet use

Web used by social scientists (including Dr Huberman) to investigate the **7** .... of social networks.

Most **8** .... intended for limited number of people – not everyone on list.

Dr Huberman has also investigated:
- **9** .... to discover how long people will spend on a particular website;
- why a small number of sites get much more **10** .... than others on same subject.

Exam advice Note completion

- Read the title of the notes and find the section of the passage which deals with the subject.
- Read the notes and decide what type of information you need for each gap.
- Be careful to copy the answer from the passage exactly.

❻ Look at Questions 11–13 below.

1 Underline the key idea in each question and find the part of the passage which deals with it.
2 Read the passage and underline the words you need to answer the questions, then copy the answers carefully.
3 Check that your answer gives the correct information, e.g. for Question 11 your answer should be a name (*Whose writing ... ?*).

Questions 11–13

Answer the questions below.

*Choose **NO MORE THAN TWO WORDS** from the passage for each answer.*

11 Whose writing improves as a result of feedback received from readers?
12 What type of writing is not reviewed extensively on the Web?
13 Which publication invited authors to publish their articles on the World Wide Web?

New media

Exam advice *Short-answer questions*
- Underline the key idea in each question and find where it is dealt with in the passage.
- Read that part carefully and underline the answer.

7 Work in small groups.
1. Do you use Facebook, Twitter or other social networking sites?
2. If so, how many 'friends' do you have? How many do you 'talk' to regularly? What sort of things do you talk about?
3. What other ways do you have of keeping in touch with your friends?

"Are you following my tweets?"

Listening Section 4

Exam information
- You hear one speaker giving a talk, lecture or presentation on an academic subject.
- The speaker will express opinions and ideas, not just facts.
- This section does not contain a break.

1 Work in small groups. You are going to hear a lecturer talking about journalism practised by people who are not professional journalists. Before you listen, discuss this question.

Where do you think amateur journalists can publish articles and reports?

2 Work in pairs. Read Questions 1–5 below.
1. What type of word (noun/verb/adjective, etc.) is needed in each gap?
2. If you need a noun, do you think it will be singular or plural?

Questions 1–5
Complete the sentences below.
Write ONE OR TWO WORDS *for each answer.*

1. Ordinary people can provide a news story, a .... or a video when no professional journalist is present.
2. Amateur journalists often report on subjects which would be of little interest to a large ....
3. In the past, someone who wanted to express an opinion used to write a .... , while now they write a blog.
4. An amateur journalist's subject is more likely to be a .... rather than national or international news.
5. Amateur news websites, such as *Ohmynews* in South Korea, earn money from ....

3 Now listen and answer Questions 1–5.

Unit 4

4 Look at Questions 6–10 below.

1 What is a *flow chart*?
2 What type of word (noun/verb/adjective, etc.) is needed in each gap?
3 If you need a noun, do you think it will be singular or plural?

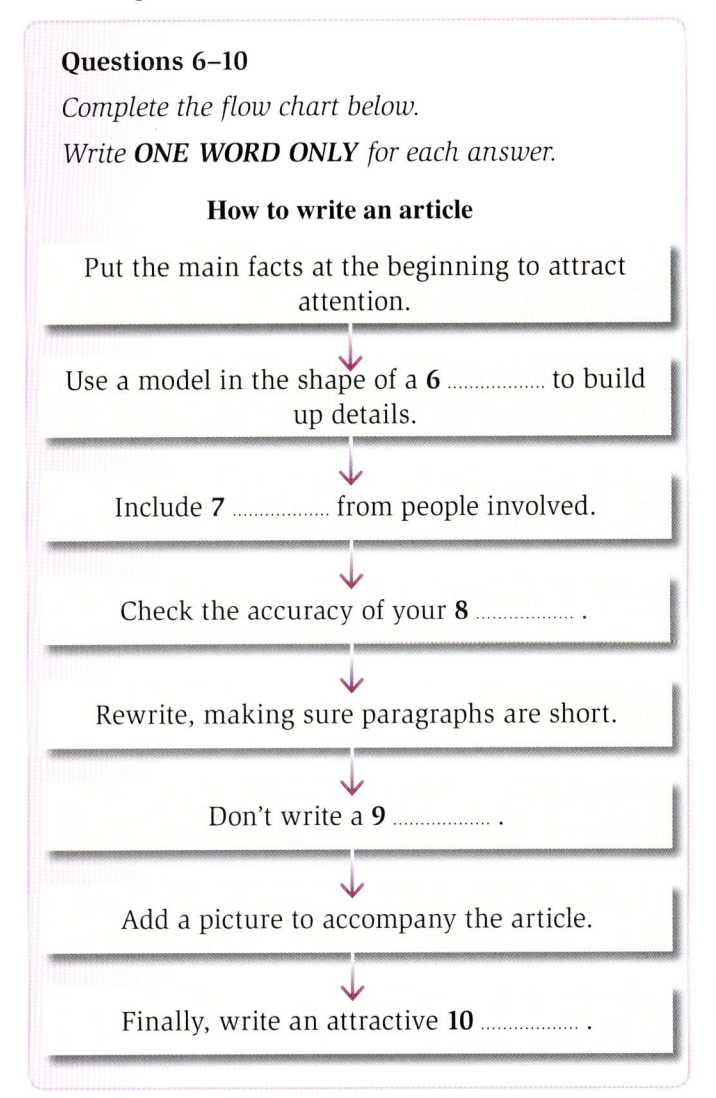

Questions 6–10

Complete the flow chart below.

*Write **ONE WORD ONLY** for each answer.*

How to write an article

Put the main facts at the beginning to attract attention.

↓

Use a model in the shape of a **6** .... to build up details.

↓

Include **7** .... from people involved.

↓

Check the accuracy of your **8** ....

↓

Rewrite, making sure paragraphs are short.

↓

Don't write a **9** ....

↓

Add a picture to accompany the article.

↓

Finally, write an attractive **10** ....

5 🔊 Now listen and answer Questions 6–10.

> **Exam advice** *Sentence and flow-chart completion*
> - Try to use words you actually hear. If not, use words which express the same idea.
> - Check your answers when you have finished.

6 Work in small groups.

Have you ever contributed to a blog, or posted a photo or video on the Internet? What was it about?

Vocabulary
Cause, factor and reason

1 IELTS candidates often confuse *cause*, *factor* and *reason*. Complete these sentences by writing one of the above words in each gap.

1 Another key .... in the process has been the mobile phone.
2 I think the main .... of this change has been the Internet.
3 Newspapers only print a few of the thousands of letters they receive each day, and the .... for this is that they just don't have enough space.

2 Check your answers by reading these extracts from *CALD*. Which words are often used before and after *cause*, *factor* and *reason*?

> **cause** the reason why something, especially something bad, happens:
> *The police are still trying to establish the **cause of** the fire.*

> **factor** a fact or situation that influences the result of something:
> *Price will be a **major/crucial factor in** the success of this new product.*

> **reason** the cause of an event or situation or something which provides an excuse or explanation:
> *The **reason for** the disaster was engine failure, not human error.*
> *The **reason why** grass is green was a mystery to the little boy.*

3 👁 Find and correct the mistakes made by IELTS candidates in these sentences.

1 Pollution is a ~~reason~~ of global warming. *cause*
2 A major reason which causes this serious problem is pressure on students.
3 The growth of big cities has its human, economic and political reasons.
4 This chart shows the main causes why agricultural land is losing productiveness.
5 We work hard throughout our student life in order to prepare for the future, although this is not the only cause.

Speaking Parts 2 and 3

1 Work in pairs. Look at this task for Speaking Part 2. Which words and phrases in the box below would you use when you do the task?

> Describe a website on the Internet that you use regularly.
>
> You should say:
>   what sort of website it is
>   what you use it for
>   what you like and dislike about it
> and explain why you use it regularly.

| site   social networking   to browse   to buy online |
| to chat   to download   to keep in touch |
| to keep up to date   to research   to visit   to watch |

2 You are going to do the task in Exercise 1. Before you talk, think about what you're going to say and make some notes.

3 Work in pairs and take turns to give your talks. You should each speak for up to two minutes.

Exam information   Speaking Part 3

- In Part 3, the examiner asks you questions on a range of topics connected with the topic of Part 2, and you discuss your opinions with him/her.
- The questions are more general and less personal than in Part 1.
- This part takes four to five minutes.

4 Look at this Part 3 question and the three answers below. Which answer do you think is best? Why?

> How does the Internet help people in their everyday lives?

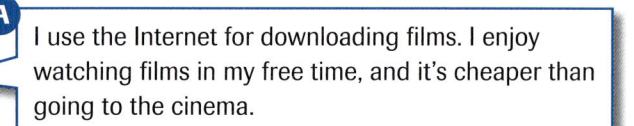

A I use the Internet for downloading films. I enjoy watching films in my free time, and it's cheaper than going to the cinema.

B Well, I think it helps people in quite a lot of ways, for instance to get information, or to book air tickets, it helps people to study and to do research for their homework and their studies or even to get advice about how to study.

C Yes, I think it helps people a lot.

5 Work in pairs. Look at these questions for Speaking Part 3.

1 What opinion or ideas would you express to answer each question?
2 What reasons and examples can you give?

> **Internet use**
>
> - How does the Internet help people in their everyday lives?
> - Do you think that some people spend too much time on the Internet? Why?
> - In your opinion, will newspapers and books disappear as a result of the Internet? Why? / Why not?

6 Read the response below given by Elena, an IELTS candidate.

1 Which question from Speaking Part 3 in Exercise 5 is she answering?
2 Underline the reasons and examples she gives.
3 Which four words and phrases does she use to show she's not certain about her answer?

> Well, I'm not sure. Some people do perhaps, for example young people who should be studying instead, but a lot of people use the Internet for their jobs or for other things. Maybe too much time chatting to friends, not enough time doing other things. Too much time sitting down. But many people leave the Internet connected all day because they use it instead of a telephone for messages or instead of going to the library, so I think it depends. For some things, it saves time.

▶ Pronunciation: *Chunking*

7 Work in pairs. Take turns to ask and answer the questions in Exercise 5.

Exam advice   Speaking Part 3

- Listen carefully to the questions and make sure you give direct and relevant answers.
- Give quite long answers to the questions, giving an example or a reason.
- If you're not certain how to answer, say so and suggest possible ideas you have.

8 Work in pairs. Take turns to ask and answer these questions.

Using the Internet

1 How can the Internet help students with their studies?
2 What dangers do you think there are connected with the Internet?
3 What are the advantages of using social networking sites instead of meeting friends face to face?
4 Do you think people should pay for music and films they download from the Internet, or should they be free? Why? / Why not?

Pronunciation
Chunking

We tend to say words in groups, almost like one word. We call this *chunking*. Between groups of words, we pause or hesitate.

1 🎧17 Listen to Elena's answer to the first question from Speaking Part 3 above and mark the pauses or hesitations / as she speaks.

> Well, I think it helps people in quite a lot of ways, for instance to get information, or to book air tickets. It helps people to study and to do research for their homework and their studies or even to get advice about how to study.

2 🎧18 Work in pairs. Read Elena's answer to the second question and decide where she will pause. Then listen and check your answers.

> Well, I'm not sure. Some people do perhaps, for example young people who should be studying instead, but a lot of people use the Internet for their jobs or for other things. Maybe too much time chatting to friends, not enough time doing other things. Too much time sitting down. But many people leave the Internet connected all day because they use it instead of a telephone for messages or instead of going to the library, so I think it depends. For some things, it saves time.

3 Now take turns to read Elena's answer aloud.

Writing Task 2

1 Work in pairs. Read this Writing task and underline the things you must deal with in your answer. Then answer the question below.

Write about the following topic.

The media should limit how much bad news they report because it discourages people from doing activities which usually involve very little risk.

To what extent do you agree or disagree?

Give reasons for your answer and include any relevant examples from your own knowledge or experience.

Which of these things should you write about in your answer?
a Whether the media report too much bad news
b What you enjoy watching on TV and reading in newspapers
c If people are really affected by the news
d Which activities you think people should avoid
e If the media should limit the amount of news they report
f How much you agree or disagree with the topic

2 Three people wrote answers to the question. Read the first paragraph of each of their answers (1–3) and match each with a description (a–c) on page 44.

1 Radio, television and the Internet repeat stories about isolated incidents, such as a murder or a robbery, 24 hours a day. As a result, many people worry about normal things such as allowing their children to play in the park. I feel this is a pity and that the media should reduce the amount of bad news they tell.

2 In the past, people used to hear the news by talking to travellers who arrived at their town or village. Today, we hear news from all over the world every day through the mass media, and it is often combined with shocking or frightening images which affect the way we think and behave.

3 The majority of news reports tend to be sensational, shocking and unpleasant. However, I believe we have a right to know what is happening in the world and I do not believe that the media should restrict what they tell us.

New media

a A general description of how the world has changed and how the situation affects us now to show why the subject is important
b A short opening sentence introducing the subject of the essay, followed by the writer's opinion given clearly and directly
c An explanation of the topic giving examples, followed by the writer's opinion

3 Work in pairs. Tick (✓) the things which all three paragraphs in Exercise 2 have in common.

a They are quite short – just two or three sentences each. ✓
b The writer's opinion is clearly stated. ☐
c The paragraphs are a clear introduction to the subject. ☐
d The writers have used their own words, not just repeated words from the question. ☐

4 Read the notes Hassan made before he started writing his answer to the Writing task in Exercise 1. Then read his answer on the right and match each paragraph (1–4) with the relevant note (a–d).

Para. 1
Para. 2
Para. 3
Para. 4

a *Conclusion: my opinion: media's duty to report + lack of info reduces freedom*

b *Introduce subject: news mainly bad + my opinion: our right to info*

c *Main idea: why reporting should not be limited. Reasons: info makes people responsible, decide themselves about risks. Supporting point: e.g. motorway accident*

d *Main idea: why people think bad news should be limited: stops people doing things Supporting points: e.g. crime and not visiting dangerous districts / plane crashes, people stop flying. Results: businesses suffer*

5 Look at how the highlighted words and phrases are used in the answer in Exercise 4. Which words and phrases:

1 start a new sentence?
2 join two sentences?

▶ page 103 *However, although, even though* and *on the other hand*

44 **Unit 4**

Most news reports tend to be sensational, shocking and unpleasant. However, I believe we have a right to know what is happening in the world and I do not believe that the media should restrict what they tell us.

People who argue that the media should not report so much bad news have one main reason for this opinion. They suggest that bad news discourages people from doing things which are normally safe, for instance, crime rates may be a major factor in discouraging people from visiting a city. Another example is when a plane crashes and many people stop flying for a while, even though it is one of the safest ways to travel. As a result of these reactions, businesses suffer because people become frightened of doing things they previously thought were harmless.

On the other hand, there are strong reasons for arguing that the media should not limit their reporting. Firstly, people have to be informed so that they can then take responsible decisions. Also, people have to be able to decide for themselves what risks are involved in doing a particular activity. For example, when there has been an accident on the motorway, I do not stop driving, although I usually drive more carefully for a few days, especially if the cause of the accident was the weather.

In short, I think the media have a duty to report all important events. If we do not receive information of this type, we cannot make responsible decisions about what we do, and this reduces our freedom to act in a way which is best for us.

(270 words)

6 Match items 1–6 with items a–f.

1 Although there are more and more channels, *f*
2 I believe we should be informed about how politicians behave.
3 I find the radio distracts me when I'm working.
4 I like to buy a newspaper on Sunday,
5 Online newspapers are widely read.
6 Television news programmes should show pictures of disasters that have happened,

a even though many people find these extremely upsetting.
b even though I can read it online for free.
c However, I don't believe they will ever completely replace printed ones.
d However, I find it entertaining when I'm driving or doing the housework.
e On the other hand, I don't think we should be told details of their private lives.
f people spend less and less time watching television.

▶ Key grammar: *Articles*

7 Read this Writing task and underline the things you must deal with in your answer.

> Write about the following topic.
>
> *The media pay too much attention to the lives and relationships of celebrities such as actors, singers or footballers. They should spend more time reporting the lives of ordinary people instead.*
>
> *To what extent do you agree or disagree?*
>
> Give reasons for your answer and include any relevant examples from your own knowledge or experience.

8 Work in small groups. Discuss to what extent you agree or disagree with the statement in the Writing task in Exercise 7. While you are discussing, note down any ideas you might use when you write your answer.

9 Write a plan for your answer, then write your complete answer. You should write at least 250 words.

- For your first paragraph, use one of the paragraphs you looked at in Exercise 2 as a model.
- Your middle paragraphs should each have a main idea and supporting points or examples.
- Your final paragraph should contain your opinion and the reasons for it.

Exam advice Writing Task 2

- Your answer should include a short introductory paragraph saying why the topic is important or what you are going to discuss.
- Each of the middle paragraphs should express one main idea with supporting points and/or examples.
- Summarise your opinion in the final paragraph.

Key grammar
Articles

1 Read these rules for when to use articles (*a, an, the* or no article) and complete each gap using one of the underlined phrases from the sample answer to the Writing task in Exercise 5. You will have to use two words twice

Use *the*
- when people know what you are talking about because you've mentioned it before or it's clear from the context: *I've been to the post office,* 1 *the accident*
- when only one of a thing exists: *the sun,* 2 ....
- with a noun which refers to a group of people or things: *the police,* 3 ....
- with superlatives: *the highest figure,* 4 ....

Use *a* or *an*
- with a singular countable noun the first time you mention it: *an example,* 5 ....

Don't use *a* or *an*
- with uncountable nouns or plural nouns: *society,* 6 ...., ...

Don't use *the*
- when you are talking in general
- with an uncountable noun or with plural nouns: *Fruit is good for you,* 7 ...., ...

▶ page 104 *Use of articles*

2 Each of these sentences contains a mistake with articles made by IELTS candidates. Correct the mistakes.

1 As ˄*the* world is changing, society is becoming more competitive.
2 I think computers play an important role in the society.
3 If students are allowed to use the computers in class, they can easily access the latest information.
4 Internet and other media benefit us in many ways.
5 It is necessary to keep in mind that the older the people get, the more experienced they are.
6 People can access the information from a computer whenever and wherever they want.
7 Some people argue that the books are the best type of media for communicating information.
8 Their parents always plan and give them a best school to study at.

New media 45

Vocabulary and grammar review Unit 3

Vocabulary

1 Complete each of these sentences with the correct form of *learn*, *teach*, *study*, *know* or *find out*.

1 Some people *learn* to speak a new language faster than others.
2 I'll .... how much the book costs and call you back.
3 This software is great – it's .... me how to pronounce some difficult English sounds.
4 Unfortunately, my brother should have .... harder for his exams.
5 My tutor was annoyed because he didn't .... why I was late for the lecture.
6 I prefer .... in the library, where it's quiet.
7 We haven't .... about phonetics with our course tutor yet.
8 I was going to tell Mark about the test, but he already ....

Grammar

2 Complete these sentences with the past simple, present perfect or present perfect continuous of the verb in brackets. In some cases, two forms are possible.

1 I *have been learning* (learn) Japanese for two years now.
2 .... (you decide) which university to apply for yet?
3 My favourite author .... (write) his first book ten years ago.
4 Not everyone in my old high school .... (come from) the local area.
5 We .... (wait) here for half an hour, but my tutor still hasn't arrived.
6 Maisie .... (feel) very nervous before the presentation, but it went well.
7 Since the heavy rains started, my sister .... (travel) to college by bus.
8 My neighbour recently confessed that he .... (never read) a newspaper in his life!

3 Study this graph and complete each sentence below using a preposition from the box. Two of the prepositions are used twice.

Full-time enrolment of students in education in Ireland (1980–2010)

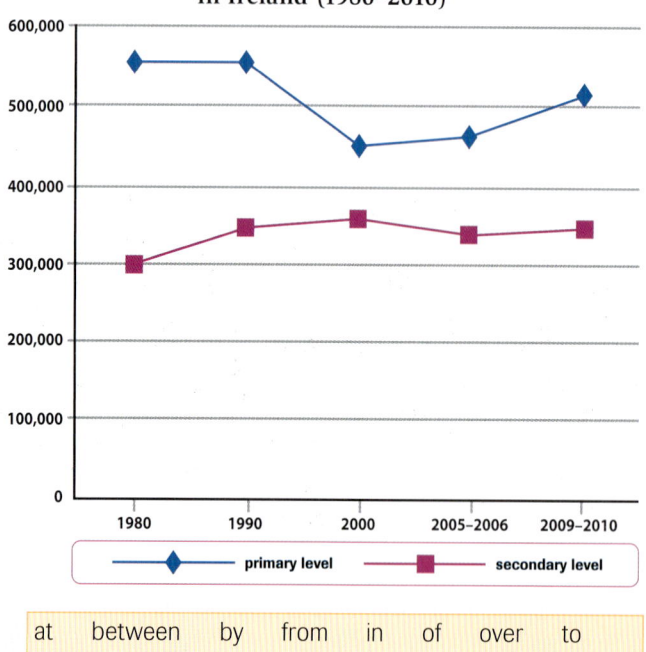

| at | between | by | from | in | of | over | to |

The chart shows changes in Irish school enrolment figures 1 ...*over*... a 30-year period.
2 .... 1980 and 2010, there were always more students at primary level than at secondary level. About 550,000 students were studying at primary level 3 .... 1980, and this figure remained stable 4 .... the next ten-year period. Enrolments fell 5 .... 100,000 after that, then rose gradually 6 .... 500,000 at the end of the first decade of the 21st century.
Enrolments in secondary education fluctuated slightly during this time period. 7 .... 1980 to 2000, there was an increase 8 .... 50,000 students, and numbers reached 350,000. The next five years showed a slight decrease 9 .... numbers, and since 2005, numbers have remained stable 10 .... 325,000. Overall, while primary school numbers have fallen slightly, secondary school enrolments have risen.

46 Vocabulary and grammar review Unit 3

Vocabulary and grammar review Unit 4

Vocabulary

1 Complete the sentences below with words connected with the Internet from the box in the correct form.

| ~~browse~~ | chat | download | go | keep | visit |

1 I _browse_ the Web to look for the information I need for my studies.
2 I .... with my friends using a social networking site.
3 Although there are millions of websites, most people just .... a few favourites frequently.
4 Facebook is a great way to .... in touch with your friends.
5 When I want to buy something, first I .... online to compare products and prices.
6 I .... films onto my computer because I find it more convenient than going to the cinema.

2 Complete each of these sentences with the correct form of *cause*, *factor* or *reason*.

1 There are several _factors_ which influence people when deciding where to go on holiday.
2 The Internet has been the main .... of the decline of conventional newspapers.
3 One .... why young people watch less television is that they have less time.
4 Online advertising is successful for a number of .... One is that people can react to it instantly.
5 You can only really deal with a problem if you understand its ....
6 Advertising is influential, but price will always be the main .... influencing your decision to buy.

Grammar

3 Complete these sentences with *however*, *although*, *on the other hand* or *even though*. In most cases, more than one answer is correct.

1 Television advertising is expensive. _However / On the other hand_ , it reaches the widest audience.
2 .... TV advertisements are often amusing, I don't like them when they interrupt films on TV.
3 Chen never uses online dictionaries .... his teacher recommends them.
4 Printed books have been around for centuries. .... , I think they will become obsolete in the next few years.
5 Printed books have been around for centuries. .... , electronic books are relatively new.

4 Complete this paragraph by writing *a*, *an*, *the* or – if you think no article is needed. In some cases, more than one answer is possible.

When you join **1** _a_ group on **2** .... social networking site, you may be revealing more than you want to. **3** .... experimental website has managed to identify **4** .... names of people who visit it by gathering **5** .... information about **6** .... groups they belong to. **7** .... website exploits **8** .... fact that your web browser keeps a list of **9** .... web addresses you have visited. **10** .... owners of websites can obtain this information by hiding **11** .... list of **12** .... web addresses in the code for their web page. When someone accesses **13** .... page, their browser will tell **14** .... website owner which of **15** .... hidden addresses they have already visited.

Unit 5 The world in our hands

Starting off

1 Work in pairs. Match the photos (1–5) with the environmental problems (a–e).

a climate change
b destruction of forests
c endangered species
d greenhouse gases
e rising sea levels

2 Match these sentence halves to form four ways of protecting the environment. Which do you think is the most urgent?

1 Driving cars with zero emissions
2 Nature reserves are a way
3 Switching to renewable energy
4 Wildlife conservation programmes

a are essential for protecting endangered species.
b will reduce our dependence on fossil fuels.
c will cut the quantity of greenhouse gases which are released into the atmosphere.
d of protecting natural habitats.

Listening Section 1

1 Work in pairs. You are going to hear a man who is interested in protecting the environment talking to a travel agent about eco-holidays. Before you listen, discuss these questions.

1 What do you think eco-holidays are?
2 Can you think of examples of eco-holidays?

2 Work in pairs. Look at Questions 1–6 and decide what type of information you need to fill each gap.

Questions 1–6

Complete the notes below.

Write NO MORE THAN TWO WORDS AND/OR A NUMBER for each answer.

Customer's name: Igor Petrov
Length of holiday: 1..........................
Will pay up to £2..........................
Told him about 3..........................for advance payments
Needs quote for 4..........................during holiday
Requires 5..........................on plane
Must check if he needs a 6..........................

48 Unit 5

3 🔊 Now listen and answer Questions 1–6.

Exam advice *Note and table completion*
- Check how many words you are allowed to use.
- Take care to spell your answers correctly.
- Write numbers as figures, not words.

4 Read Questions 7–10 below and decide what information you might need for each gap.

Questions 7–10

Complete the table below.

Write **ONE OR TWO WORDS** *for each answer.*

Eco-holidays

	type of holiday	accommodation	advantage
Dumbarton Tablelands	watching animals	house in a **7**	close to nature
Bago Nature Reserve	live with a **8**	village house	learn about way of life
San Luis Island	working in a **9**	hostel	holiday location without **10** ....

5 🔊 Now listen and answer Questions 7–10.

6 Work in pairs.
1 Would you enjoy an eco-holiday?
2 Which of the eco-holidays in Exercise 4 would interest you? Why?

Vocabulary

Nature, the environment or *the countryside?*
Tourist or *tourism?*

1 IELTS candidates often confuse *nature, the environment* and *the countryside,* and *tourist* and *tourism.* Match the words (1–5) with their definitions from *CALD* (a–e).

1 nature
2 the environment
3 countryside
4 tourism
5 tourist

a [U] land where there are no towns or cities
b [U] all the things in the world which exist naturally and were not created by people
c [U] the land, water and air that animals and plants live in. It is usually used when talking about the way people use or damage the natural world.
d [C] someone who visits a place for pleasure and interest, usually while they are on holiday
e [U] the business of providing services such as transport, places to stay or entertainment for people who are on holiday

The world in our hands 49

2 Complete these sentences from the Listening section by writing the correct form of a word from Exercise 1 in each gap. You will have to use one word twice.

I phoned you earlier about an eco-holiday, you know, one of those holidays where you don't damage
1 *the environment* at all and you get close to
2 ....

You get to stay in a quite luxurious house or cabin built high up in a tree and surrounded by lovely
3 ....

You go and stay with a local family in their house in a small mountain village away from other
4 .... and the usual 5 .... spots.

You might like it because international
6 .... hasn't spoilt it yet.

3 ⊙ Four of these sentences contain a mistake made by IELTS candidates in the exam. Find and correct the mistakes.

1 As far as I am concerned, the increase in the amount of ~~tourist~~ is inevitable. *tourism*
2 In conclusion, the nature we live in is very important to us and therefore we should all try to protect it.
3 There is also a very positive side to tourists because it brings money and business to places.
4 They live in a lovely old house surrounded by beautiful countryside.
5 People from the city leave their rubbish in the nature and spoil it as a result.

Reading Section 2

1 Work in pairs. You are going to read an article about a form of renewable energy. Before you read, look at the title and the subheading and answer these questions.

1 What do you think the article will be about?
2 What problems do you think there might be with producing electricity in this way?

2 Now read the article quite quickly to find three problems with producing electricity in the Sahara.

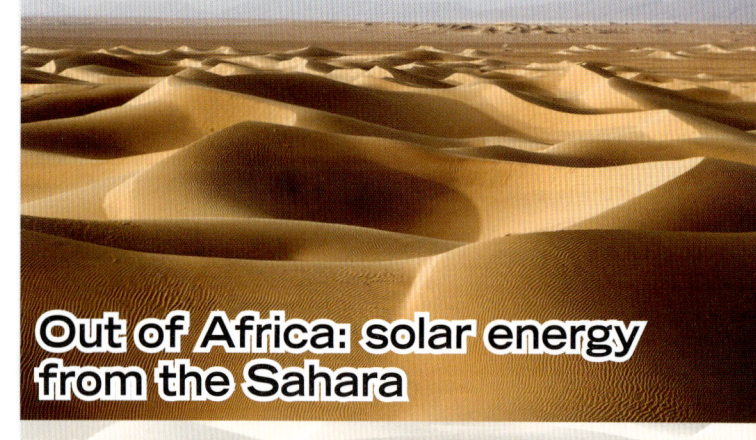

Out of Africa: solar energy from the Sahara

Vivienne Walt reports on how the Sahara Desert could offer a truly green solution to Europe's energy problems

A   For years, the Sahara has been regarded by many Europeans as a *terra incognita** of little economic value or importance. But this idea may soon change completely. Politicians and scientists on both sides of the Mediterranean are beginning to focus on the Sahara's potential to provide power for Europe in the future. They believe the desert's true value comes from the fact that it is dry and empty. Some areas of the Sahara reach 45 degrees centigrade on many afternoons. It is, in other words, a gigantic natural storehouse of solar energy.

B   A few years ago, scientists began to calculate just how much energy the Sahara holds. They were astonished at the answer. In theory, a 90,600 square kilometre chunk of the Sahara – smaller than Portugal and a little over 1% of its total area – could yield the same amount of electricity as all the world's power plants combined. A smaller square of 15,500 square kilometres – about the size of Connecticut – could provide electricity for Europe's 500 million people. 'I admit I was sceptical until I did the calculations myself,' says Michael Pawlyn, director of Exploration Architecture, one of three British environmental companies comprising the Sahara Forest Project, which is testing solar plants in Oman and the United Arab Emirates. Pawlyn calls the Sahara's potential 'staggering'.

C   At the moment, no one is proposing the creation of a solar power station the size of a small country. But a relatively well-developed technology exists, which proponents say could turn the Sahara's heat and sunlight into a major source of electricity – Concentrating Solar Power (CSP). Unlike solar panels, which convert sunlight directly into electricity, CSP utilises mirrors which focus light on water pipes or boilers to produce very hot steam to operate the turbines of generators. Small CSP plants have produced power in California's Mojave Desert since the 1980s. The Sahara Forest Project proposes building CSP plants in areas below sea level (the Sahara has several such depressions) so that sea water can flow into them. This water would then be purified and used for powering turbines and washing dust off the mirrors. Waste water would then supply irrigation to areas around the stations, creating lush oases – hence the 'forest' in the group's name.

50   Unit 5

D But producing significant quantities of electricity means building huge arrays of mirrors and pipes across hundreds of miles of remote desert, which is expensive. Gerry Wolff, an engineer who heads DESERTEC, an international consortium of solar-power scientists, says they have estimated it will cost about $59 billion to begin transmitting power from the Sahara by 2020.

E Building plants is just part of the challenge. One of the drawbacks to CSP technology is that it works at maximum efficiency only in sunny, hot climates – and deserts tend to be distant from population centres. To supply Europe with 20% of its electricity needs, more than 19,300 kilometres of cables would need to be laid under the Mediterranean, says Gunnar Asplund, head of HVDC research at ABB Power Technologies in Ludvika, Sweden. Indeed, to use renewable sources of power, including solar, wind and tidal, Europe will need to build completely new electrical grids. That's because existing infrastructures, built largely for the coal-fired plants that supply 80% of Europe's power, would not be suitable for carrying the amount of electricity generated by the Sahara. Germany's government-run Aerospace Centre, which researches energy, estimates that replacing those lines could raise the cost of building solar plants in the Sahara and sending significant amounts of power to Europe to about $465 billion over the next 40 years. Generous government subsidies will be needed. 'Of course it costs a lot of money,' says Asplund. 'It's a lot cheaper to burn coal than to make solar power in the Sahara.'

F Meanwhile, some companies are getting started. Seville engineering company Abengoa is building one solar-thermal plant in Algeria and another in Morocco, while a third is being built in Egypt by a Spanish–Japanese joint venture. The next step will be to get cables in place. Although the European Parliament has passed a law that aids investors who help the continent reach its goal of getting 20% of its power from renewable energy by 2020, it could take years to create the necessary infrastructure.

G Nicholas Dunlop, secretary-general of the London-based NGO e-Parliament, thinks companies should begin transmitting small amounts of solar power as soon as the North African plants begin operating, by linking a few cable lines under the Med. 'I call it the Lego method,' he says. 'Build it piece by piece.' If it can be shown that power from the Sahara can be produced profitably, he says, companies and governments will soon jump in. If they do, perhaps airplane passengers flying across the Sahara will one day count the mirrors and patches of green instead of staring at sand.

adapted from *Time Magazine*

terra incognita – Latin, meaning 'an unknown land'

❸ Read the instructions for Questions 1–5 below and answer these questions. Then underline the key ideas in Questions 1–5.

1 Will you need to use all the letters, A–G, in your answers?
2 Can you use the same letter for more than one answer?

Questions 1–5

The reading passage has seven paragraphs, **A–G**.

Which paragraph contains the following information?

Write the correct letter, **A–G**.

NB You may use any letter more than once.

1 a mention of systems which could not be used
2 estimates of the quantity of power the Sahara could produce
3 a suggestion for how to convince organisations about the Sahara's potential
4 a short description of the Sahara at present
5 a comparison of the costs of two different energy sources

❹ Now read the article and answer Questions 1–5.

Exam advice *Matching information*
- Read the instructions carefully.
  - You will not need all the paragraphs for your answers.
  - You may be able to find two of the answers in the same paragraph.
- Read the questions carefully.
  - Underline the key ideas in each of them.
  - Quickly find the right part of the passage and read carefully to make sure it covers the information.

The world in our hands

5 **Look at Questions 6–9 and the list of organisations below.**

1 Read the passage very quickly and underline where each organisation on the list is mentioned.
2 Read the statements and underline the key ideas.
3 Carefully read the parts of the article where each organisation is mentioned and decide whether a statement matches this.

Questions 6–9

Look at the following statements (Questions 6–9) and the list of organisations below.

Match each statement with the correct organisation, A–G.

6 They have set a time for achieving an objective.
7 They believe that successful small-scale projects will demonstrate that larger projects are possible.
8 They have a number of renewable energy projects under construction.
9 They are already experimenting with solar-energy installations in other parts of the world.

List of Organisations
A Exploration Architecture
B DESERTEC
C ABB Power Technologies
D Aerospace Centre
E Abengoa
F The European Parliament
G e-Parliament

Exam advice *Matching features*
- Sometimes there are more options than questions; they are listed in the order they appear in the passage. Quickly locate them and underline them.
- Underline the key ideas in each question.
- Read carefully what the passage says about each option and match each question to one option.

6 **Look at Questions 10–13 below.**

1 What type of information do you need to complete each gap?
2 Which paragraph in the article deals with Concentrating Solar Power? Read it and complete the gaps.

Questions 10–13

Complete the summary below.

*Choose **NO MORE THAN TWO WORDS** from the passage for each answer.*

Concentrating Solar Power (CSP)

Unlike solar panels, CSP concentrates the sun's rays on boilers by using **10** .... The resulting heat produces high-temperature **11** .... , which in turn moves the turbines which generate electricity. CSP plants will be situated in **12** .... to allow sea water to run in. This, when purified, can be used to wash the equipment. The resulting dirty water will be used for **13** .... around the power plant, and in this way oases will be formed.

Exam advice *Summary completion*
- Read the summary carefully first.
- Use the title to find the correct section of the passage, then read it carefully.
- Check your summary when you have finished.

7 **Work in small groups.**
- What renewable energy is used in your country?
- Why is renewable energy better than other sources of energy?
- What disadvantages does renewable energy have?

Speaking Parts 2 and 3

1 Look at this task for Speaking Part 2 and make notes about the place you would like to describe.

> **Describe a beautiful place you have visited in your country.**
>
> You should say:
>   when you visited it
>   who you went with
>   what you did there
> and explain why you think the place is so beautiful.

2 Listen to Jamila doing the task in Exercise 1. While you listen, complete the notes she made beforehand by writing one of the adjectives from the box in each of the gaps.

| fantastic | fresh | lovely | spectacular | steep |
| unspoilt | warm | wonderful | | |

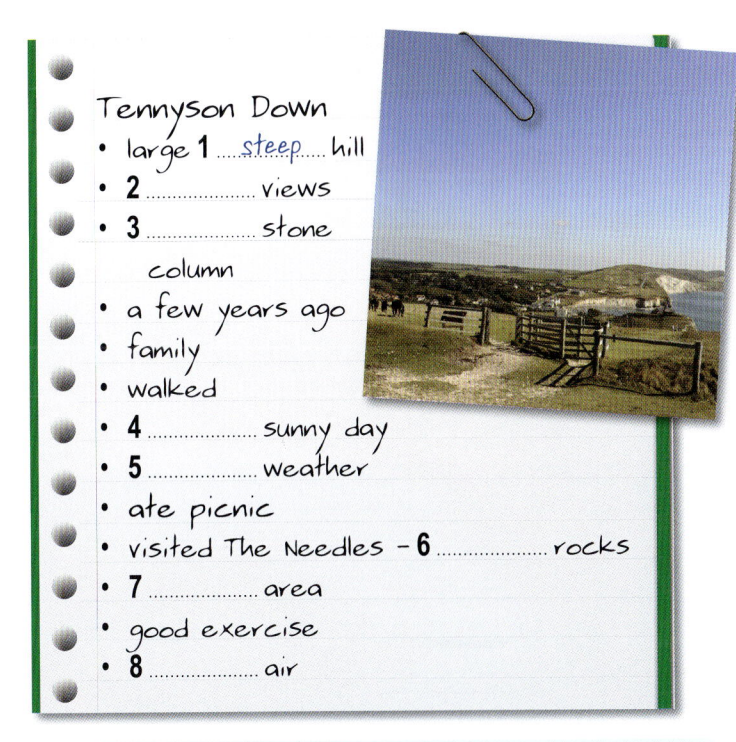

Tennyson Down
- large 1 ...steep... hill
- 2 .... views
- 3 .... stone column
- a few years ago
- family
- walked
- 4 .... sunny day
- 5 .... weather
- ate picnic
- visited The Needles – 6 .... rocks
- 7 .... area
- good exercise
- 8 .... air

3 Work in pairs. Take turns to give your talk. You should try to speak for two minutes.

4 Work in pairs. Discuss how you could answer this Speaking Part 3 question.

> What things attract tourists to a place?

5 Read and listen to Jamila's response.
1. How many ideas does she express in her answer?
2. Which ideas do you agree with?

> Well, I think in general people like to go to places which are well-known tourist destinations because you know, generally people like to feel safe when they're on holiday, especially when they travel to a foreign country. I think usually people choose places where there are plenty of hotels, so they can get good accommodation and plenty of things to do, so they don't get bored. Also people tend to choose places where they think the weather will be good, especially if they want to do things outdoors.

6 Jamila gives a general answer to the question.
1. Which tense does she use?
2. Find four words or phrases in her answer which she uses to say that she is making a generalisation.

7 Work in pairs. Look at the Part 3 questions below and think of ideas you could use to give general answers to each question.

Beautiful places
- What things attract tourists to visit a place?
- How do places change when too many tourists visit them?
- What can individual people do to protect beautiful places?

The environment
- Apart from tourism, what other environmental problems are common in the world today?
- Whose responsibility is it to deal with these problems?
- What can ordinary people do to protect the environment?

Exam advice   Speaking Part 2
- You may be asked to talk about something you enjoy or like. Sound enthusiastic and think of positive adjectives to describe the topic.
- Where possible, use your own words instead of the words given in the task, as this shows your ability to create language.

▶ page 54 Pronunciation: *Sentence stress 2*

8 Change partners and take turns to ask and answer the questions in Exercise 7.

Exam advice Speaking Part 3
- Give general answers to Part 3 questions; don't talk about yourself.
- Use words and phrases which show that you are making general points.

Pronunciation
Sentence stress 2

You can stress words which express how you feel about something, for example positive adjectives to express enthusiasm or negative adjectives to express annoyance.

1 Work in pairs. Look at these extracts from Jamila's answer. Underline the words which you think should be stressed. Then listen and check which words Jamila stressed.

1 … there are these <u>fantastic</u> <u>views</u> across the sea in all directions …
2 At the top of the hill, there's this wonderful stone column …
3 It was a lovely sunny day and there weren't too many people around.
4 … until you reach the Needles, which are some spectacular rocks standing out in the sea, very spectacular …
5 Why is the place so beautiful? I think it's particularly beautiful because it's such an unspoilt area, it's protected.
6 … it's a wonderful day out, good exercise, fresh air, fantastic views and very, very relaxing.

2 Work in pairs.

1 What types of word does Jamila tend to stress (nouns, adjectives, etc.)?
2 Why does she stress words like *fantastic*, *spectacular* and *wonderful*?

3 Work in pairs. Take turns to read the sentences in Exercise 1 aloud, trying to put the stress in the same places.

Writing Task 1

1 Work in pairs. Look at the diagrams in the Writing task below.

1 What is the machine used for?
2 How does it work?
3 Where can it be placed?
4 What comparisons can you make about the two locations?

The diagrams below show the design for a wave-energy machine and its location.

Summarise the information by selecting and reporting the main features, making comparisons where relevant.

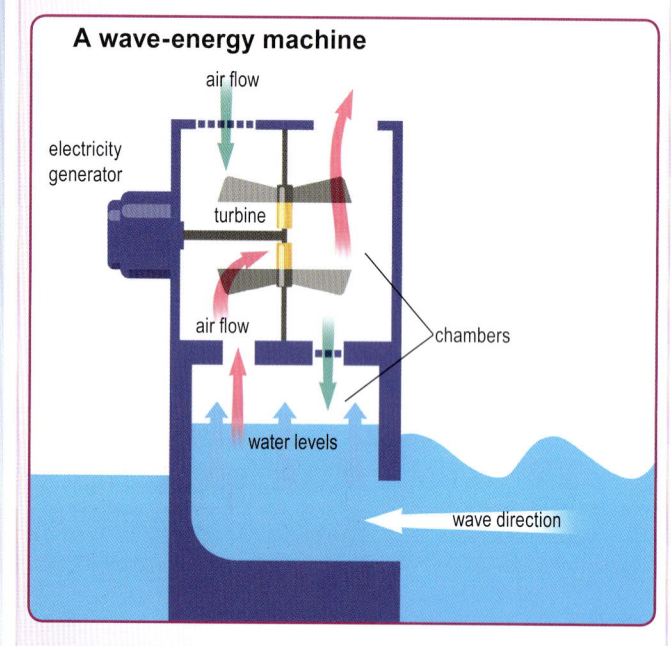

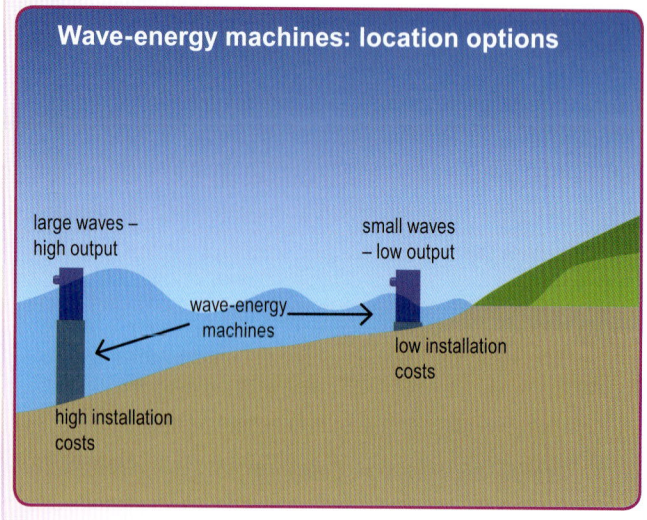

A wave-energy machine
- air flow
- electricity generator
- turbine
- air flow
- chambers
- water levels
- wave direction

Wave-energy machines: location options
- large waves – high output
- small waves – low output
- wave-energy machines
- high installation costs
- low installation costs

Unit 5

2 Complete this answer to the Writing task using verbs from the box. In some cases, more than one answer may be possible.

| connected | ~~consists~~ | sucked | turns | enters |
| generated | installed | passes | produced | rises |

The diagrams show a machine for generating electricity from waves and where it can be placed. The machine 1 consists of two chambers, one above the other. The process starts when a wave 2 .... the lower chamber. As a result, the water level inside the chamber 3 .... and air is pushed up into the chamber above. As the air 4 .... through the upper chamber, it moves a turbine which is 5 .... to a generator. When the wave goes down, air is 6 .... in from outside and this also 7 .... the turbine. The machine can be placed near the coast, and in this case it can be 8 .... at a lower cost. However, waves near the coast tend to be smaller and so less electricity is 9 .... Alternatively, the machine can be placed in deeper water where the waves are larger and more electricity can be 10 .... However, in this case, it will cost more to install. In general, while the machine appears to be a simple way of harnessing renewable energy, its installation may cause a number of problems related to its cost and its location.

3 Work in pairs. Divide the answer in Exercise 2 into paragraphs. Write // where you think there should be a new paragraph. Then discuss the purpose of each paragraph.

Key grammar
The passive

1 **The passive is formed with the verb *to be* + past participle (*opened, done, eaten*, etc.). Which verb in this sentence is passive?**

As a result, the water level inside the chamber rises and air is pushed up into the chamber above.

2 Underline other examples of the passive in the sample answer in Writing Exercise 2.

3 Which reasons (a–c) apply to the example sentence in Exercise 1? You can choose more than one.

We use the passive when:
a we don't know who or what does/did something.
b we don't need to say who or what does/did something.
c what happens/happened is more important than who or what does/did it.

▶ page 104 *The passive*

4 Rewrite each of these sentences using a verb in the passive and starting with the words given.

1 They generate 20 percent of the nation's energy using renewable energy sources.
Twenty percent of the nation's energy *is generated using renewable energy sources.*
2 They have closed down some nuclear power plants.
Some nuclear power plants …
3 They can use the electricity for lighting homes.
The electricity …
4 The government will subsidise new wind-turbine installations.
New wind-turbine installations …
5 In the first stage of the process, they heat the air which will inflate the balloon.
In the first stage of the process, the air which will inflate the balloon …
6 In tropical countries, people tend to consume more electricity in summer months.
In tropical countries, more electricity tends …

5 ⊙ IELTS candidates often make mistakes when they use the passive. Correct the mistake in each of these sentences.

1 Children are easily ~~influence~~ by others, by their environment or by their parents. *influenced*
2 I think some problems which exist in this world can solve by money.
3 In my country, few schools teach students by computer but not all subjects teach by computer.
4 Moreover, unnecessary restrictions should reduce by the government.
5 The primary reason for their disapproval is the damage to the environment which caused by mass tourism.
6 The result of this research shows that in the UK a great proportion of household tasks are doing by women.
7 This diagram presents the process of brick manufacturing which is used for the building industry.

The world in our hands 55

4 When describing a process, it is a good idea to use words and phrases which explain the order in which things happen. Find these phrases in the sample answer, then write them in the correct column of the table below.

as a result   as   the process starts when   when the wave goes down

introduces the first part of the process	explains that one thing happens after another	explains that two things happen simultaneously
	as a result	

5 Add these words and phrases to the table in Exercise 4.

as a consequence   at the same time   first
following this   in the first stage of the process
in the next stage   meanwhile   next   then

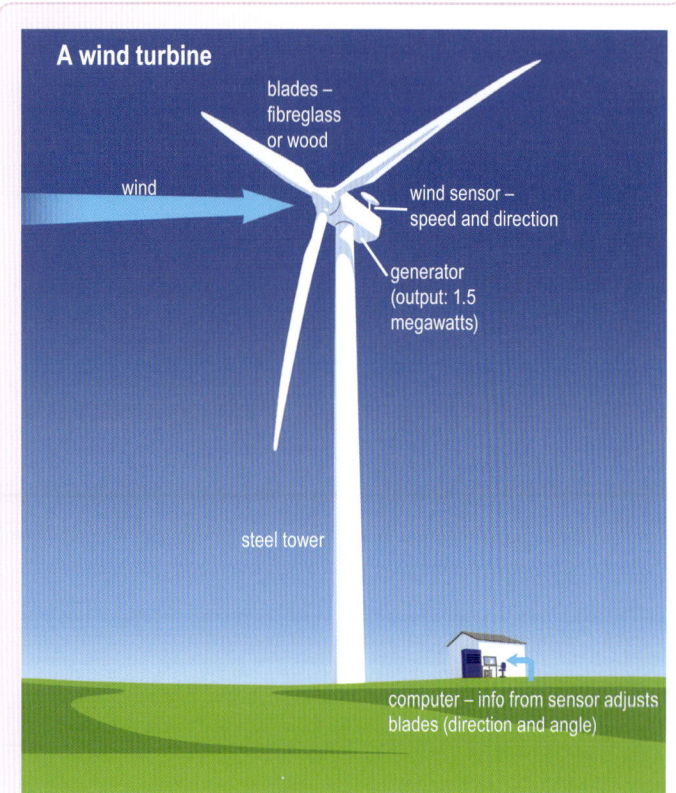

Exam advice   *Diagram summary*

When you have to describe a diagram or diagrams:
- describe the key stages in a logical order.
- compare information and include a short, general overview.

6 Work in pairs. Look at the Writing task below.

1. Decide what the main features of the machines are and how they work.
2. Decide what comparisons you can make.
3. Write a plan: decide how many paragraphs you need and what information to include in each paragraph.
4. Work alone to write your answer. You should write at least 150 words.

The diagrams below show the design for a wind turbine and its location.

Summarise the information by selecting and reporting the main features, and make comparisons where relevant.

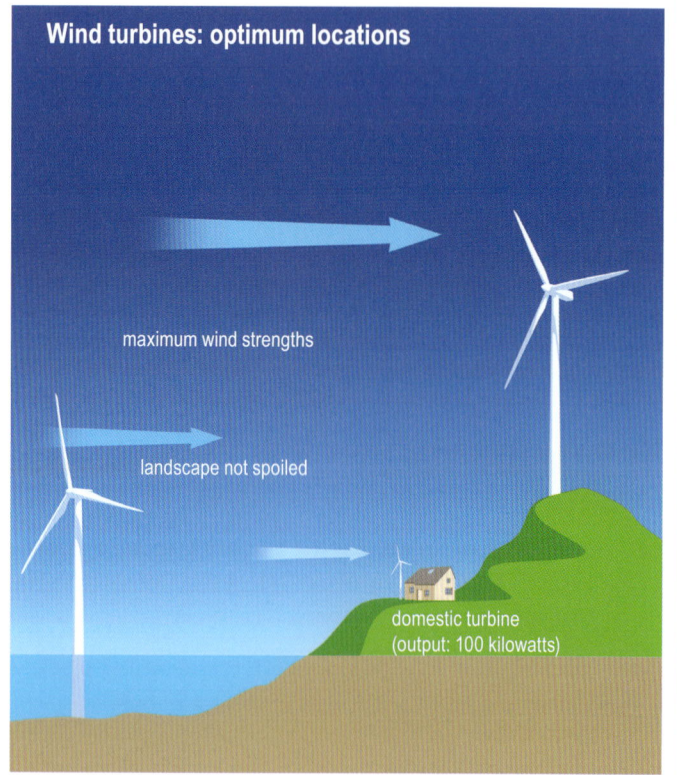

A wind turbine

- blades – fibreglass or wood
- wind
- wind sensor – speed and direction
- generator (output: 1.5 megawatts)
- steel tower
- computer – info from sensor adjusts blades (direction and angle)

Wind turbines: optimum locations

- maximum wind strengths
- landscape not spoiled
- domestic turbine (output: 100 kilowatts)

Unit 5

Unit 6 Making money, spending money

Starting off

Work in pairs.

1 Which of these shops would you prefer to shop at? Why?
2 What things attract you to some shops more than others?

Reading Section 1

1 Work in small groups. You are going to read a passage about supermarkets. Before you read, match these words and phrases (1–7) with their definitions from Cambridge dictionaries (a–g).

1 aisle
2 bargain
3 branded product
4 own-label product
5 promotion
6 purchase
7 retailer

a a person, shop or business that sells goods to the public
b a long, narrow space between the rows of shelves in a large shop
c a product with the name of the shop where you buy it, rather than the name of the company that made it
d a product made by a particular company
e activities to advertise something
f something on sale at a lower price than its true value
g something that you buy

2 Work in pairs. Read the title and subheading of the passage on the next page. What aspect of supermarkets do you think the passage will describe?

3 Read the passage quite quickly. Find three methods supermarkets use to persuade customers to spend more money.

Making money, spending money 57

The way the brain buys

Supermarkets take great care over the way the goods they sell are arranged. This is because they know a lot about how to persuade people to buy things.

When you enter a supermarket, it takes some time for the mind to get into a shopping mode. This is why the area immediately inside the entrance of a supermarket is known as the 'decompression zone'. People need to slow down and take stock of the surroundings, even if they are regulars. Supermarkets do not expect to sell much here, so it tends to be used more for promotion. So the large items piled up here are designed to suggest that there are bargains further inside the store, and shoppers are not necessarily expected to buy them. Walmart, the world's biggest retailer, famously employs 'greeters' at the entrance to its stores. A friendly welcome is said to cut shoplifting. It is harder to steal from nice people.

Immediately to the left in many supermarkets is a 'chill zone', where customers can enjoy browsing magazines, books and DVDs. This is intended to tempt unplanned purchases and slow customers down. But people who just want to do their shopping quickly will keep walking ahead, and the first thing they come to is the fresh fruit and vegetables section. However, for shoppers, this makes no sense. Fruit and vegetables can be easily damaged, so they should be bought at the end, not the beginning, of a shopping trip. But psychology is at work here: selecting these items makes people feel good, so they feel less guilty about reaching for less healthy food later on.

Shoppers already know that everyday items, like milk, are invariably placed towards the back of a store to provide more opportunity to tempt customers to buy things which are not on their shopping list. This is why pharmacies are also generally at the back. But supermarkets know shoppers know this, so they use other tricks, like placing popular items halfway along a section so that people have to walk all along the aisle looking for them. The idea is to boost 'dwell time': the length of time people spend in a store.

Having walked to the end of the fruit-and-vegetable aisle, shoppers arrive at counters of prepared food, the fishmonger, the butcher and the deli. Then there is the in-store bakery, which can be smelt before it is seen. Even small supermarkets now use in-store bakeries. Mostly these bake pre-prepared items and frozen ingredients which have been delivered to the supermarket previously, and their numbers have increased, even though central bakeries that deliver to a number of stores are much more efficient. They do it for the smell of freshly baked bread, which arouses people's appetites and thus encourages them to purchase not just bread but also other food, including ready meals.

Retailers and producers talk a lot about the 'moment of truth'. This is not a philosophical idea, but the point when people standing in the aisle decide to buy something and reach to get it. At the instant coffee section, for example, branded products from the big producers are arranged at eye level while cheaper ones are lower down, along with the supermarket's own-label products.

But shelf positioning is fiercely fought over, not just by those trying to sell goods, but also by those arguing over how best to manipulate shoppers. While many stores reckon eye level is the top spot, some think a little higher is better. Others think goods displayed at the end of aisles sell the most because they have the greatest visibility. To be on the right-hand side of an eye-level selection is often considered the very best place, because most people are right-handed and most people's eyes drift rightwards. Some supermarkets reserve that for their most expensive own-label goods.

Scott Bearse, a retail expert with Deloitte Consulting in Boston, Massachusetts, has led projects observing and questioning tens of thousands of customers about how they feel about shopping. People say they leave shops empty-handed more often because they are 'unable to decide' than because prices are too high, says Mr Bearse. Getting customers to try something is one of the best ways of getting them to buy, adds Mr Bearse. Deloitte found that customers who use fitting rooms in order to try on clothes buy the product they are considering at a rate of 85% compared with 58% for those that do not do so.

Often a customer struggling to decide which of two items is best ends up not buying either. In order to avoid a situation where a customer decides not to buy either product, a third 'decoy' item, which is not quite as good as the other two, is placed beside them to make the choice easier and more pleasurable. Happier customers are more likely to buy.

adapted from The Economist

4 Work in pairs. Look at the diagram below.
1 What does it show?
2 What information might you need to complete each gap (1–4)?

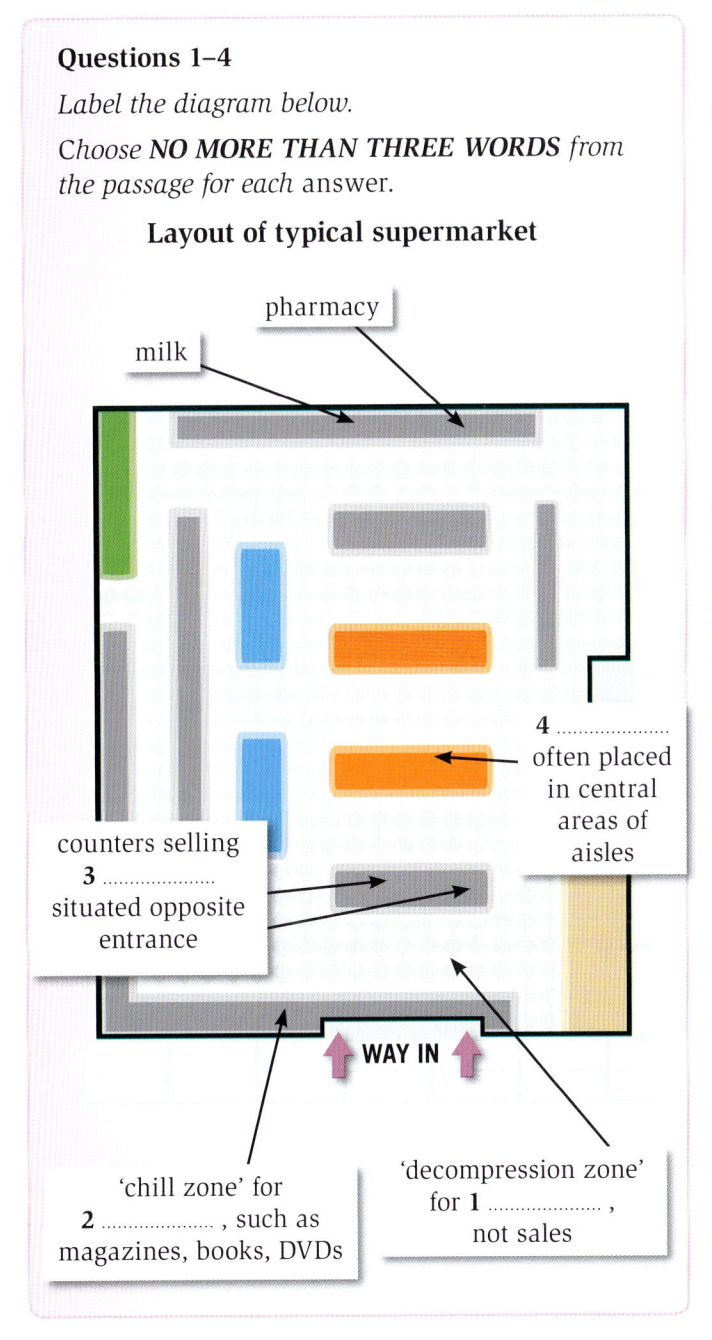

Questions 1–4

Label the diagram below.

Choose **NO MORE THAN THREE WORDS** from the passage for each answer.

Layout of typical supermarket

- pharmacy
- milk
- 4 .... often placed in central areas of aisles
- counters selling 3 .... situated opposite entrance
- WAY IN
- 'chill zone' for 2 ...., such as magazines, books, DVDs
- 'decompression zone' for 1 ...., not sales

5 Find the relevant paragraphs in the passage and read these carefully, underlining the words which give you the answers. Then label the diagram.

Exam advice   *Labelling a diagram*
- Use the title of the diagram to find the right part of the passage.
- Check how many words you need for each gap.
- Write the answers exactly as they appear in the passage.

6 Look at Questions 5–10 below.
1 Underline a word or phrase in each statement which you think will help you find the right part of the passage.
2 Read the passage quite quickly to find where each answer is dealt with.
3 Read those parts of the passage carefully to answer the questions, and where possible, underline the words which give you the answers.

Questions 5–10

Do the following statements agree with the information given in the reading passage?

Write

TRUE if the statement agrees with the information

FALSE if the statement contradicts the information

NOT GIVEN if there is no information on this

5 The 'greeters' at Walmart increase sales.
6 People feel better about their shopping if they buy fruit and vegetables before they buy other food.
7 In-store bakeries produce a wider range of products than central bakeries.
8 Supermarkets find right-handed people easier to persuade than left-handed people.
9 The most frequent reason for leaving shops without buying something is price.
10 'Decoy' items are products which the store expects customers to choose.

Exam advice   *True / False / Not Given*
Don't read the whole passage again. Find the sections that answer each question.

Making money, spending money

7 Read Questions 11–13 below and describe what the flow chart shows in your own words.

Questions 11–13

Complete the flow chart below.

*Choose **NO MORE THAN TWO WORDS** from the passage for each answer.*

In-store bread production process

The supermarket is sent **11** .... and other items which have been prepared earlier.

↓

Baking bread in-store produces an aroma.

↓

Shoppers' **12** .... are stimulated.

↓

They are then keener to buy food, including bread and **13** ....

---

8 Find the paragraph of the passage which deals with the subject, then read it carefully and complete the flow chart.

Exam advice   **Flow-chart completion**

- Use the title of the flow chart to find the right part of the passage.
- Check how many words you need to fill each gap.
- <u>Underline</u> the words you need and copy them onto the answer sheet.

Listening Section 2

1 You are going to hear a worker from the Citizen's Advice Bureau talking to people who have arrived recently in the country about the banking system in Britain. Before you listen, match these words and phrases (1–8) with their definitions (a–h).

1 account   _b_
2 balance   ☐
3 branch   ☐
4 direct debit ☐
5 in credit ☐
6 interest rate ☐
7 overdraft ☐
8 savings   ☐

a arrangement that allows an organisation to take money from your bank account to pay for something
b arrangement with a bank to keep your money there
c exact amount of money you have in a bank account
d extra money that you must pay to a bank which has lent you money
e having money in your bank account
f money which you have saved and not spent
g one of the offices of a bank
h when you have taken more money out of your bank account than you had in it

2 Read Questions 1–4 and <u>underline</u> the key idea in each.

Questions 1–4

Which bank provides the following?

*Choose **FOUR** answers from the box and write the correct letter, **A–F**, next to questions **1–4**.*

1 a branch on the campus   ....
2 a free gift for new customers ....
3 special interest rates for students ....
4 no bank charges for certain customers ....

A Evergreen	D International Union
B Finley's	E Moneysafe
C Great Western	F Northern Star

---

3 🔊 Now listen and answer Questions 1–4.

Exam advice   **Matching**

- <u>Underline</u> the key idea in each question. Sometimes you will have to underline the whole phrase.
- Write only one letter for each question – you will not need to use all the letters.

Unit 6

4 Work in pairs. Look at Questions 5–10 and the diagram below. What information do you think you need to complete the labels?

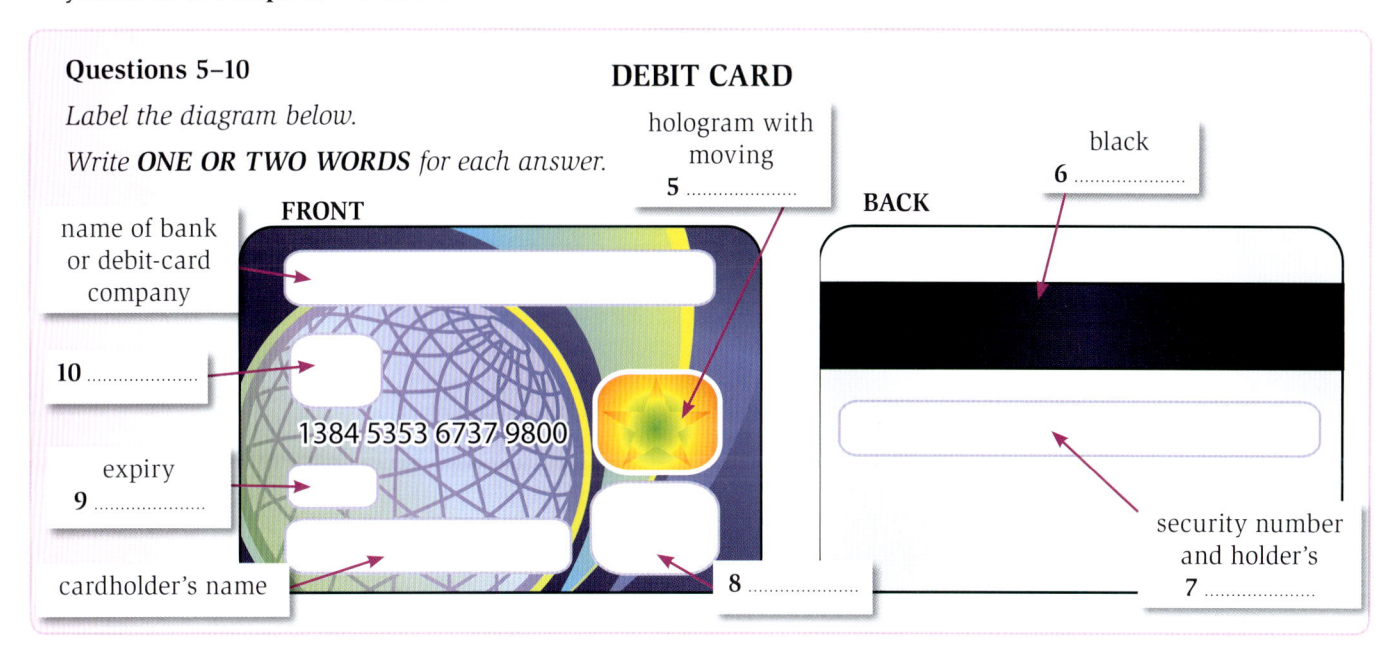

Questions 5–10

Label the diagram below.

Write ONE OR TWO WORDS for each answer.

DEBIT CARD

FRONT — name of bank or debit-card company; 10 ....; 1384 5353 6737 9800; expiry 9 ....; cardholder's name; 5 hologram with moving ....; 8 ....

BACK — 6 black ....; security number and holder's 7 ....

5 🔊 02 Now listen and answer Questions 5–10.

Exam advice   **Labelling a diagram**

- Look at the title of the diagram to see what it is about.
- Find the first gap you need to label: this will be the first piece of information you hear.
- The gaps you need to label are arranged in a logical order on the diagram. You will hear the information in the same order.

6 Work in small groups.

1 What things are important to you when choosing a bank?
2 Which do you prefer to use: a credit card or cash? Why?

Vocabulary

Verb + *to do* / verb + *doing*

1 Look at these extracts from the Reading passage and circle the correct verb form in each one.

1 … they know a lot about how to persuade people *(to buy)* / *buying* things.
2 Supermarkets do not expect *to sell* / *selling* much here, so it tends *to be* / *being* used more for promotion.
3 … a 'chill zone', where customers can enjoy *to browse* / *browsing* magazines …
4 … the smell of freshly baked bread encourages people *to purchase* / *purchasing* not just bread but also other food …
5 Often a customer ends up *not to buy* / *not buying* either.
6 In order to avoid a situation where a customer decides *not to buy* / *not buying* either product, …

▶ page 105 *Verbs + infinitive and verbs + –ing*

2 ⊙ Six of these sentences contain mistakes made by IELTS candidates. Two are correct. Find and correct the mistakes.

1 When people think in terms of shopping, they always think of ~~buy~~ something pleasant. *buying*
2 I strongly recommend using small local shops.
3 I suggest to improve the situation by spending more money to solve the problem.
4 Many people cannot afford buying expensive clothes, so they tend to look for bargains.
5 I don't think spending money on your child will make him become irresponsible with money as an adult.
6 In conclusion, oil prices are forecast increasing in the medium term.
7 Parents should give their children pocket money to enable them buying the things they want.
8 Some people will spend all their spare time to shop.

Making money, spending money

3 ◉ These sentences were all written by IELTS candidates. Complete them with the correct form of the verb in brackets.

1 We enjoy *buying* (buy) many different kinds of food.
2 Some people cannot afford .... (go) shopping in such expensive stores.
3 Young people should spend less time .... (watch) television.
4 Firstly, the money could help poorer nations .... (improve) their economies.
5 We enjoy .... (have) more money than in the past.
6 In summary, it's a good idea to encourage tourists .... (come) to our country.
7 Some people spend a lot of money .... (buy) high-quality clothes.
8 Improvements in people's living standards are allowing more people .... (get) whatever they want.

4 Work in pairs. Take turns to ask and answer these questions.

1 Do you enjoy shopping at your local supermarket? Why? / Why not?
2 How does your supermarket try to persuade you to spend more money?
3 Where would you recommend visitors to your town or city go shopping?

Speaking Parts 2 and 3

1 Look at this Speaking Part 2 task and think about what you could say. Make some notes.

> Describe an advertisement which you found very persuasive.
>
> You should say:
>   what the advertisement was for
>   where you saw or read it
>   what the advertisement consisted of
> and why you found it so persuasive.

2 🎧 03 Listen to Irina doing the task in Exercise 1. As you listen, take notes on her answer for each of the points.

◉ Pronunciation: *Word stress*

3 Work in pairs. Take turns to do the Speaking task in Exercise 1.

4 Work in pairs.

1 How would you answer the questions below from Part 3?
2 What reasons and examples could you give to support each answer?

Company advertising

- How important do you think it is for companies to advertise their products?
- How do advertisements influence people to buy things?
- How effective is advertising as a way of persuading people to buy things?

The wider implications of advertising

- Apart from advertising, what other factors influence people's decisions to buy things?
- In what ways can advertising be bad or harmful to society?
- Why do you think that some people say advertising is a form of art?

5 (04) Listen to Irina answering the first question in Exercise 4. Note down the reasons and examples she gives for her answer.

6 (04) Listen again. Which of the phrases below does Irina use:

1 to express the same idea again more clearly?
2 to correct something she has said?
3 when she's looking for the correct word?

| I mean | in other words | how do you say |
| what's the word |

7 Work in pairs. Take turns to ask and answer the questions in Exercise 4.

Exam advice *Speaking Parts 2 and 3*

- If you think you haven't expressed yourself clearly, express the idea again using other words.
- If you think you've made a mistake, correct yourself.

Pronunciation
Word stress

With words which have more than one syllable, e.g. *actually*, we stress one syllable more than the others. *Actually* contains three syllables:

• • •
ac tua lly

1 (05) Listen to the first sentence of Irina's answer again. Which syllable is stressed in *actually*?

2 Work in pairs. How many syllables does each of these words have?

1 advertisements 4
2 persuasive
3 energy
4 activity
5 television
6 generally
7 advertising
8 usually
9 product
10 person
11 famous
12 successful
13 university
14 expensive
15 energetic

3 (06) Decide which syllable in each word in Exercise 2 has the main stress. Then listen again to Irina's talk to check your answers.

4 Answer these questions about the words in Exercise 2.

1 What do you notice about *advertisements* and *advertising*, and *energy* and *energetic*?
2 Look at the words again. Which syllable is *not* usually the stressed syllable?

5 Work in pairs. Take turns to practise saying the words in Exercise 2.

Making money, spending money

Writing Task 2

1 Work in pairs. Read this Writing task and make a list of advantages and disadvantages.

> Write about the following topic.
>
> *Buying things on the Internet, such as books, air tickets and groceries, is becoming more and more popular.*
>
> *Do the advantages of shopping in this way outweigh the disadvantages?*
>
> Give reasons for your answer and include any relevant examples from your own knowledge or experience.

2 Divide this sample answer into paragraphs by writing // where you think the writer should start a new paragraph.

> It is becoming increasingly common for people to go online to buy what they need rather than going to a shop or travel agent to do so. Although there are some dangers and disadvantages to internet shopping, I believe that the convenience often outweighs any drawbacks. There are two main dangers and disadvantages to buying things on the Internet. The one that attracts the most publicity is the problem of internet fraud. Unless the website is secure, hackers may be able to copy your credit card details and steal your money. A further disadvantage is that you cannot examine what you are buying until after you have bought it. This means you may sometimes buy something that you do not really want. On the other hand, shopping for certain things on the Internet has several points in its favour. The main one is its convenience. People who want to compare products and prices can look at all this information on a website without having to go from shop to shop. Also, they can make their purchases at any time of day or night and from any part of the world. The other advantage is that because internet companies do not need a shop, the products which they sell are often cheaper. All in all, I think that the advantages of using the Internet for buying things such as books, computers and air tickets are greater than the disadvantages. However, someone that wants to buy clothes should visit shops because they need to see and touch them before buying them, and I would not recommend purchasing them online.

3 Read the sample answer again.

1 Which of the things on your list from Exercise 1 are mentioned in the answer?
2 Would it be possible to include everything on your list in an answer? If not, how do you decide what things to include and what things to leave out?
3 What is the purpose of these two sentences?
There are two main dangers and disadvantages to buying things on the Internet.
On the other hand, shopping for certain things on the Internet has several points in its favour.

▶ Key grammar: *Relative pronouns and relative clauses*

4 <u>Underline</u> any words and phrases in the sample answer which you think might be useful when you do a Writing task.

> *Exam advice*   Writing Task 2
>
> - Each paragraph should cover a different aspect of what you want to say.
> - If you're not sure how to begin a paragraph, start it with a short sentence saying what the paragraph is about.

5 Work in pairs. Look at this Writing task and brainstorm a list of advantages and disadvantages.

> Write about the following topic.
>
> *Some people decide to start their own business instead of working for a company or organisation. Do the advantages for people working for their own business outweigh the disadvantages?*
>
> Give reasons for your answer and include any relevant examples from your own knowledge or experience.

Unit 6

6 Work in pairs. Look at the opening sentences below of paragraphs 2 and 3 of the Writing task.

1 Discuss how you would complete the paragraphs.
2 Working alone, write one of the paragraphs using phrases you underlined in the sample answer in Exercise 2.
3 When you have finished, compare what you have written with your partner.

There are two main advantages to starting your own business instead of being employed by another organisation.

On the other hand, many people prefer not to be self-employed or to start their own company, and they give two reasons for this.

7 Work in pairs. Look at the Writing task below.

1 Brainstorm a list of advantages and disadvantages.
2 Write a plan for your answer.
   • Decide how many paragraphs you will need and what will be the subject of each paragraph.
   • Think of examples and consequences to support your points.
   • Decide what your opinion is and which paragraph(s) you will express it in.

Write about the following topic.

Some suggest that young people should take a job for a few years between school and university.

Discuss what the advantages and disadvantages might be for people who do this.

Give reasons for your answer and include any relevant examples from your own knowledge or experience.

---

8 Write your complete answer to the Writing task in Exercise 7. You should write at least 250 words.

Key grammar
Relative pronouns and relative clauses

1 Look at the highlighted words in the sample answer in Writing Exercise 2. Which word:

1 is used to refer to people? *who*
2 is used to refer to things?
3 is used to refer to both people and things?
4 means *the thing(s) which*?

▶ page 105 *Relative clauses and relative pronouns*

2 IELTS candidates often make mistakes with relative clauses. Correct the mistake in each of these sentences.

1 It is not difficult for young people to spend money on ~~which~~ they want. *what*
2 Internet shopping is not easy in places who do not have good delivery services.
3 People from all walks of life generally like shopping, so shopping is one activity where families can enjoy doing together.
4 The Internet can also be used by people who they are travelling.
5 There has been continuous debate on the advantages and disadvantages of what we can do on the Internet, especially those who are related to buying things and using credit cards.
6 We would like to spend our money on something what makes us happy.

3 Complete these sentences by writing *who*, *which*, *what* or *that* in each gap. In some cases, more than one answer is possible.

1 I like browsing in shops *which/that* sell the latest fashions.
2 Kiri doesn't enjoy shopping because she can never afford .... she likes.
3 There's an excellent boutique on Main Street .... always seems to have .... I'm looking for.
4 People .... pay for their purchases with a credit card often spend more than they should.
5 .... you can buy on this website are things .... you can't find in the shops.

Making money, spending money 65

Vocabulary and grammar review Unit 5

Vocabulary

1 Complete the sentences below with words connected with the environment, then use the words to complete this crossword.

1 Many animals are now protected as a result of wildlife conservation ..*programmes*.. .
2 We need to reduce the quantity of .... gases we release into the atmosphere.
3 Politicians talk a lot about .... change, but don't do enough to prevent it.
4 Rising sea .... may mean that some islands will disappear.
5 I believe it's time to reduce our dependence on .... fuels.
6 Solar power and wind power are two forms of .... energy.
7 The ideal situation would be to drive cars with zero ....
8 Tigers and pandas are .... species.

2 Complete each of these sentences with the correct form of *nature, the environment, the countryside, tourist* or *tourism*.

1 The town I live in is surrounded by beautiful unspoilt *countryside* .
2 Governments should do more to protect .... by limiting pollution, especially in big cities.
3 .... is a big industry in my country, and people come here from all over the world. On the other hand, when our holidays come along, we local people become .... ourselves and go off to visit other parts of the world.
4 I love to go walking in the country; it makes me feel in harmony with .... and the natural world.

Grammar

3 Rewrite the passage below putting the verbs in the underlined phrases into the passive. Make any other necessary changes.

Example: Could asphalt and concrete eventually be replaced by solar panels?

Could solar panels eventually replace asphalt and concrete?

These days, we can find solar panels just about everywhere. People have suggested that if we laid down a gigantic number of solar panels over a wide area, they could absorb enough sunlight to power entire cities, effectively ending our energy crisis. The problem is that they would spoil the countryside if we covered large areas of it with these things.

On the other hand, there is a network of roads all over the country, and now they are even manufacturing cars with solar panels on them. If you put the two together, you get a unique solution: solar panels on our highways. This could mean that we could place the panels along roadways as sound barriers, or an even more extreme idea – that we will make the roads themselves out of solar panels.

adapted from www.science.howstuffworks.com

Vocabulary and grammar review Unit 6

Vocabulary

1 Circle the correct option in each of these sentences.

1 The majority of people choose *(to go)* / *going* shopping in large shopping centres.
2 Many employers will avoid *to employ* / *employing* someone who has never had a job, but they will consider *to offer* / *offering* work to someone with a little work experience.
3 For people who want *to buy* / *buying* clothes, I would recommend them *not to do* / *not doing* so online.
4 Governments should encourage people *to save* / *saving* money rather than spending it.
5 I believe that every young person should consider *to work* / *working* for a year before going to university.
6 Many young people waste a lot of time *to play* / *playing* online games instead of studying.
7 Some students fail *to save* / *saving* enough money, so they are forced *to take out* / *taking* out a loan from the bank.
8 The number of shoppers paying by credit card seems *to be* / *being* rising.

2 Find seven more words and phrases in the grid connected with banks and banking. You can find the words horizontally, vertically and diagonally – and in any direction (forwards and backwards). When you have finished, you can read a hidden message in the first three lines.

I	G	O	O	D	L	U	S	C	E	T	K
N	W	I	T	H	I	A	E	C	L	N	T
T	S	T	Q	I	V	K	N	M	K	U	T
E	M	T	L	I	N	A	L	L	L	O	P
R	R	M	N	N	L	C	F	D	Y	C	L
E	K	G	F	A	Y	L	R	V	R	C	R
S	S	M	B	R	Q	W	R	E	X	A	V
T	V	T	P	T	W	K	Z	Z	D	C	P
R	D	I	R	E	C	T	D	E	B	I	T
A	V	M	R	M	K	N	M	R	R	Y	T
T	G	O	V	E	R	D	R	A	F	T	H
E	D	C	L	B	R	A	N	C	H	J	W

Grammar

3 Complete these sentences with *who*, *which*, *that*, *whose*, *what*, *where*, *when* or *why*. In some cases, more than one answer is possible.

1 I believe ....*that*.... the idea that money makes people happy is only partly true.
2 It is important to understand .... motivates people to work hard.
3 Many banks seem to make large profits and pay low rates of interest, and this is the reason .... they are often unpopular.
4 .... most people dream of is a secure, well-paid job.
5 My parents moved from the town .... I was born to live in the capital when I was nine years old.
6 Parents should only give pocket money to children .... help with the housework.
7 Students' results are better in countries .... teachers are well paid.
8 Young people need the work experience .... will make them attractive to employers.

4 Join these pairs of sentences using *who*, *which*, *that*, *whose*, *what*, *where*, *when* or *why*.

1 School leavers can find jobs. The jobs are badly paid.
   School leavers can find jobs which are badly paid.
2 Some jobs take up too much time. For that reason, students often leave them.
   The reason ...
3 Young people are often in a hurry to go to university. Their parents are ambitious for them.
4 Students often take a part-time job. The job helps pay their university fees.
5 Students work. Students often find this distracts them from their studies.
6 Students often find it difficult to find a job near their college. They study at the college.
7 I got my first job at the age of 18. I left school at the age of 18.
8 I got my first job in a town. My cousin lives in the town.

Unit 7 Relationships

Starting off

Work in pairs. Look at the photos of people in different situations and discuss these questions. You can use the vocabulary in the box to help you express your views.

1 What does their body language suggest about how they feel?
2 What sort of conversation do you think they are having?

> The man/woman is looking …
> annoyed   anxious   bored   concerned   interested
> unhappy   upset
> The man/woman is being …
> argumentative   helpful   irritating   persuasive   reassuring

Listening Section 3

1 Work in small groups. You are going to hear two students talking about a project on human relationships. Before you listen, discuss these questions.

1 How do you think doing projects can help people to learn?
2 Do you enjoy doing project work?

2 <u>Underline</u> the key ideas in Questions 1–5 (but not options A–C).

Questions 1–5

Choose the correct letter, A, B or C.

1 <u>What problem</u> does <u>Fumiko have</u> with her <u>psychology project</u>?
   A She isn't interested in the topic.
   B She can't find enough information.
   C She doesn't know what to focus on.

2 What point does Victor make about Fumiko's tutor?
   A He explores his students' key interests.
   B He is a very hard-working member of staff.
   C He uses a limited range of project titles.

3 What has Fumiko already read on her topic?
   A book extracts
   B journal articles
   C internet material

4 According to Mr Dresden, Fumiko's project must include
   A some graphic data.
   B a bibliography.
   C a public survey.

5 Victor and Fumiko arrange to
   A get in contact in half an hour.
   B meet up in the library.
   C have lunch together.

3 Speakers in IELTS Listening tests often use signals to help candidates know when the answer to a question is coming. Match Questions 1–5 above to these signals (a–e).

a The thing about Mr Dresden is … ☐
b That's the trouble … ☐
c He said that the important thing was … ☐
d Look, tell you what, I'll text you … ☐
e So what reading have you done so far? ☐

Exam advice — Listening Sections 1–4

- Look quickly at the number of tasks and the number of questions in each task.
- Use the signals you hear and the key ideas you <u>underline</u> to help you answer the questions.
- Leave any questions you cannot do; try to answer them when the recording has finished.

4 Quickly read through Questions 6–10 and think about the type of word and type of information that you will need.

Questions 6–10

Complete the flow chart below.

*Write **NO MORE THAN TWO WORDS** for each answer.*

Fumiko's plan

Define **6** .... using a diagram
↓
Background: relationships in the **7** ...., e.g. apes
↓
Present an overview of the **8** .... for human relationships, e.g. work, home
↓
Look at six **9** .... involved in a friendship (plus survey)
↓
Predict the future **10** .... on friendship

5 (07) Now listen and do Questions 1–10.

6 (08) Complete the speaker's signals for each of the answers in Questions 6–10 by writing one word in each gap. Then listen again to check your answers.

6 I think the very .... thing you need to do is …
7 After ...., you could do …
8 'You mean … ?' 'Yes, ... the word.'
9 The .... thing might be to …
10 Why don't I .... by … , or better still, …

7 Work in pairs. Take turns to speak for a minute or two on this topic.

Describe someone who is a really good friend. Say who they are, how you met them and why they are such a good friend.

Relationships 69

Vocabulary
age(s) / aged / age group

1 IELTS candidates often confuse these words: *age(s) / aged / age group*. Read these dictionary extracts. Then circle the correct word in the sentences below from the Listening section.

> **age** a noun that refers to the number of years someone has lived, or that something has existed:
> *The show appeals to people **of all ages**.*
> *She left India **at the age of 12**.*
> *Children **under ten years of age** must be accompanied by an adult.*

> **aged** an adjective that means 'having a particular age or age range':
> *They have one daughter, **aged three**.*
> *The toys are for children **aged four to six**.*

> **age group** a noun that refers to people of a particular age (note that the ages come first):
> *We should provide job training for people **in the 16–24 age group**.*

1 I want to do a survey and interview some people of different (ages)/ age group.
2 Are you going to target a particular *group of age / age group*?
3 Even toddlers *aged / age* 18 months or under have relationships.
4 I could examine the 21–30 *age group / aged group*.
5 It might be good to get some opinions from people over *age / the age* of 60.

2 These sentences each contain a mistake made by IELTS candidates. Correct the underlined mistakes by reorganising, changing or adding words.

1 I met my best friend at ^the age of 16.
2 People <u>ages between</u> 35 and 40 have a wide range of relationships.
3 Many babies <u>10–20 months</u> begin to form strong relationships with siblings.
4 Most of the people I work with are in the 20–35 <u>aged group</u>.
5 Children in the <u>age group 5 to 11</u> tend to change their friends quite frequently.
6 Relationships are very important for the <u>group age</u> 60 and above.

Reading Section 2

1 Work in pairs. How much do you remember about the Reading Test? Say whether these statements are true (T) or false (F). If you think a statement is false, correct it.

1 There are four sections to the Reading paper; each section has 13 questions.
2 You need to understand the whole passage before doing any of the questions.
3 The answers do not have to be spelled correctly.
4 The passages gradually get harder.
5 You get extra time to transfer answers onto the answer sheet.
6 Written answers must be copied exactly from the reading passage.

2 Work in groups. You are going to read an article about lying. Before you read, discuss these questions.

1 What things do people generally lie about?
2 Why do people lie? What advantage do they gain from lying?
3 How can you tell when someone is lying?

3 Now read the passage and answer Questions 1–6 below and Questions 7–13 on page 72.

> **Questions 1–6**
> The reading passage has six paragraphs, **A–F**.
> *Choose the correct heading for each paragraph from the list of headings below.*
>
> **List of Headings**
> i Some of the things liars really do
> ii When do we begin to lie?
> iii How wrong is it to lie?
> iv Exposing some false beliefs
> v Which form of communication best exposes a lie?
> vi Do only humans lie?
> vii Dealing with known liars
> viii A public test of our ability to spot a lie
>
> 1 Paragraph A ....   4 Paragraph D ....
> 2 Paragraph B ....   5 Paragraph E ....
> 3 Paragraph C ....   6 Paragraph F ....

Exam advice   Reading Sections 1–3

- If there are any questions you can't do, make a note of possible answers and come back to them later.
- Make sure you leave time to do the other questions.

Unit 7

THE TRUTH ABOUT LYING
by Dan Roberts

Over the years Richard Wiseman has tried to unravel the truth about deception – investigating the signs that give away a liar.

A In the 1970s, as part of a large-scale research programme exploring the area of interspecies communication, Dr Francine Patterson from Stanford University attempted to teach two lowland gorillas called Michael and Koko a simplified version of Sign Language. According to Patterson, the great apes were capable of holding meaningful conversations, and could even reflect upon profound topics, such as love and death. During the project, their trainers believe they uncovered instances where the two gorillas' linguistic skills seemed to provide reliable evidence of intentional deceit. In one example, Koko broke a toy cat, and then signed to indicate that the breakage had been caused by one of her trainers. In another episode, Michael ripped a jacket belonging to a trainer and, when asked who was responsible for the incident, signed 'Koko'. When the trainer expressed some scepticism, Michael appeared to change his mind, and indicated that Dr Patterson was actually responsible, before finally confessing.

B Other researchers have explored the development of deception in children. Some of the most interesting experiments have involved asking youngsters not to take a peek at their favourite toys. During these studies, a child is led into a laboratory and asked to face one of the walls. The experimenter then explains that he is going to set up an elaborate toy a few feet behind them. After setting up the toy, the experimenter says that he has to leave the laboratory, and asks the child not to turn around and peek at the toy. The child is secretly filmed by hidden cameras for a few minutes, and then the experimenter returns and asks them whether they peeked. Almost all three-year-olds do, and then half of them lie about it to the experimenter. By the time the children have reached the age of five, all of them peek and all of them lie. The results provide compelling evidence that lying starts to emerge the moment we learn to speak.

C So what are the tell-tale signs that give away a lie? In 1994, the psychologist Richard Wiseman devised a large-scale experiment on a TV programme called *Tomorrow's World*. As part of the experiment, viewers watched two interviews in which Wiseman asked a presenter in front of the cameras to describe his favourite film. In one interview, the presenter picked *Some Like It Hot* and he told the truth; in the other interview, he picked *Gone with the Wind* and lied. The viewers were then invited to make a choice – to telephone in to say which film he was lying about. More than 30,000 calls were received, but viewers were unable to tell the difference and the vote was a 50/50 split. In similar experiments, the results have been remarkably consistent – when it comes to lie detection, people might as well simply toss a coin. It doesn't matter if you are male or female, young or old; very few people are able to detect deception.

D Why is this? Professor Charles Bond from the Texas Christian University has conducted surveys into the sorts of behaviour people associate with lying. He has interviewed thousands of people from more than 60 countries, asking them to describe how they set about telling whether someone is lying. People's answers are remarkably consistent. Almost everyone thinks liars tend to avert their gaze, nervously wave their hands around and shift about in their seats. There is, however, one small problem. Researchers have spent hour upon hour carefully comparing films of liars and truth-tellers. The results are clear. Liars do not necessarily look away from you; they do not appear nervous and move their hands around or shift about in their seats. People fail to detect lies because they are basing their opinions on behaviours that are not actually associated with deception.

E So what are we missing? It is obvious that the more information you give away, the greater the chances of some of it coming back to haunt you. As a result, liars tend to say less and provide fewer details than truth-tellers. Looking back at the transcripts of the interviews with the presenter, his lie about *Gone with the Wind* contained about 40 words, whereas the truth about *Some Like It Hot* was nearly twice as long. People who lie also try psychologically to keep a distance from their falsehoods, and so tend to include fewer references to themselves in their stories. In his entire interview about *Gone with the Wind*, the presenter only once mentioned how the film made him feel, compared with the several references to his feelings when he talked about *Some Like It Hot*.

F The simple fact is that the real clues to deceit are in the words that people use, not the body language. So do people become better lie detectors when they listen to a liar, or even just read a transcript of their comments? The interviews with the presenter were also broadcast on radio and published in a newspaper, and although the lie-detecting abilities of the television viewers were no better than chance, the newspaper readers were correct 64% of the time, and the radio listeners scored an impressive 73% accuracy rate.

adapted from *The National Newspaper*

Questions 7–10

Look at the following statements and the list of experiments below.

Match each statement with the correct experiment, **A–C**.

You may use any letter more than once.

7 Someone who was innocent was blamed for something.
8 Those involved knew they were being filmed.
9 Some objects were damaged.
10 Some instructions were ignored.

List of Experiments
A the gorilla experiment
B the experiment with children
C the TV experiment

Exam advice **Matching features**

- Sometimes there are more questions than options, so you will need to use some of the options more than once.
- Quickly locate and underline the options.
- Read what the passage says about each option carefully and match each question to one option.

Questions 11–13

Complete the sentences below.

Choose **ONE WORD ONLY** from the passage for each answer.

11 Filming liars has shown that they do not display .... behaviour.
12 Liars tend to avoid talking about their own ....
13 Signs of lying are exposed in people's .... rather than their movements.

Exam advice **Sentence completion**

- Copy the words you need exactly.
- Don't use too many words.
- Check that the completed sentence is grammatically correct.

❹ IELTS candidates often make mistakes when doing completion tasks. Here are some wrong answers to Questions 11–13. Why were they marked wrong? There may be more than one reason.

Q	answer	reason it was marked wrong
11	body language	*two words / a noun / wrong answer*
11	nervously	
12	their feelings	
12	themsleves	
12	feeling	
13	real clues	
13	use	

❺ Discuss these questions.

1 How do you feel when someone lies to you?
2 Are all lies equally wrong/bad, or is lying sometimes justified?

Speaking Part 1

❶ Work in pairs. How much do you remember about Speaking Part 1? Complete the sentences below with a word from the box.

| familiar | ~~five~~ | question | three | vocabulary | word |

1 It can last up to ...*five*... minutes.
2 The questions are about .... topics.
3 You should aim to answer in two or .... sentences.
4 It is important to use some topic-related ....
5 The examiner can explain a .... that you don't understand.
6 Each .... is based on a theme, e.g. shopping.

❷ (09) Work in pairs. It can be useful to begin a Part 1 answer with an opening phrase, or 'opener'. Listen to two people talking about the same topic and answer these questions.

1 How do the speakers begin their answers?
2 Which speaker produces a better answer? Why?
3 How does the opener help the better speaker?

3 Work in pairs. Match each of these 'openers' (1–5) with their function (a–e).

1 That's an interesting question. *d*
2 Let me see … it's hard to remember …
3 I'm sorry, could you repeat the question?
4 It depends on what you mean by … If you mean …, then …
5 Generally speaking, I …

a needs some thinking time
b can interpret the question in different ways
c wants to talk about what usually happens or what he/she usually does/feels
d likes the question or is amused by it
e hasn't fully understood the question

4 Look at these Part 1 questions. Which one(s) can you answer quickly without needing an opener? Which 'openers' from Exercise 3 could you use with the other questions?

1 Do you come from a large or small family?
2 When did you last visit relatives?
3 What don't you like about visiting relatives?
4 Who in your family has been most successful?
5 Do you think you're similar to this person?

▶ page 74 Pronunciation: *Sentence stress 3*

5 Listen to Dominic answering the questions in Exercise 4. Which 'openers' does he use?

6 Work in pairs. Take turns to ask and answer these questions on friendship using openers.

1 Are friends important to you? Why? / Why not?
2 How often do you go out with friends?
3 How do you communicate with friends?
4 What makes someone a special friend?
5 Did you have a lot of friends when you were a child?

7 Listen again to Dominic.

1 Which of these words does Dominic not know?
   a park   c suburbs
   b underground d countryside
2 Dominic uses other language to express the word that he doesn't know (X). Which two of these paraphrasing strategies does he use?
   a state what X is not
   b explain what X is made of
   c describe what X looks like
   d use words that have a similar meaning to X
   e explain how X makes you feel
   f describe what X is used for or does
   g give a definition of X

8 Listen to some students paraphrasing words they have forgotten or do not know and answer these questions.

1 Which picture shows what each student is paraphrasing?
2 Which strategy/strategies from Exercise 7 does each student use to paraphrase?

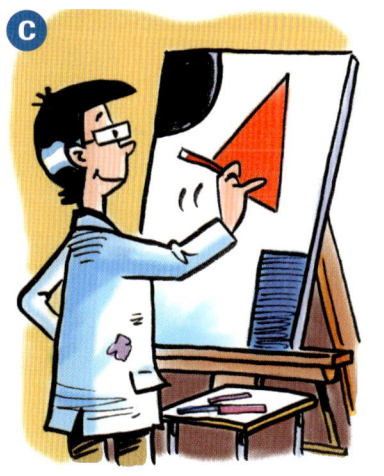

A

B

C

D

9 Work in pairs. Take turns to interview each other using the questions in Exercise 4.

Exam advice Speaking Part 1

- Use openers to avoid hesitation and repetition.
- Paraphrase when you can't think of the word(s).
- Use stress to emphasise points or make a contrast.
- If you don't understand a question, ask the examiner to repeat it.

Relationships 73

Pronunciation
Sentence stress 3

Speakers use stress to emphasise a point they are making and show that it is important or that they feel strongly about it. They also use stress to make a contrast and show how points differ.

1 🎧12 **Listen to these two sentences from Dominic's interview and <u>underline</u> the stressed words in each.**

1 When I was younger, I hated going to see them – yeah – I thought it was so boring.
2 My sister's very hard-working. She knows what she wants, whereas I'm still trying to make some decisions about that.

In which sentence (1 or 2) does Dominic use stress to emphasise how strongly he felt? In which sentence does he use stress to make a contrast?

2 🎧13 **Look at these extracts from another student's interview. <u>Underline</u> the words you would stress for emphasis and the words you would express for contrast. Then listen and check your answers.**

1 Being an only child has its advantages – I mean, I get all my parents' attention.
2 Before I left home and came here to study, I used to visit my grandparents about twice a week, but now it's much more difficult.
3 My gran, who lives on her own, is always so pleased to see me.
4 Both my parents are architects, but my mum gets more work than my dad!

3 Think about how you could answer these questions. Write down some ideas you could emphasise and some you could contrast.

Example: 1 Well, I remember my <u>family's</u> birthdays, but often forget my <u>friends'</u> birthdays.

1 How good are you at remembering other people's birthdays?
2 Do you arrive on time when you arrange to meet someone? Why? / Why not?
3 How do you feel if someone is late meeting you?
4 When was the last time you forgot something important?
5 What do you do if you need to remember something?

4 Work in small groups and take turns to ask and answer the questions in Exercise 3.

Writing Task 1

1 Work in pairs. How much do you remember about Writing Task 1? Choose the correct option to complete each of these sentences.

1 You should allow *20 / 25* minutes to write your answer.
2 There will *always / not always* be a chart to summarise.
3 You *should / should not* copy the headings.
4 You *should / should not* include data in your answer.
5 You *should / should not* give your opinion on the diagrams.
6 You should use *your own words / words from the question paper* as far as possible.
7 If you have a diagram question, you *need / do not need* to write an overview.

2 Work in pairs. Look at the task below.

1 How are the graph and the chart linked? What features do they have in common?
2 What trends does the graph show?
3 What trends does the chart show?
4 What overall conclusions can you draw from each one?
5 Which would you describe first?

The graph below and the chart on the next page show the answers people gave about the extent to which they are satisfied with their lives and what they think would make them happiest.

Summarise the information by selecting and reporting the main features, and make comparisons where relevant.

How satisfied are you with your life?

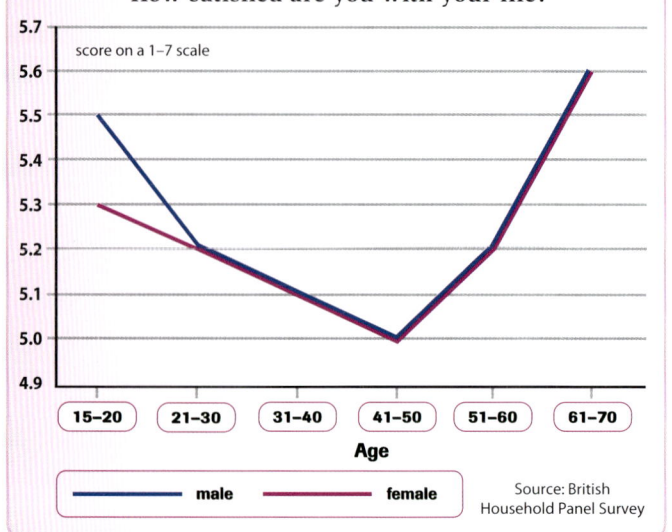

score on a 1–7 scale

Age: 15–20, 21–30, 31–40, 41–50, 51–60, 61–70

— male — female

Source: British Household Panel Survey

Unit 7

What would make you happiest?

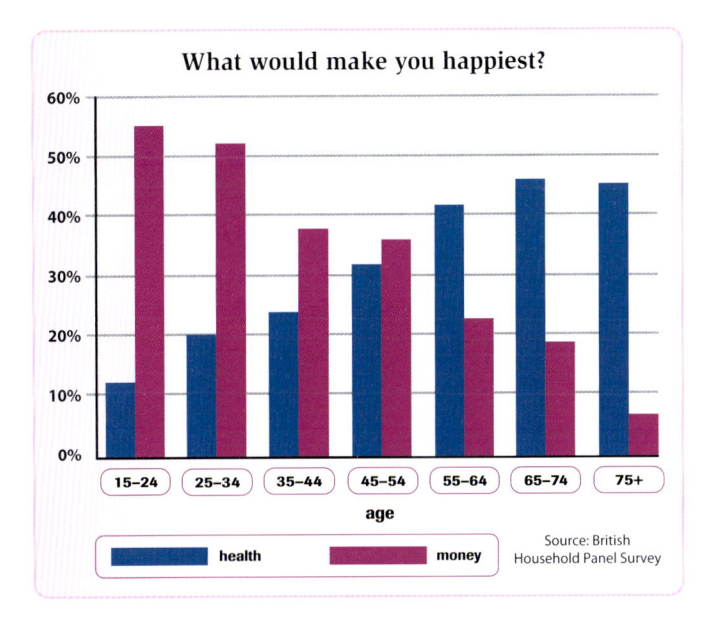

(Bar chart showing percentages across age groups 15–24, 25–34, 35–44, 45–54, 55–64, 65–74, 75+ for health and money. Source: British Household Panel Survey)

3 Read these three introductory paragraphs and answer the questions below.

a The graph and chart provide information about general feelings of happiness in life. The graph compares people's levels of life satisfaction at different ages. The chart looks at factors that people think might make them happy and compares these across age groups.

b There are two graphs about people's average life satisfaction and what might make them happiest. They clearly show that men and women are the same. However, different things make them happy.

c The graph is about satisfaction with life. It shows the data across different age groups. The chart is about people and happiness. It shows the data in percentages.

Which introduction(s):
1 begin with a general introductory statement?
2 provide a brief description of the content of each chart/graph?
3 are written as far as possible in the student's own words?

4 Work in pairs. Read the second paragraph of a student's answer to the task in Exercise 2 (ignore the underlined words for now). Is the student summarising the chart or graph? Circle the parts of the chart/graph which the sentences describe.

The trend in life satisfaction is similar for men and women. However, **1** <u>it</u> differs slightly during the teenage years, when men's score is 5.5, while women's is 5.3. So between the ages of 15 and 20, women are less satisfied with **2** <u>their</u> lives. After **3** <u>this</u> period, scores fall gradually to **4** <u>their</u> lowest point of 5.0 for everyone aged 41–50. **5** <u>They</u> then rise significantly to a peak of around 5.6 for those in the 61–70 age group.

5 Read the paragraph in Exercise 4 again and say what each of the underlined words (1–5) refers back to.

▶ page 106 *Reference devices*

▶ page 76 *Key grammar: Zero, first and second conditionals*

6 Complete the third and final paragraphs below with the words in the box. You will need to use some of them more than once. Then say what each pronoun refers back to.

| it | one | their | ~~them~~ | these | they | this |

Although 55% of the youngest age group say that money would make **1** *them* happiest, **2** .... figure falls as people get older, and by the age of 75, **3** .... is relatively low. On the other hand, only 12% of the 15–24 age group worry about **4** .... health, but it becomes a key concern as **5** .... get older. So the trends for **6** .... two features cross in middle age and **7** .... is the opposite of the other.

Overall, it seems that people are most satisfied at the start and end of **8** .... lives. For young people, happiness comes from money, while for older people **9** .... is linked to health.

Exam advice   Chart/graph summary
- If you have more than one chart or graph, look at the similarities and differences between them and pick out the key features.
- Introduce both charts/graphs, then compare the information within them.
- Use some referencing to avoid repetition.

7 Work in pairs. Look at this task and discuss the questions in Exercise 2.

The charts below show the results of a survey on happiness ratings for married and unmarried people in the US, and the effect of children on the overall ratings of married couples.

Summarise the information by selecting and reporting the main features, and make comparisons where relevant.

Happiness ratings: married and unmarried people

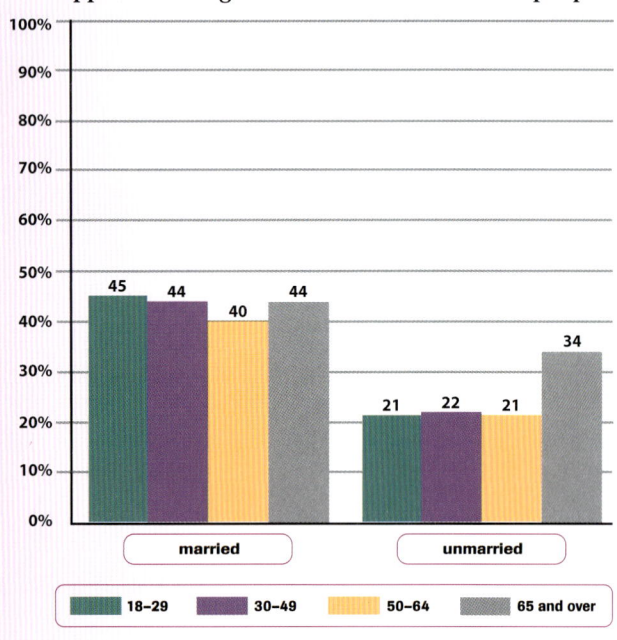

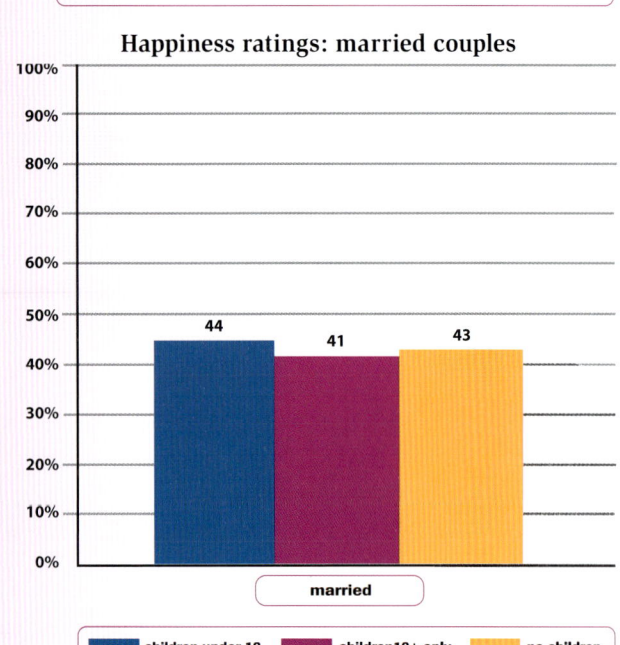

married: 18–29: 45, 30–49: 44, 50–64: 40, 65 and over: 44
unmarried: 18–29: 21, 30–49: 22, 50–64: 21, 65 and over: 34

Happiness ratings: married couples

married: children under 18: 44, children 18+ only: 41, no children: 43

8 Write your answer to the task in Exercise 7. You should write at least 150 words.

Key grammar
Zero, first and second conditionals

1 Work in pairs. Look at these extracts (1–3) from Dominic's answers to Speaking Exercise 5. Which answer refers to something that:

a always happens?
b will probably happen?
c is not likely to happen?

1 I'd do well if I worked harder.
2 If I don't go out this evening, for example, I'll eat dinner and chat with her.
3 We meet up in the city if there's a birthday or something …

2 What tenses are used in each sentence in Exercise 1?

▶ page 106 *Zero, first and second conditionals*

3 Complete these sentences by writing the correct form of the verb in brackets.

1 My father's very decisive – if he says he's going to do something, he *means* (mean) it.
2 If Jayne told the truth more often, people .... (like) her better.
3 If I .... (be) rich, I'd give a lot of money to charity.
4 You'll find it hard to write a good essay if you .... (not plan) it first.
5 If I take 50 driving lessons, I still .... (not pass) my test.
6 If politicians .... (stop) talking, they might learn something!
7 Where would you live if you .... (have) the choice?
8 If I keep quiet about the mistake, no one .... (find out).

4 ☉ IELTS candidates often make mistakes using conditional sentences. Correct the underlined errors in these sentences.

1 Globalisation can only happen if people <u>will all think</u> the same way. *all think*
2 If people <u>would agree</u> with each other all the time, the world would be a boring place.
3 Some youngsters think that <u>if they leave</u> home, they <u>would</u> be unhappy.
4 Some people will not smile if they <u>did not</u> want to.
5 People have more friends if they <u>were</u> rich.
6 If you only think about yourself, you <u>never understood</u> other people.

76 Unit 7

Unit 8 Fashion and design

Starting off

1 Work in pairs. Look at these photos of people wearing different clothes and briefly describe what they are wearing.

- How are their clothes suitable for what they are doing?
- Where do you think these photographs were taken?

2 Now discuss these questions.

1. What dress is traditional in your country? When do people wear it?
2. Do you think it is important for a country to have traditional clothes? Why?

Reading Section 3

1 Work in pairs. You are going to read an article about a project to restore a dress. Before you read, look at the painting in the article on page 78.

1. How old do you think the painting is?
2. What do you think the person in the painting is doing?
3. Why might some old clothes become valuable items?

2 Read the subheading to find out what the article is about. Then read the article quickly to find three reasons why the dress is being restored.

Fashion and design 77

An astonishingly intricate project is being undertaken to restore a legendary theatrical dress, Angela Wintle explains.

On December 28th, 1888, the curtain rose on a daring new stage revival of Shakespeare's *Macbeth* at the Lyceum Theatre in London. Topping the bill, playing Lady Macbeth, a main character in the play, was Ellen Terry. She was the greatest and most adored English actress of the age. But she didn't achieve this devotion through her acting ability alone. She knew the power of presentation and carefully cultivated her image. That first night was no exception. When she walked on stage for the famous banqueting scene, her appearance drew a collective gasp from the audience.

She was dressed in the most extraordinary clothes ever to have graced a British stage: a long, emerald and sea-green gown with tapering sleeves, surmounted by a velvet cloak, which glistened and sparkled eerily in the limelight. Yet this was no mere stage trickery. The effect had been achieved using hundreds of wings from beetles. The gown — later named the 'Beetlewing dress' — became one of the most iconic and celebrated costumes of the age.

Terry was every bit as remarkable as her costumes. At 31, she became a leading lady at the Lyceum Theatre and for two decades, she set about bringing culture to the masses. The productions she worked on were extravagant and daring. Shakespeare's plays were staged alongside blood-and-thunder melodramas and their texts were ruthlessly cut. Some people were critical, but they missed the point. The innovations sold tickets and brought new audiences to see masterpieces that they would never otherwise have seen.

However, it was a painter who immortalised her. John Singer Sargent had been so struck by Terry's appearance at that first performance that he asked her to model for him, and his famous portrait of 1889, now at the Tate Gallery in London, showed her with a glint in her eye, holding a crown over her flame-red hair. But while the painting remains almost as fresh as the day it was painted, the years have not been so kind to the dress. Its delicate structure, combined with the cumulative effects of time, has meant it is now in an extremely fragile condition. Thus, two years ago, a fundraising project was launched by Britain's National Trust[1] to pay for its conservation.

It turned to textile conservator Zenzie Tinker to do the job. Zenzie loves historical dress because of the link with the past. 'Working on costumes like the Beetlewing dress gives you a real sense of the people who wore them; you can see the sweat stains and wear marks. But it's quite unusual to know who actually wore a garment. That's the thing that makes the Beetlewing project so special.'

Before any of Zenzie's conservation work can begin, she and her team will conduct a thorough investigation to help determine what changes have been made to the dress and when. This will involve close examination of the dress for signs of damage and wear, and will be aided by comparing it with John Singer Sargent's painting and contemporary photographs. Then Zenzie and the National Trust will decide how far back to take the reconstruction, as some members feel that even the most recent changes are now part of the history of the dress.

The first stages in the actual restoration will involve delicate surface cleaning, using a small vacuum suction device. Once the level of reconstruction has been determined, the original crocheted[2] overdress will be stitched onto a dyed net support before repairs begin. 'It's going to be extraordinarily difficult, because the original cloth is quite stretchy, so we've deliberately chosen net because that has a certain amount of flexibility in it too,' says Zenzie. 'When the dress is displayed, none of our work will be noticeable, but we'll retain all the evidence on the reverse so that future experts will be able to see exactly what we've done — and I'll produce a detailed report.'

Zenzie has estimated that the project, costing about £30,000, will require more than 700 hours' work. 'It will be a huge undertaking and I don't think the Trust has ever spent quite as much on a costume before,' she says. 'But this dress is unique. It's very unusual to see this level of workmanship on a theatrical costume, and it must have looked spectacular on stage.' If Terry was alive today, there's no doubt she would be delighted. Unlike many other actresses, she valued her costumes because she kept and reused them time and time again. 'I'd like to think she'd see our contribution as part of the ongoing history of the dress,' says Zenzie.

[1] A conservation organisation whose work includes the funding of projects designed to protect and preserve Britain's cultural heritage

[2] Produced using wool and a special needle with a hook at the end

adapted from *Sussex Life* magazine

a beetle

❸ Answer Questions 1–10 below.

Questions 1–6

Choose the correct letter, A, B, C or D.

1 What do you learn about Ellen Terry in the first paragraph?
   A Lady Macbeth was her first leading role.
   B The Lyceum was her favourite theatre.
   C She tried hard to look good on stage.
   D She wanted to look young for her audience.

2 What is the writer's purpose in paragraph 2?
   A to describe different responses to the Beetlewing dress
   B to explain why the Beetlewing dress had such a big impact
   C to consider the suitability of the Beetlewing dress for the play
   D to compare the look of the Beetlewing dress on and off the stage

3 According to the writer, the main effect of the Lyceum productions was to
   A expose more people to Shakespeare's plays.
   B reduce the interest in other types of production.
   C raise the cost of going to the theatre.
   D encourage writers to produce more plays.

4 In the fourth paragraph, what comparison does the writer make between Sargent's portrait and the Beetlewing dress?
   A The dress has attracted more attention than the painting.
   B The dress is worth more money than the painting.
   C The painting took longer to produce.
   D The painting looks newer.

5 Zenzie says the Beetlewing project is particularly special because
   A the dress is very old.
   B people know who wore the dress.
   C the dress was designed by someone famous.
   D there is evidence that the dress has been used.

6 Which of the following is the most suitable title for the passage?
   A A lesson from the past
   B A challenging task
   C An unusual fashion show
   D An unexpected discovery

Exam advice   **Multiple choice**

- Find the option which expresses the same idea; don't just match words.
- If you have a question on the title of the passage, read the subheading again, then skim each paragraph quickly to check the overall theme.

Questions 7–10

Do the following statements agree with the views of the writer in the reading passage?

Write

YES   if the statement agrees with the views of the writer

NO   if the statement contradicts the views of the writer

NOT GIVEN   if it is impossible to say what the writer thinks about this

7 The National Trust conducted useful research to assist Zenzie's plans for the dress.
8 There will be some discussion over the changes that Zenzie's team should make to the dress.
9 Zenzie's estimate for the timing of the project is realistic.
10 Ellen Terry's attitude towards her dresses was typical of her time.

Exam advice   **Yes / No / Not Given**

- Remember that the ideas in the passage may be worded differently in the questions.
- Once you have found the right place in the passage, read it carefully before you decide on the answer.
- Make sure your choice reflects the writer's opinion or claim.

❹ Look at Questions 11–14 on page 80. Underline the key ideas in the questions and the box of endings.

❺ Use key words in Questions 11–14 to find the relevant sentences in the passage. Read these carefully and match each question to the correct ending.

Fashion and design 79

Questions 11–14

Complete each sentence with the correct ending, A–F, below.

11 Pictures will be used
12 A special machine will be used
13 A net material has been selected
14 Work will be visible on one side

A to show how the team did the repairs on the dress.
B to reduce the time taken to repair the dress.
C to remove the dirt from the top layer of the dress.
D to demonstrate the quality of the team's work on the dress.
E to match a quality of the original fabric used in the dress.
F to help show where the dress needs repair work.

Exam advice **Matching sentence endings**

- Underline the key words in the questions and use these to find the right place in the passage. (You will find them in the same order.)
- Read the completed sentences to check they make sense.

Vocabulary

dress (uncountable) / *dress(es)* (countable) / *clothes* / *cloth*

❶ **IELTS candidates often confuse these words: *dress* / *dresses* / *clothes* / *cloth*. Circle the correct word in each of these two sentences from the Reading passage. Then check your answers by reading the definitions below.**

1 She was dressed in the most extraordinary *cloth* / *clothes* ever to have graced a British stage.
2 Zenzie loves historical *dress* / *dresses* because of the link with the past.

cloth (n) [U] material that can be used to make clothes and furnishings:
*The **cloth** used to make this dress was very expensive.*

clothes (n) [plural] Items that are worn, such as skirt, trousers, socks, etc. *Clothes* is always plural:
*I packed my **clothes** in the suitcase.*
*I need some new **clothes**.*

dress (n) [C] an item of clothing worn by women
dress (n) [U] a style of clothing, e.g. *formal dress, traditional dress*, etc.

❷ ⊙ **Four of these sentences contain mistakes made by IELTS candidates; one is correct. Find and correct the mistakes.**

1 Young men and women tend to wear similar ~~dresses~~. *clothes*
2 People need shelter, cloth to wear and food to eat.
3 Famous people attract thousands of fans, who imitate their style of dresses.
4 People who travel may adopt the culture, dresses and customs of another country.
5 Indian saris are usually made using very colourful cloth.

❸ **Work in pairs. Take turns to ask and answer these questions.**

1 How important is fashion to you?
2 When did you last buy some new clothes?
3 Have you ever had your clothes made for you?
4 What's the oldest item of clothing that you own?

Listening Section 4

❶ **Work in pairs. How much do you remember about the Listening Test? Complete the sentences below with the words in the box.**

| answers | break | correct | ~~once~~ | one |
| questions | ten | ten | | |

1 You hear the script *once*.
2 You have time to read the .... before the start of each section.
3 There is no .... in Section 4.
4 There are .... questions in every section.
5 There is .... mark per question.
6 You will hear the .... in the same order as the questions.
7 Spellings must be ....
8 At the end of the test, you get .... minutes to complete the answer sheet.

80 Unit 8

2 Work in pairs. You are going to hear someone giving a lecture on a traditional Japanese form of stitching called *sashiko*. Before you listen, work in pairs and take turns to describe the items below.

1 What are they? What features do they have in common?
2 Who do you think made them and why?
3 Where would you expect to see them?

3 Work in pairs. <u>Underline</u> the words or phrases in Questions 1–10 below that have a similar area of meaning to these words from the script.

1 translates as
2 origins
3 material/cloth
4 stitch together
5 patterns
6 dressed (in)
7 skill
8 no longer necessary
9 nowadays
10 ancient garments

4 🎧 Listen and answer Questions 1–10.

Questions 1–10

Complete the sentences below.

Write NO MORE THAN TWO WORDS *for each answer.*

1 The word *sashiko* <u>means</u> '……………'.
2 In the beginning, *sashiko* was …………… rather than decorative.
3 In the past, warm fabrics such as …………… were not available in some parts of Japan.
4 Warm clothes were produced by using *sashiko* to join …………… of material.
5 Traditional *sashiko* designs included one called '……………'.
6 In the towns of ancient Japan, workers such as …………… wore *sashiko* garments.
7 It used to be essential for someone married to a …………… to know how to do *sashiko*.
8 *Sashiko* was not needed when …………… began in northern Japan.
9 Modern *sashiko* patterns include stripes and …………… shapes.
10 Unfortunately, …………… are not as interested in old clothes as in other ancient craft objects.

Exam advice — Sentence completion

- The words in the questions will not always be exactly the same as what you hear; listen for the same meaning.
- You will hear the exact word(s) you need to complete the sentences.
- Read the completed sentences to check they make sense.

5 Work in small groups.

1 Why is it important to preserve old things from the past?
2 What ancient things are kept in museums in your culture?

Exam information

The words used in Listening questions are often synonyms or paraphrases of words used in the script.

Fashion and design

Speaking Parts 2 and 3

1 Work in pairs. How much do you remember about Speaking Parts 2 and 3? Say whether these statements are true (T) or false (F). If you think a statement is false, correct it.

Part 2

1 I can use my notes and the topic card during my talk. T
2 There is a choice of topics.
3 I need to talk about the points in order.
4 It is a good idea to prepare a talk beforehand.
5 I can talk about myself.
6 I don't need to speak for the full two minutes.

Part 3

7 The questions are similar to Part 1.
8 Part 3 is longer than Part 1.
9 The questions gradually get more challenging.
10 I can ask the examiner to rephrase the question.

2 Work in pairs. Look at this topic and discuss what you could say, making notes as you speak. Then change partners and take turns to give your talks.

> Describe a museum or exhibition that you particularly enjoyed visiting.
>
> You should say:
>   where the museum or exhibition is/was
>   who you went with
>   what you saw there
> and explain why you enjoyed visiting this museum or exhibition.

3 Work in pairs. Read the questions below and decide which one(s) invite you to:

  a make comparisons.
  b provide a number of advantages.
  c support an opinion with reasons.

Then discuss how you could answer each of them.

> **Museums and education**
>
> 1 What benefits can schoolchildren gain from visiting museums?
> 2 How do you think most children feel about visiting a museum?
> 3 Are museums more educational now than they were when your parents were young?

4 (15) (16) (17) Listen to David and Lin answering the questions from Exercise 3 and put a tick (✓) or cross (✗) beside the appropriate points for each question below.

Who:		David	Lin
question 1	a presents benefits?		✓
	b explains benefits?		
	c keeps strictly to the question?	✗	
	d structures their answer clearly?		
question 2	a presents a view?		
	b gives reasons?		
	c uses general, not personal, arguments?		
	d structures their answer clearly?		
question 3	a makes comparisons?		
	b supports points?		
	c covers past and present?		
	d structures their answer clearly?		

5 Who do you think gives the best answer to each question: David or Lin? Why?

▶ Pronunciation: *Linking and pausing*

6 Work in pairs. Take turns to ask and answer the questions from Exercise 3 yourselves. Give your partner feedback using the checklist in Exercise 4.

7 Work in pairs. Take turns to ask and answer these questions.

> **Fashion and history**
>
> • Why do many people like to wear fashionable clothes?
> • How do fashions vary for different age groups?
> • What factors cause adult fashions to change?

Exam advice Speaking Part 3

• Listen carefully to the question: you may have to compare / explain / list points / give an argument, etc.
• Make sure your answer is clear, relevant and well developed.
• Try to use a range of vocabulary and sentence types.

Pronunciation
Linking and pausing

Speakers tend to link certain words together and pause between others. This gives their speech a characteristic rhythm and flow, and helps the listener follow what they say.

1 🎧 **Listen to this extract from one of David's answers in Speaking Exercise 4 and answer the question below.**

> Museums are sometimes a bit expensive, but if the school pays, it's OK and there's such a lot to see.

Where does he tend to link words?
a   Between words which end with a vowel and begin with a consonant
b   Between words which end with a consonant and begin with a vowel

2 **Work in pairs. Look at part of Lin's answer to Questions 1 and 3 in Speaking Exercise 3.**

1   Which words would you link when speaking? Underline them.
2   Where would you pause when speaking? Put / between the words.

1
> First of all, they can experience things directly … you know, they're not in the classroom any more, they're in a different environment.

3
> I don't think there's any doubt that museums are much better at educating children now … In the past, I think museums had a different function, um they were just places to keep ancient objects like coins or pots, but now they're … well, there are many interactive displays.

3 🎧 **Listen and check your answers to Exercise 2. When you have finished, take turns to read Lin's answers aloud.**

Writing Task 2

1 **Work in pairs. How much do you remember about Writing Task 2? Choose the correct options in each of these sentences.**

1   You should allow *30 / 40* minutes to write your answer.
2   You get *twice as many marks as / the same marks as* Task 1 for this answer.
3   If you write fewer than 250 words, *you will lose marks / it doesn't matter*.
4   You *must / needn't* give your own opinion.
5   You *should try to / needn't* express opinions the examiner will agree with.
6   Paragraphing *is / is not* important.
7   It is better to *keep your language simple but correct / try to use complex language and risk making mistakes*.

2 **Work in pairs. Underline the two opinions you have to deal with in this task.**

> Write about the following topic.
>
> *Some people argue that fashion items cost too much money. Others say that this is acceptable because fashion is an important part of life.*
>
> *Discuss both these views and give your own opinion.*
>
> Give reasons for your answer and include any relevant examples from your own knowledge or experience.

3 **Work in small groups. Discuss how these people might feel about the opinions in Exercise 2.**

1   a celebrity   4   a parent
2   a teenager   5   a fashion designer
3   a young adult   6   an elderly person

Fashion and design   83

4 Read the sample answer below and find two sentences that introduce the opinions expressed in the task. Then <u>underline</u> the sentences that express the writer's own opinion.

> Throughout history, people have always been interested in fashion. When you read magazines these days, you see many advertisements for the latest fashions, and some of these are very expensive. So, is this a good thing?
>
> Some people say that prices should be lower in shops, and I can understand their point of view. Before youngsters start work, they depend on their parents for money. Although many parents are not wealthy, they are often pressurised into buying things like designer jeans for their children. After they have started earning money, young adults can still find it hard to afford fashionable clothes because they are saving up for other items.
>
> However, there are other people who say they are happy to pay for designer clothes. Teenagers look forward to doing this when they have their own income. Celebrities have plenty of money, so they might say that they do not worry about how much clothes cost. They know they need to look after their image while they are famous. Surely fashion designers would also argue that the cost is fine. According to people in the fashion business, you cannot criticise until you have seen how hard it is to be original and set new trends.
>
> Personally, I think the question depends on how important fashion is to you. If you are not interested in fashion, you needn't spend a lot of money because these days there are many clothes shops around. On the other hand, if you like to look good, you have to buy fewer clothes and pay more money for them.

5 Work in pairs. Write these phrases introducing opinions in the correct column of the table below.

> Other people disagree.   X may argue that …
> According to X, …   In X's opinion, …
> Personally, I agree.

A suggesting what might be someone else's view	B giving a clear opinion of your own	C introducing an opposing argument	D giving someone else's view
			in X's opinion

6 Find six other phrases in the sample answer in Exercise 4 which introduce opinions, and write them in the correct column in the table in Exercise 5.

7 The sample answer in Exercise 4 is missing a concluding paragraph. Which of these items would be appropriate for this part of the essay?

1 a statement expressing your personal opinion
2 a repetition of the argument in paragraph 2
3 a reference to the views of people not mentioned previously in the essay
4 a summary of the views discussed in the essay
5 a quote
6 a new argument about the subject
7 a logical link to the previous paragraph

8 Which items 1–7 from Exercise 7 can you find in this concluding paragraph?

> Although clothes have become quite expensive, I think there is enough choice these days for everyone. Parents just have to be strict with children about what they can afford, and people have to buy within their budget.

▶ Key grammar: *Time conjunctions:* until/before/when/after

9 Work in small groups. Look at this Writing task. Write a list of people or organisations who would have opinions on each side of the issue, then write a plan for your answer.

> Write about the following topic.
>
> *Some organisations believe that their employees should dress smartly. Others value quality of work above appearance.*
>
> *Discuss both these views and give your own opinion.*
>
> Give reasons for your answer and include any relevant examples from your own knowledge or experience.

Unit 8

10 Write an answer to the task in Exercise 9. You should write at least 250 words.

Exam advice **Writing Task 2**
- Check how many opinions you should write about.
- Consider who might have the opinions and express them using your own words.
- Make your own opinion clear, too.
- Summarise your points and draw a conclusion.

Key grammar
Time conjunctions: *until/before/when/after*

1 Complete these sentences by writing a conjunction (*until*, *before*, *when* or *after*) in each gap. Then check your answers by referring to the sample answer on page 84.

1 *When* you read magazines these days, you see many advertisements for the latest fashions.
2 .... youngsters start work, they depend on their parents for money.
3 .... they have started earning money, young adults can still find it hard to afford fashionable clothes.
4 Teenagers look forward to doing this .... they have their own income.
5 You cannot criticise .... you have seen how hard it is to be original.

▷ page 107 *Time conjunctions*

2 Join each pair of sentences using the conjunction in brackets and starting with the words given. You may need to reorganise the sentence and add, change or remove some words.

1 New fashions reach the shops. Prices often go up. (*when*)
When new fashions *reach the shops, prices often go up.*
2 Staff must leave the building first. Then they can smoke. (*until*)
Staff cannot …
3 You wear casual clothes to work. Then it is hard to wear a suit. (*after*)
After you …
4 The sales start. Then some people go shopping. (*until*)
Some people …
5 Employees put on a uniform. They all look the same. (*when*)
Employees all …
6 Customers spent less money on clothes. Designer brands were introduced. (*before*)
Before designer brands …
7 I spend all my money. I go home. (*when*)
When I …

3 IELTS candidates often make mistakes with tenses following time conjunctions. Circle the correct verb form in each of these sentences.

1 I go shopping when I *was* / *am* upset by somebody.
2 The customer was aware of the price before she *buy* / *bought* the dress.
3 After *graduate* / *we graduate*, we need to compete for a good job.
4 We must set goals and not stop until *achieved* / *we achieve* them.
5 When children *will grow up* / *grow up*, they face many problems.
6 Some parents don't want their children to work before they *reach* / *will reach* adulthood.

Fashion and design 85

Vocabulary and grammar review Unit 7

Vocabulary

1 Complete each conversation below with a word from the box.

| bored | concerned | irritating |
| persuasive | reassuring | ~~upsetting~~ |

A: I cried when I watched the programme about the baby gorilla that died.
B: I know, it was so **1** *upsetting*.

A: I've been worrying about Gina's new job.
B: Me too – but it's **2** .... to know that she's getting on well with her colleagues.

A: Whenever I get to the bus stop, one's just left!
B: That must be really **3** ....!

A: Telling people that they will save money if they buy a more expensive phone makes no sense.
B: Mmm, but it's a very **4** .... argument.

A: He's yawning again.
B: I guess he's **5** ....

A: I'd like to give more money to charity.
B: Yes, but you can't be **6** .... about everyone.

2 Complete the sentences below about US Facebook users using the expressions in the box. You will need to use some expressions more than once.

| age | age group | aged | ages | the age(s) |

1 Facebook is used by people of all *ages*.
2 Just over 50 percent of users are under .... of 26.
3 The 18 to 25 .... is the largest single group of users.
4 People between .... of 26 and 34 make up the second largest group of users.
5 More youngsters .... 13 to 17 use Facebook than people over 44.
6 Twelve percent of Facebook users are under 17 years of ....
7 Ninety-seven percent of users are under .... of 55.
8 The 55 to 65 .... represents the smallest category of users.

US Facebook users by age group (insideFacebook.com)

13–17 12%
18–25 43%
26–34 23%
35–44 14%
45–54 14%
55–65 3%

Grammar

3 Circle the correct option in each of these sentences.

1 Petra said she'd join us for lunch if she (finished) / would finish her work in time.
2 If you asked people, most of them *will said / would say* that lying is wrong.
3 The old woman won't get across the road if someone *didn't / doesn't* help her.
4 Harim's changed so much that if I *met / will meet* him now, I wouldn't recognise him.
5 Research shows that children will disobey an instruction if they *think / thought* no one is watching them.
6 In England, people say 'Pardon' if they *cannot / could not* hear someone clearly.
7 If you get on with your colleagues, work *is / was* more enjoyable.
8 I'll tell you what I think, but you *might / would* not agree with me.
9 You shouldn't give up the course unless *you find / you'll find* it too hard.

4 Find five other referencing mistakes in this paragraph and correct them using the words in the box.

| it | its | ~~other~~ | they | this | this |

In every society, people need to build relationships with ~~another~~ *other* people. These relationships can take place at work, school or home. Wherever it occur, it is important that people understand each other. An organisation will not function well if their members are unhappy. Good managers understand the point and make sure they reward employees for good work. In fact, when you take time to understand what people want and why they want them, it is usually possible to solve most problems. These results in a happy environment where people progress well.

Vocabulary and grammar review Unit 8

Vocabulary

1 Match the words from the Reading passage on page 78 (1–8) with a synonym (a–h).

1	ability	a	well known
2	famous	b	garments
3	clothes	c	new
4	extraordinary	d	connection
5	seen	e	skill
6	fresh	f	state
7	condition	g	observed
8	link	h	unusual

2 Complete these sentences with words connected with fashion and design, then use the words to complete the crossword below.

1 You should wear ...*smart*... clothes to the graduation ceremony.
2 I've bought some beautiful silk .... to make a shirt.
3 .... often set the trends for young people.
4 More and more businesswomen are wearing a .... to work.
5 The school .... was very expensive.
6 Are you .... yet? It's time to go out.
7 The .... is a traditional Indian garment for women.
8 Jeans have been .... for many years.

3 Complete these sentences with *dress*, *dresses*, *cloth* or *clothes*.

1 If Marc had more money, he could afford some new ...*clothes*... .
2 It's formal .... at the party tonight, so I'm going to wear my suit.
3 Different textiles are woven into .... using a machine called a loom.
4 There are many different styles of .... for women, to suit a range of different occasions.
5 Fortunately, the .... that was used to make these curtains is fire-resistant.
6 The shop sells a variety of hand-made .... for men and women.
7 Some women prefer to wear skirts and tops to ....
8 People can sometimes find it hard to throw away their old ....

Grammar

4 Circle the correct verb in each sentence. Then underline the time conjunctions.

1 <u>When</u> you don't have much money, it (*is*)/ *will be* hard to afford new clothes.
2 I'm not leaving this shop until I *will buy* / *have bought* something.
3 Sashiko had a functional purpose before it *has become* / *became* a decorative art form.
4 The textiles are spun into cloth after they *have been* / *were* dyed.
5 Woollen fabrics sometimes shrink when you *wash* / *washed* them.
6 It's important to check the quality of a garment before you *will buy* / *buy* it.
7 Until I went to India, I *have had* / *had* no idea how colourful the traditional clothes were.
8 When I *go* / *have been* to the fashion museum, I'll go shopping.
9 I promise *we* / *we'll* go out after the show has finished.

Speaking reference

What to expect in the exam

The Speaking Test is normally held on the same day as the other tests. It is the last part of the exam.

- The Speaking Test lasts 11–14 minutes and has three parts.
- You do the test on your own.
- There is one examiner in the room who gives you the instructions, asks the questions and assesses your performance.
- It is recorded for administrative purposes.

Part 1: Introduction and interview

Part 1 lasts between four and five minutes. It consists of:

- a short introduction in which the examiner asks you your name and where you come from, and checks your identification;
- some initial questions about what you do or where you live;
- some questions on topics such as your hobbies and activities, places you know, family celebrations, holidays, etc.

You studied and practised Part 1 in Units 1 and 7.

How to do Part 1

1 Listen carefully to each question the examiner asks you. Think about the topic and the tenses that you need to use.
2 Give relevant replies and try to provide some reasons for your answer.
3 Aim to answer each question in about two or three sentences.
4 Don't memorise answers, but make sure you know the sort of topics that are often used in Part 1 and learn some vocabulary related to these.
5 Speak clearly so that the examiner can hear and understand you.
6 Try to look confident and relaxed; look at the examiner when you are speaking.
7 If you don't understand a question ask the examiner to repeat it: *I'm sorry, could you repeat the question, please?*

Topics and questions

Match each of these questions (1–12) to a topic (a–l).

1 Do you prefer to study by yourself or in a class? Why? [d]
2 Which form of transport did you use last? ☐
3 When did you last celebrate something in your home? ☐
4 How often do you watch a play or film? ☐
5 Are there any sports you want to play in the future? ☐
6 Do you do the same activities every day? ☐
7 What special types of dish are there in your culture? ☐
8 How did you find out about the news last week? ☐
9 Have you ever lived in a different place? ☐
10 What influences the way you dress? ☐
11 Do you plan to go on holiday in the future? ☐
12 Have the weather patterns changed recently in your country? ☐

Typical Part 1 topics

a Forms of entertainment
b Fashion
c Daily routines
d ~~Education and learning~~
e The media
f Tourism
g Health and fitness
h Family occasions
i Cooking
j Your home town or city
k Daily travel
l The seasons

Exercise

Work in pairs. Discuss which of these tenses you would be likely to use to answer each question 1–12 above.

Tense	Question
a Present simple	1, …
b Present continuous	
c Past simple	
d Present perfect	

Then take turns to ask and answer the questions.

Part 2: Long turn

Part 2 lasts between three and four minutes. The examiner gives you a topic to talk about. The topic is written down and includes some bullet points to guide you. The examiner also gives you some paper and a pencil. You have one minute to prepare for the talk and two minutes to give the talk. When you have finished, the examiner may ask you a short yes/no question about the talk.

You studied and practised Part 2 in Units 2, 3, 4, 5, 6 and 8.

How to do Part 2

1. Listen carefully to the instructions. The examiner will tell you how long you have to prepare and to talk. He/She will also read the first line of the topic to you, before giving you the written instructions.
2. Read the topic carefully, including all the bullet points, which help give you ideas and a structure for your talk.
3. Make full use of the minute's preparation time and write down some key points.
4. Introduce your talk at the start. Link your points together and use an appropriate ending.
5. Don't memorise a talk; the examiner will know if you do.
6. Aim to speak for two minutes. You don't need to stop until the examiner says 'Thank you'.
7. If the examiner asks you a short question at the end, you only need to give a very brief answer.

Useful language

Introducing your talk

I'm going to talk about …

The X I'm going to talk about is …

Giving a reason/detail/explanation

The reason (why) …

In other words, …

What I mean is …

What else can I tell you about …

Introducing a new point

So let me tell you …

The next thing …

Describing the stages in a story

At that time, …

Then …

Before/After …

When …

Eventually, …

Referring back to something you said earlier in the talk

As I mentioned before, …

As I said before, …

Ending the talk

So, all in all, …

In the end, …

So I guess that's …

Why did/do I …?

Exercise

In pairs, read the instructions and the sample topic below and discuss your ideas. Afterwards, spend a minute making some notes on your own and then take turns to give your talk. Try to talk for about two minutes.

Examiner's instructions

Now I'm going to give you a topic and I'd like you to talk about it for one to two minutes. Before you talk, you'll have one minute to think about what you're going to say. You can make some notes if you wish. Do you understand?

Here's a paper and pencil for making notes and here's your topic.

I'd like you to describe a new country or town you have visited.

Describe a new country or town you have visited. You should say:

- where this country/town is
- why you visited this country/town
- what you did there

and explain how you felt about visiting this country or town.

Part 3: Two-way discussion

Part 3 lasts between four and five minutes. The examiner leads a discussion that is based on the Part 2 topic. You have to give your opinions on general, abstract topics, not personal topics as in Part 1. This is your opportunity to show the examiner the full range of your language.

You studied and practised Part 3 in Units 4, 5, 6 and 8.

How to do Part 3

1. Listen carefully to the instructions and questions. Consider what the examiner is expecting you to do, e.g. give reasons, explain something, compare two things, agree or disagree, etc.
2. Make sure your replies are relevant and try to extend your answers (more than you did in Part 1).
3. Don't use memorised answers, but make sure you know the sort of topics that come up in Part 3 (e.g. environmental issues, language and communications, human relationships, education and learning, etc.) and learn some vocabulary and phrases related to them.
4. Speak clearly so that the examiner can understand you; try to answer the questions as you would in a discussion.
5. Remember that there are no right or wrong answers. The examiner is interested in hearing whether you can talk fluently about abstract topics and organise your points in a logical way.

Useful language

Starting your response

I think that …

Well, in my view/opinion, …

Giving reasons

This is because …

This is why …

The main reason is …

Comparing and contrasting

In the past, … but nowadays …

Many years ago, … but now …

However, …

On the other hand, …

While …

Agreeing/Disagreeing

I agree that …

I'm not sure I agree that … / I don't think/believe that …

Exercise

In pairs, read these instructions and discuss the sample questions. Think about what sort of reply you need to give and write down some useful vocabulary.

Examiner's instructions

We've been talking about a new country/town you have visited and I'd like to ask you one or two more general questions related to this. Let's consider first of all moving to a new place.

- *Can you tell me some reasons why someone might have to go to a new city or country?*
- *What sort of things would you organise before going somewhere new?*
- *Is it easier to go somewhere new now than it used to be in the past? Why?*

Let's move on to talk about living in a new place.

- *What sort of changes might you have to deal with when you move to a new place?*
- *How can these changes affect people?*
- *What is the best way to get used to circumstances that are different?*

Ask each other the questions. Try to give extended answers.

How are you rated?

The examiner listens very carefully to your speech and gives you a Band Score from 1 to 9 for the whole test. This means that the three parts are not rated separately. However, there are levels of performance that you need to reach in order to achieve a certain band.

As the examiner is talking to you, he/she considers these questions:

1 How long are your answers? How well can you link your ideas and structure your points?

2 How much vocabulary can you use, and how accurate is it?

3 How many grammatical structures can you use, and how accurate are they?

4 How well can you use standard features of pronunciation?

Exercise

Here are some things you should try to do in the Speaking Test. Match each of them (a–j) to one the questions above (1–4).

a be understood, even though you make grammatical mistakes

b give quite long answers in Part 3

c be understood, even though some words are mispronounced

d use a range of different words and phrases

e use a range of linkers

f use some accurate intonation and stress

g be understood, even though you sometimes use the wrong word

h paraphrase when you cannot find the right word

i use a mix of simple and complex sentences

j pause naturally as you speak

Preparing for the Speaking Test

Part 1

- Build up a list of vocabulary that will help you to talk about the topics that are often used in this part of the test. Start by looking back at page 88 and underlining the topic vocabulary in the questions. You can also go back to Units 1 and 7 and note down some vocabulary from the exercises.

- Practise making statements about yourself in relation to Part 1 topics, e.g. talk about your likes, dislikes and preferences; your activities and when you do them; what you are studying and why; your favourite shop / animal / type of clothing; things you did as a child; where you would like to live/travel in the future, etc.

- Keep a list of topics and useful words and phrases in a Speaking notebook or file, and add to this list whenever you can.

Part 2

- Practise talking on your own on a topic for two minutes. There are plenty of examples of topics in IELTS practice materials. You can also use the topics in Units 2, 3, 4, 5, 6 and 8 of this book, but think of a different idea from the one you used in the classroom.
- Make a collection of topics for your IELTS preparation. Brainstorm some ideas and vocabulary, and keep a record of this under a topic heading in your notebook.
- Study the model talks in the units. They will show you how to structure a Part 2 talk and how to link ideas. Make a note of any useful vocabulary and linkers.
- Record yourself and practise using some of the Useful language in this section. Also try to include some of the grammatical structures that you have learned on this course, such as conditionals, relative clauses, time conjunctions, etc. When you first practise, allow yourself the time you need.
- As the test date approaches, use Practice Tests and try to spend only a minute preparing for your talk. When the test date is near, make sure you have a fairly good idea of how much you need to say to fill two minutes.

Part 3

- Build up a list of abstract Speaking topics in your notebook and record some vocabulary that you can use to talk about them. Start by re-reading the articles in this book and checking the relevant Vocabulary reviews. Topics like language, the media, the environment, health and nutrition, etc. are common Part 3 topics.
- Develop your ideas by reading some articles on international topics such as city life, pollution, nature, the rich and poor, etc.
- Practise expressing views on topical issues, using some of the structures on page 90. Write a list of questions, with a friend or classmate if possible, and then practise answering them, e.g.:

  1 Should parents pay for their children's education?

  I think it depends on how rich the parents are. If they have a lot of money, they can afford to pay, but if they don't, it isn't fair to expect them to pay.

  2 Should air travel be more expensive than it is?

  3 What are the benefits of knowing more than one language?

For all parts, record yourself speaking and ask a teacher / native speaker to point out:

- how clearly you speak;
- any individual sounds or words that you don't pronounce clearly;
- how effectively you group words and phrases;
- how well you use stress to emphasise words;
- whether you need to use more or less intonation.

On the test day

Remember these important points because they may affect your mark.

- **Listen carefully to the examiner's questions and instructions**
  Each answer you give should be relevant. If you cannot understand the examiner, ask him/her to repeat the question.

- **Smile at the examiner and look interested**
  Communication works better for everyone if people are interested in what they are saying.

- **Make sure the examiner can hear you**
  If you speak too softly, too quickly or not clearly enough, the examiner may mark you down for pronunciation and may be unable to judge your true language level.

- **Provide enough language for the examiner to assess**
  Examiners can only rate what they hear. Even if you know a lot of English, you won't get a high mark if you don't say enough to demonstrate your true language ability.

- **Use your imagination**
  There are no right or wrong answers to the questions. If you don't have any experience of the Part 2 topic, think about something you have read or seen on television, or make something up. Similarly, if you don't have a view on a Part 3 question, imagine one that someone else might have.

- **Be prepared and be confident**
  The Speaking Test materials are designed to help you talk as much as possible. During the test, the examiner will cover a number of different topics and will encourage you to speak. If you are well prepared, you should feel confident enough to do your best.

Writing reference

What to expect in the exam

The Writing Test is the third paper in the exam and it takes place after the Reading Test.

You do two tasks in one hour:

- Task 1 is a summary of one or more charts or diagrams on the same subject.
- Task 2 is a discursive essay. There is only one topic.

Task 1

In this task, you must summarise and compare information from a graph, chart, table or diagram, or a combination of these.

Your summary must be at least 150 words long. You may write more than this, but if you write less, you will lose some marks. You need to spend about 20 minutes on this task.

You should try to:

- include all the key points;
- include some details or data to support the key points;
- compare relevant features of the information;
- include an overview;
- organise your answer in a logical way;
- use relevant vocabulary;
- use your own words where possible, rather than copying from the question;
- write grammatically correct sentences;
- use accurate spelling and punctuation;
- write in a formal academic style (not bullet points or note form).

You studied and practised Writing Task 1 in Units 1, 3, 5 and 7.

How to do Task 1

1. Read the instructions and study the headings and information carefully. Find at least three key points and decide which features you should compare. (Allow between two and three minutes.)
2. Decide how many paragraphs to write and what to put in each one. Decide what will go in your overview. (Allow between two and three minutes.)
3. Write your answer, allowing a couple of minutes to check it through afterwards. (15 minutes)

Graphs, charts and diagrams

There are different types of visual information that you will have to deal with.

1 Graphs: showing trends over time

Look at the Writing task below and answer these questions.

1. What do the figures on the vertical axis represent?
2. What period of time does the graph cover?
3. What overall trends does the graph show?
4. Find three key points that you can compare on the graph.

The graph below shows population figures for India and China since the year 2000 and predicted population growth up until 2050.

Summarise the information by selecting and reporting the main features, and make comparisons where relevant.

Population growth in India and China

5. Read the sample answer on page 93. Underline the writer's key points and the comparisons the writer makes.
6. Are the data that support the key points accurate?

[Start with a sentence that introduces the summary. Use your own words as far as possible.]

Sample answer

The graph shows how the populations of India and China have changed since 2000 and how they will change in the future.

In 2000, there were more people living in China than in India. The number of Chinese was 1.25 billion, while India's population was about 1 billion. Between 2000 and the present, there has been a 0.2 billion rise in the number of Indian citizens. Over the same period, China's population has increased by 0.1 billion to reach over 1.35 billion.

According to the graph, the population in India will increase more quickly than in China, and experts say that by 2030, both countries will have the same population of 1.45 billion. After this, China's population is likely to fall slightly to 1.4 billion in 2050, while India's population will probably increase and reach 1.6 billion.

Thus, over the 50-year period, India is going to experience steady growth in its population and it will overtake China. On the other hand, China's population will peak in 2030 and then begin to fall.

[Note the change in tense to summarise points about the future.]

[The paragraphs cover different time periods on the graph. In this answer, the second paragraph goes up to the present day and the third paragraph deals with the future.]

[The overview is at the end and forms the final paragraph. It gives an overall picture of the trends.]

7 Read the sample answer again. Underline any verbs, nouns and phrases that the writer uses to describe trends. (Include the prepositions.)

2 Pie charts: showing how 100% of something is divided up into smaller percentages

Look at the Writing task below and answer these questions.

1 Say what the pie chart shows (tell a partner in your own words). What does the bar on the right represent?

2 What are the key points in the charts?

3 How could you organise the information into paragraphs?

The chart below shows the world's energy use in 2010.

Summarise the information by selecting and reporting the main features, and make comparisons where relevant.

Global breakdown of energy consumption 2010

- petroleum 39%
- nuclear electric power 8%
- renewable 7%
- coal 22%
- natural gas 23%

sectors or categories

- solar 5%
- hydroelectric 36%
- geothermal 5%
- biomass (wood, straw, etc.) 53%
- wind 1%

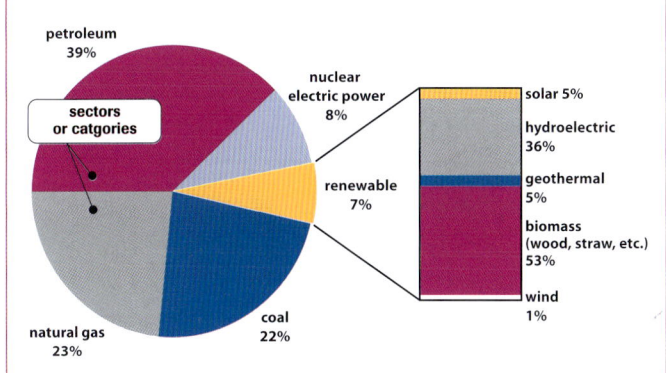

4 Read the sample answer on the right. Which sentence sums up the first key point?

5 Find the overview.

6 Read the sample answer again. Underline the phrases the writer uses to make comparisons.

7 Underline the linkers.

Sample answer

The chart illustrates the world's use of different forms of energy in 2010 and provides a breakdown of the use of renewable energy.

By far the biggest source of power is petroleum. Thirty-nine per cent of the world's energy comes from this source. Also, natural gas and coal together contribute 45 per cent of our energy sources. Clearly, we are very dependent on these three main energy supplies.

Similar but much smaller amounts of energy are consumed from nuclear power (8 per cent) and renewable sources (7 per cent). Within the renewable sector, there are a number of different energy sources. Wood-based sources and hydroelectric power are the largest of these and account for 53 and 36 per cent respectively, while solar energy is the smallest, at one per cent. In addition, very small percentages of wind and geothermal energy are used.

Although we use some renewable energy, our reliance on these forms is still minimal compared to the significant consumption of fossil fuels

[Notice how the writer avoids repeating the same words and phrases.]

[It is fine to use words from the task if you put them in your own sentence.]

[Include relevant vocabulary to improve your score.]

Writing reference 93

3 Tables and bar charts: showing items and related values in columns

Look at the Writing task below and answer these questions.

1 How are the table and chart related? (Which would you summarise first?)
2 What comparisons could you make?
3 What should you put in your overview?

The table and chart give the results of surveys in Australia about the use of the Internet. The table provides information on the reasons for use. The chart shows use in relation to age.

Summarise the information by selecting and reporting the main features, and make comparisons where relevant.

Internet uses Trends – all Australians 2008

Internet uses	%
Banking	62%
Phone calls	22%
Blogs	10%
Ordering goods and services	57%
Bills	63%

Internet use (in %)

Age group	%
Total people over 14	89%
14–17	100%
18–19	98%
20–29	99%
30–39	97%
40–49	96%
50–64	91%
65+	58%

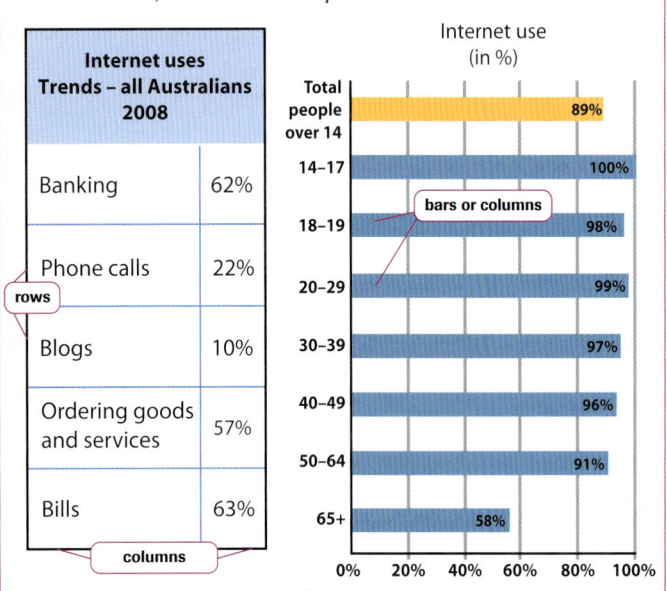

Sample answer

The table and chart provide details about who uses the Internet in Australia and what it is used for.

First, the chart indicates that an average of 89 per cent of Australians use the Internet. However, all 14–17-year-olds go online, and 99 per cent of the 20–29 age group. This figure is a few percent lower between these two age groups and then decreases to 91 per cent up to the age of 64. After that age, the percentage of people who use the Internet dips to 56.

According to the table, people use the Internet most for paying bills and banking, at 63 and 62 per cent respectively. The next most popular reason why the Internet is used is to purchase products and services. In contrast, only 22 per cent of use is for making phone calls, and even less for writing blogs.

Overall, internet use is very high among most age groups, but it is less popular among older people. Among adults, its highest level of use is related to financial activities.

Note how the writer has changed the words in the task to his/her own vocabulary.

4 Read the sample answer on the right. How has the writer organised the information?
5 Which figures are included, and why?

4 Diagrams: showing a process and/or how something works

Look at the Writing task on the right and answer these questions.

1 What are the key stages in the process? (Explain them to a partner.)
2 What verbs and verb forms will you use?
3 What comparisons could you make?
4 Read the sample answer on page 95. Has the writer included all the key stages? In which paragraph(s) are they? Where is the overview?
5 Underline the words/phrases used to mark the stages in the process.
6 Read the answer again and underline the verb forms the writer uses to describe the process.

The diagram below shows how household waste is turned into energy. Summarise the information by selecting and reporting the main features, and make comparisons where relevant.

Waste-to-energy plant diagram

Pollution control systems
a nitrogen oxide removal system
b mercury and dioxin removal systems
c acid gas removal system

94 Complete IELTS Bands 5–6.5

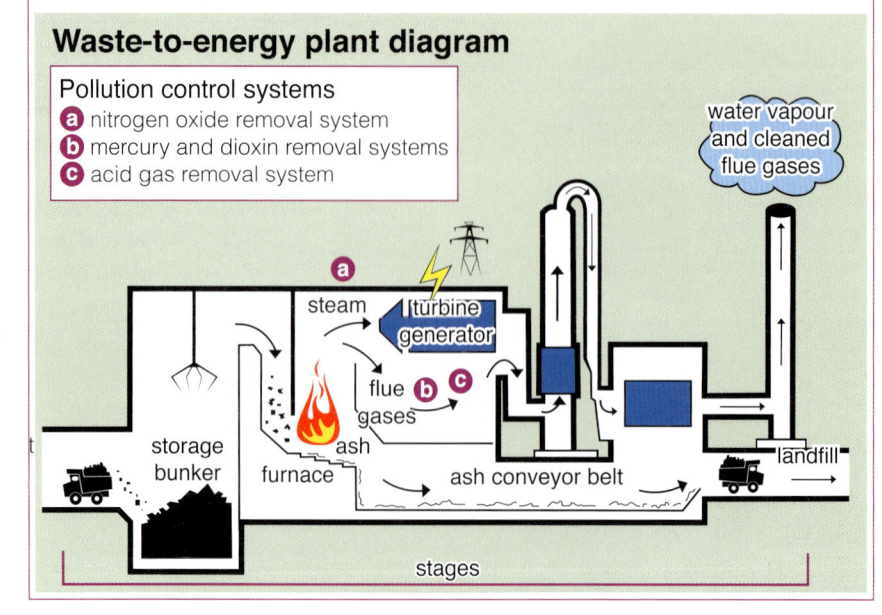

> Note the use of the passive because what happens to the waste is the important information.

Sample answer

The diagram illustrates how rubbish from homes is used to create energy. The process is quite straightforward, but there are several important stages to complete and a number of safety controls.

When the waste truck arrives at the plant, the waste is tipped into a bunker where it can be stored until it is needed. Eventually, the waste is collected and burned in a furnace, and this produces steam, flue gases and ash. Unlike the steam, the ash is not useful, so it is sent by a conveyor belt to another truck and taken to a landfill site.

Before the steam is used, it must be treated by removing any nitrogen oxide. Then the steam is separated from the flue gases and used to drive a turbine and generate electricity.

The flue gases are also cleaned by removing <u>pollutants</u> such as mercury and acid gas. Finally, clean gases and any remaining water vapour are released into the air.

> Use other forms of key words if you know them.

Useful language

Starting your answer / Introducing a key point

The graph/chart/table/diagram shows …

The graph/chart/table/diagram gives/provides information about/on …

The graph/chart/table/diagram indicates …

The diagram illustrates …

According to the graph/chart/table/diagram, …

Linking ideas and sentences

In addition / Also, …

However, …

Comparing and contrasting

While …

On the other hand, …

However, …

Although …

Similarly, …

In contrast/comparison, …

Unlike …

Summarising the stages in a diagram

First/Before/When

Next / Then / After that, …

Finally/Lastly/Eventually, …

Describing trends

a(n) … increase/decrease/rise/fall/drop in

to increase/decrease/rise/fall/drop by

to fluctuate

to remain stable/steady

to dip

to peak

Introducing the overview

Overall, …

Thus, …

Clearly, …

Task 2

This task is in the form of a statement and question(s). There may be more than one part to discuss, and you need to give your own opinion.

Your answer must be at least 250 words long. You can write more than this, but if you write less, you will lose some marks. You need to spend about 40 minutes on this task. There are twice as many marks for Part 2 as for Part 1.

You should try to:

- discuss all the questions or issues in the task;
- present main ideas and provide some supporting ideas or examples;
- include relevant examples from your own experience;
- draw a logical conclusion;
- organise your answer, using paragraphs;
- link your ideas together in a logical way;
- use your own words where possible and avoid copying from the question;
- write grammatically correct sentences;
- use accurate spelling and punctuation;
- write in a formal academic style.

You studied and practised Writing Task 2 in Units 2, 4, 6 and 8.

How to do Task 2

1 Read the instructions carefully. Decide how many parts there are to the question and underline them. Decide what your view is on the topic. (Allow between two and three minutes.)

2 Quickly brainstorm some ideas and write a plan. Make sure you know how many paragraphs to write and what to put in each one. Decide what will go in your conclusion. (Allow between three and four minutes.)

3 Write your answer, allowing up to five minutes to check it through afterwards. (34 minutes)

Task 2 questions

In addition to writing about a single question or statement, there are other types of task you may have to deal with.

Two questions

Read the Writing task below and answer these questions.

1 What does *these changes* refer back to?
2 What are the issues you must write about? Describe them in your own words.

> In today's world, many people use mobile phones and the Internet to communicate with others. This has resulted in the use of new words and different forms of spelling and grammar.
>
> Why do you think these changes have happened?
>
> Are they a positive or negative development?
>
> Give reasons for your answer and include any relevant examples from your own knowledge or experience.

Both questions must be covered.

3 Read the sample answer on the right and complete this plan for the essay. Has the writer dealt with all parts of the task? In which paragraph(s) is each part dealt with?

para. 1	Introduction	1 Communication has changed – this affects language
para. 2	Main idea + supporting idea	2 .... + examples
para. 3	Main idea + supporting idea	3 .... + examples
para. 4	Main idea + supporting idea	4 .... + reasons
para. 5	Conclusion	5 Cannot stop change but still need to be accurate

4 Read the sample answer again and underline the linkers the writer uses.

5 What idea links paragraphs 2 and 3?

Sample answer

There have been many changes in the way we communicate over the last 20 years, and it is understandable that these changes have affected the way we speak and write. Is this a good thing or a bad thing?

In the past, people communicated by writing letters and speaking on the phone. However, technology has changed this, and now emails, texts and the Internet are the most common communication tools, especially for young people. These methods of communication are much faster than the old ones, and this means that people write more quickly and communicate more frequently.

Unfortunately, the speed of modern communication systems has reduced the accuracy of our messages. This is because people make up their own words and abbreviations, and some of these can become quite popular. In my country, for example, LOL means 'laugh out loud', and children write this and say it. What is more, punctuation may be missing, and people worry less about how they spell words.

Yet language change is not necessarily a bad thing. Informal texts and emails are just messages between friends. It does not matter too much how they are written. The important thing is that people can switch to more accurate language when they need to. However, if they lose this ability, and formal communication becomes too careless, then there will be problems.

All in all, I do not think that you can stop change and you cannot prevent new ways of communicating. On the other hand, it is still necessary to make sure that everyone can appreciate and use correct grammar and vocabulary.

Write a short introduction to the essay.

A question often works well at the start

Link new paragraphs to previous paragraphs using topic vocabulary or linkers

Sum up your points – don't add anything new.

Two opposing views

Read the Writing task below and answer these questions.

1 Express the two opposing views in your own words.

> *Some people find history a fascinating subject. Others say it is dull and has no place in modern life.*
>
> *Discuss <u>both these views</u> and <u>give your own opinion</u>.*
>
> *Give reasons for your answer and include any relevant examples from your own knowledge or experience.*

2 Read the sample answer below. How many different views are presented? Whose are they?

3 In which paragraph(s) is each part of the task dealt with? How are the views used to support each argument?

4 Read the sample answer again and say what the underlined words refer to.

Sample answer

People do not all feel the same about history. For some people, it is very interesting and they like seeing old things and talking about how different life once was. For <u>others</u>[1], it is just a boring subject. Personally, I think the past is very interesting and there is a lot we can learn from <u>it</u>[2].

State your view clearly and stick to it.

Historians often talk about how people lived long ago because it shows us that society has moved forward. For example, whereas one person may have taken a week to make a pair of trousers in the 18th century, we can now make hundreds of pairs over the same period of time. <u>They</u>[3] believe this is important evidence of human progress.

Many tourists really enjoy going to museums when they visit other countries. There, they see objects from centuries ago. For example, my country is well known for its beautiful arts and crafts, and we see <u>these</u>[4] as cultural treasures. Other people like reading about inventors or travellers. All these types of people would say that history is a wonderful subject.

Note how the writer uses reference words to avoid repetition.

On the other hand, not everyone agrees with their views. Youngsters in particular feel that the past is too far away to think about. They are more interested in the future and in how things will change. For <u>them</u>[5], going to a museum can be very boring because they feel no connection with the exhibits, while reading about history seems meaningless.

You need to cover both arguments but you do not have to write exactly the same number of words on each one.

In my view, this is a pity. Everyone should have an interest in the past because it has made us what we are now. However, sometimes we just have to accept that people like and dislike different things, and <u>one</u>[6] example is history.

To what extent do you agree?

Read the Writing task below and answer these questions.

1 What does the statement in the task mean?

   a Learning about the environment is more important than learning to read and write.

   b Learning to read and write is more important than learning about the environment.

   c Teaching children to protect the environment and teaching them to read and write are equally important.

2 How many questions are there to discuss?

> *It is as important to teach children to protect the environment as it is to teach them to read and write.*
>
> *To what extent do you agree with this statement?*
>
> *Give reasons for your answer and include any relevant examples from your own knowledge or experience.*

To what extent means 'how much?'. You can agree completely or disagree completely, or you can present both sides of the argument.

Writing reference

3 Read the sample answer below and replace each of the highlighted words with one of the words in the box. What improvement do they make?

children ~~concern~~ deeply food matter
skills subjects topics totally world

Sample answer

There is no doubt that the environment has become a significant thing[1] over the past few years. However, I am not sure we can compare looking after it with learning to read and write. In my opinion, the two areas seem to be so[2] different, but, generally, I think reading and writing are more important.

concern

Caring about the environment is really a social thing[3]. In my country, many parents encourage their children to pick up litter and not waste stuff[4]. These are good habits, and it is important to develop them early. When youngsters go to school, they study things[5] like science. During these lessons, I think it is very important for teachers to discuss things[6] like pollution and global warming and help youngsters understand how they can reduce their effects.

> Write in an academic style and use precise words.

> Try to use words that explain exactly what you mean.

Reading and writing, on the other hand, are things[7] that everyone needs. Most pupils start to learn to read and write before they can think much[8] about life. They improve as they get older and by the time they leave school, they can understand complex issues and express their thoughts and feelings about them. As everyone knows, this is very important if they want to go to university or get a good job.

I believe that learning to take care of the environment should be part of our education, but it is not as important as literacy. Today, people[9] need to learn many things at school, but if they cannot read and write, they will be unprepared for the future and the place[10] around them.

4 Read the sample answer again. Which of a, b or c in Question 1 on page 97 is the writer's view? Where is it stated?

5 Underline the two main ideas. What are the supporting arguments?

Useful language

Giving your opinions

In my view/opinion, …

(Personally,) I think/believe …

From my point of view, …

I am not sure / I do not believe …

Introducing other people's opinions

Experts/Scientists etc. argue/say/suggest/believe/think (that) …

People sometimes say/argue …

For some people, …; for others, …

Introducing general arguments

The main argument in favour of / against …

It is (certainly) true that …

It is (generally) believed/felt that …

In the past, …; nowadays, …

Presenting reasons/examples

The main reason why …

There are a number of reasons …

This is because …

For this reason, …

For example/instance, …

Adding support

Also …

What is more, …

In addition, …

Giving personal experience

In my country/town/home/family/experience, …

Where I grew up, …

Drawing a conclusion

Overall, …

All in all, …

In conclusion, …

To conclude, …

Complete IELTS Bands 5–6.5

How are you rated?

The two tasks are rated separately, but Task 2 is worth twice as many marks as Task 1. The marks are combined to produce one Band Score from 1 to 9 for the whole test.

There are levels of performance that you need to reach in order to achieve a certain band.

The examiner considers the following questions:

Task 1
- Have you understood the task and the data/diagram?
- Have you included all the key points?
- Have you included some relevant data?
- Is there an overview?

Task 2
- Have you understood the task?
- Have you covered all the parts/questions in the task?
- Is your opinion clear?
- Have you presented relevant ideas?

Both tasks
- How well have you organised the answer? Is there a range of linkers? Can you use referencing?
- How adequate is your vocabulary, and how accurate is it?
- How many different grammatical structures can you use, and how accurate are they?

Preparing for the Writing Test

For Task 1, practise summarising the information in a range of different charts and diagrams. For Task 2, practise writing arguments on a range of different topics.

Before you write, brainstorm some ideas and then organise them into paragraphs. The sample answers in the units and in this Writing reference have been written to show you how to structure an answer and how to link ideas.

Try to use some of the grammatical structures that you have learned on this course. Don't be over-ambitious, but include some complex sentences, e.g. conditionals, relative clauses, time clauses, etc.

On the test day
Remember these important points because they affect your mark.

Task 1
- **Make sure you fully understand the data**
  Study the task first and make sure you understand it.
  - If it is a graph or chart, look carefully at the axes, labels and any keys.
  - If it is a table, look at all the headings.
  - If it is a diagram, look at all the steps or stages and get a mental image of the process or structure.
- **Include the key points**
  Decide on at least three key points and make sure you highlight these in your answer.
- **Include data and make sure they are accurate**
  Make sure that the figures or details that you include to illustrate your key points are accurate.
- **Include an overview of the information**
  The overview is like a conclusion and it gives your reader a simple picture of what the graphic shows overall. It is not the same as the introduction, which states what the information is about. The overview usually goes at the end of the answer, but it doesn't have to. As long as it is there, you will get credit for it. If it is not there, you will lose marks.

Task 2
- **Make sure you understand the question**
  Take time to read the question very carefully. Underline the parts you have to write about and ask yourself:
  - What is the main topic?
  - How many parts are there?
  - Do I need to present arguments for and against?
  - What is my opinion?
- **Introduce your essay**
  The introduction sets the scene for your reader. It tells them what you are going to discuss, what the issues are, and often what your opinion is.
- **Make your opinion on the topic clear to the reader**
  Decide on your view and state this, either in the introduction or during the course of your essay. Keep your position clear and don't change it.
- **Include some main ideas**
  Decide on at least three main ideas and some supporting points. Build your paragraphs around your main ideas. Ideas can come from other people's opinions, your own opinions, facts, etc.
- **Include some personal experience**
  Make sure this is relevant to the question. You only need to write a sentence on this, and if you have no personal experience, you do not need to worry. Just say *Although I have no personal experience of this, I think …*'.
- **Draw a conclusion**
  At the end of your essay, you need to write one or two sentences that summarise your arguments and your point of view.

Language reference

Unit 1

Making comparisons

To compare information, you can use comparative and superlative forms of adjectives and adverbs.

- Use comparative adjectives (+ *than*) to compare people, things, places or events:
  People in their 50s find learning a language **more difficult than** young people.
- Use comparative adverbs (+ *than*) to compare actions:
  People in their 50s make friends **more quickly than** young people.
- Use *the* + a superlative adjective or adverb to compare one person or thing with everyone or everything else in the group:
  The most difficult thing is learning the local language.

Forming comparative and superlative adjectives and adverbs

- Add *-er* and *-est* to:
  - one-syllable adjectives:
    slower (than), the highest
  - two-syllable adjectives ending in *-y*:
    easier (than), the happiest (changing *-y* to *i*)
  - one-syllable adverbs:
    faster (than), the hardest
- Add *more* and *most* to:
  - adjectives with two or more syllables (except two-syllable adjectives ending in *-y*):
    more important (than), the most complicated
  - adverbs with two or more syllables:
    more easily (than), the most successfully
- Some adjectives have irregular comparative and superlative forms:
  good, better, best
  bad, worse, worst
  far, farther/further, farthest/furthest
  many, more, most
  much, more, most
  little, less, least
- Some adverbs have irregular comparative and superlative forms:
  badly, worse, worst
  well, better, best
- To say one thing is less than another, use *less* and *least*:
  Children find learning to read less complicated than mathematics.

Spelling

- When there is only one vowel (*a, e, i, o* or *u*) before the final consonant (*b, c, d*, etc.), the final consonant is doubled:
  big – bigger, thin – thinner (BUT *safe – safer, clean – cleaner*)

  Note: when the final consonant is *w*, it does not double:
  low – lower
- Final *y* becomes *i*:
  friendly – friendlier

Unit 2

Word formation

Adding prefixes

Some words can be given the opposite meaning by adding a prefix (e.g. *dis-* + *appear* = *disappear*) to the beginning of a word. Here are some common prefixes which give the opposite meaning:

dis-	**dis**appear	un-	**un**usual
in-	**in**efficient	mis-	**mis**leading

Adding suffixes

Verbs, nouns, adjectives and adverbs can be formed from other related words by adding a suffix (e.g. *appear* + *-ance* = *appearance*) to the end of a word.

There are no clear rules – each word and the words which can be formed from it must be learned individually. Some of the most common are listed below.

verb → noun		
suffix	**verb**	**noun**
–ment	move	movement
–ation/–tion/–sion	rotate inform obsess	rotation information obsession
–er/–or	consume supervise	consumer supervisor
–ance	appear	appearance

adjective → noun		
suffix	**adjective**	**noun**
–ance/–ence	important absent	importance absence
–ness	fresh	freshness
–ity	popular	popularity

Complete IELTS Bands 5–6.5

noun → adjective		
suffix	noun	adjective
–y	wealth	wealthy
–ful	harm	harmful
–ous	nutrition	nutritious
–less	care	careless
–al	nature	natural

noun → verb		
suffix	noun	verb
–ify	class	classify
–ise/–ize	critic	criticise/criticize

adjective → verb		
suffix	adjective	verb
–ify	simple	simplify

verb → adjective		
suffix	verb	adjective
–ed	educate	educated
–ing	care	caring
–able/–ible	notice respond	noticeable responsible

adjective → adverb
Adverbs are almost always formed by adding –ly. If the adjective ends in –ic, you change it to an adverb by adding –ally

suffix	adjective	adverb
–ly/–ally	simple organic	simply organically

Spelling rules for adding prefixes and suffixes

Adding prefixes

When a prefix is added, the spelling does not change, e.g. *appoint – disappoint, satisfied – dissatisfied, like – unlike, necessary – unnecessary*.

Notes:

The prefix *in–* is not used in front of certain letters:

- Before words beginning with *r–*, use *ir–*:
  irrelevant
- Before words beginning with *m–* or *p–*, use *im–*:
  immature, impatient
- Before words beginning with *l–* use *il–*:
  illogical, illiterate

Adding suffixes
Doubling consonants

- Double the final consonant:
  - when you add *–ed, –ing, –er* or *–est* to a one-syllable word which ends in a consonant–vowel–consonant:
    shop – shopper, big – bigger
  - in verbs of two or more syllables which end in consonant–vowel–consonant and the final syllable is stressed:
    oc'cur – occurrence, for'get – forgetting, ad'mit – admitted (but *'happened, de'veloping*)
  - in words which end in l after one vowel in British English (in American English they may not double):
    travel – traveller, cancel – cancellation
- Final *–w, –x* and *–y* are never doubled:
  slower, relaxed, buyer
- Don't double the final consonant when:
  - there are two final consonants:
    depend – depending
  - there are two vowels before the final consonant:
    disappear – disappearance
  - the verb ends in a vowel:
    share – shared
  - the stress is not on the final syllable:
    open – opening

y → i and i → y

- For words ending in –y after a consonant, the *y* becomes *i* when a suffix is added (except –ing – see below):
  happy – happiness, try – tries, family – familiar, rely – reliance
- Note this exception:
  day – daily
- *–ing*: *i* becomes *y* with *–ing*; *y* does not change:
  lie – lying, study – studying, try – trying

When to drop the final -e

- The final *–e* is dropped if there is a consonant before it and the suffix begins with a vowel (*–er, –ed, –ing, –ance, –ation*, etc.):
  amaze – amazing, fame – famous
- The final *–e* is not dropped when the suffix begins with a consonant:
  safe – safety, arrange – arrangement
  (exception: *argue – argument*)

Adding –ly to form adverbs

Adjectives ending in *–l* end in *–lly* when the adverb is formed:
beautiful – beautifully, magical – magically

Language reference 101

Countable and uncountable nouns

Nouns are either countable [C], uncountable [U] or both countable and uncountable.
If they are both countable and uncountable, there is a difference in meaning:
It will take time [U] (= months, years) *to change people's opinions on the subject.*
I visited Sydney several times [C] (= on several occasions) *during my stay in Australia.*

Countable and uncountable nouns have different grammar rules:

Countable nouns:	Uncountable nouns:
• use *a* or *an* when they are singular: *a job, an opinion*	• do not use *a* or *an*: *work, research*
• have a plural form: *jobs, opinions*	• do not have a plural form (and so the verb is always singular): *Their experience is very useful.*
• can use *some* and *any* in the plural: *some ideas, any students*	• can use *some* and *any*: *some information, any food*
• can use *few* and *many* in the plural: *few teachers, many suggestions*	• can use *little* and *much*: *little help, much discussion*
	• may use other countable nouns to refer to a quantity: *a piece of research, a large amount of money.*

Some common uncountable nouns which IELTS candidates often make mistakes with are:

advice	food	research
aid	furniture	shopping
attention	garbage	software
behaviour	help	spending
countryside	homework	stuff
damage	information	transport
dirt	knowledge	work
equipment	pollution	

Phrases to express quantity

countable nouns	uncountable nouns	both countable and uncountable nouns
• a (large/small) number of: *A large number of people came to the meeting.* • a wide range of: *The students expressed a wide range of points of view.*	• a (large/small/considerable) amount of: *The storm produced a considerable amount of damage.* • a great deal of: *A great deal of research is being done.*	• a lot of: *They ate a lot of food.* • plenty of: *He has plenty of qualifications, but little experience.* *She has plenty of experience, but few qualifications.*

Complete IELTS Bands 5–6.5

Unit 3

Prepositions

In time expressions

- For months and years, use *in*: *in August, in 2011*
- For periods of time, use:
  - *between ... and*: *between August and October*
  - *from ... to*: *from 2005 to 2010* (= *between 2005 and 2010*)
  - *over* + a number of months or years + period: *over a 20-year period*
  - *during* + a word or phrase that represents a period of time*: *During the summer holidays / the lesson / the period between March and May / the five-year period, ...*

* Note that *during* means 'for part of the time mentioned'. *Over* means 'for the whole time mentioned': *Faisal stayed at the hotel for two weeks during the summer. The graph shows information about hotel staff over a ten-year period.*

In phrases expressing trends

- To say what has changed, use a noun + *in* (*a change in, a rise in, a decrease in*, etc.): *There has been a rise in the number of students studying Mandarin.*
- To say how much something changed, use:
  - a noun + *of*: *There has been an increase of 3 percent.*
  - a verb + *by*: *The number fell by 3,000.*
  - a verb or noun + *from ... to*: *The average rose from 0.7 to 1.3.*
- To express a level, use a verb + *at*: *Unemployment peaked at 11 percent.*
- To say the level something reached, use a verb + *to*: *The number rose to 21,000.*

Tenses: past simple, present perfect simple and continuous

	form
past simple	verb + *-ed* *did not* + verb
present perfect simple	*have/has* + verb + *-ed* *have not* + verb + *-ed*
present perfect continuous	*have/has been* + verb + *-ing* *have/has not been* + verb + *-ing*

Use the **past simple** for:

- actions or events in the past where the time you refer to is clear:
  *A couple of years ago, I **went** on holiday with a friend.*
- a series of past actions or events which happened one after the other:
  *We **hired** a car, which we **picked** up when we **reached** the airport.*
- things which were clearly finished in the past:
  *I **went** to a different primary school from my brothers.*

Use the **present perfect simple** for:

- situations or states (not actions or activities) which started in the past and are still continuing now:
  *I'**ve** always **enjoyed** travelling.*
- things which happened in the past, but no time is given and they have a result in the present:
  *Great news! I'**ve passed** the exam!*

Use the **present perfect continuous** for:

- actions and situations which started in the past and are still continuing now:
  *He **has been working** on the project for three months.*

Unit 4

However, *although*, *even though* and *on the other hand*

However, *although*, *even though* and *on the other hand* are used to contrast ideas or information.

Although and *even though*

- Use *although* and *even though* to contrast ideas in the same sentence:
  Although television is not as popular as in the past, it is still the most influential form of media.
  Many people still buy newspapers even though they have little time to read them.
- Use a comma when *although* or *even though* are placed at the beginning of the sentence:
  Although the website was expensive to design, very few people visit it.
- Don't use a comma when *although* or *even though* are placed in the middle of the sentence:
  Many people are afraid of flying even though it is very safe.
- *Even though* is stronger than *although*.

However and *on the other hand*

- Use *however* and *on the other hand* to contrast ideas or information in separate sentences. *However* and *on the other hand* start the second sentence:
  Air travel is the fastest form of travel. However, you can waste a lot of time at airports.
- *On the other hand* is often used to start a new paragraph which expresses the opposite point of view:
  On the other hand, there are strong arguments against reporting details of crimes on television.
- *However* and *on the other hand* are both followed by commas:
  However, I believe stronger measures are necessary.

Use of articles

The

Use *the*:

- when people know what you are talking about because you've mentioned the thing before or it's clear from the context:
  He had an excellent idea. **The** *idea was to post the list on the web.*
- when only one of a thing exists:
  the world, the Internet
- with a singular noun which refers to a group of people or things:
  the police, the government
- with superlatives (see *Making comparisons* on page 100):
  the highest figure, the best solution
- with *the first, the second*, etc.:
  the first difficulty
- with adjectives which refer to groups:
  the rich
- with nationalities:
  the Chinese

Don't use *the*:

- when you are talking in general with an uncountable noun or with plural nouns:
  Life *was more difficult for our grandparents.*
  People *are often afraid of taking risks*
- in these common expressions: *at home, in/to hospital, in/to prison, at/to school, at/to university, at/to work*:
  I'm hoping to go to university in Australia.
  He's at work at the moment.

A and *an*

- Use *a* or *an* with a singular countable noun the first time you mention it:
  A teacher who influenced me when I was at school was …
- Don't use *a* or *an* with uncountable nouns or plural nouns:
  freedom, arguments
- Use *an* before words beginning with:
  - *a, e, i, o* and *u*:
    an impression
  - *h* when *h* is not pronounced:
    an hour
- Use *a*, not *an*, before words beginning with *e-* and *u-* when they are pronounced *y*:
  a university, a European bank

Unit 5

The passive

The passive is formed by *to be* + past participle (*done/changed/spoken*).
With verbs like *can, should, must*, etc., the passive is formed by *can/should/must* + *be* + past participle:
The equipment **must be placed** *in the right environment.*

Look at these sentences in the active and the passive:

active	passive
The wind **moves** *the turbine.*	*The turbine* **is moved** *by the wind.*
They **raised** *the price of cigarettes last year.*	*The price of cigarettes* **was raised** *last year.*
The government **has reduced** *the tax on petrol.*	*The tax on petrol* **has been reduced**.
People **can argue** *that travel is an essential part of education.*	*It* **can be argued** *that travel is an essential part of education.*

The passive is used:

- when we don't know who or what does/did something:
  The price of cigarettes was raised last year.
- when it's not necessary to say who/what did something (because it's obvious):
  The tax on petrol has been reduced.
  (obviously by the government)
- when what happens/happened is more important than who/what does it:
  The turbine is moved by the wind.
- in formal styles of writing:
  It can be argued that travel is an essential part of education.

Unit 6

Verbs + infinitive and verbs + –ing

- **verb + infinitive**

    (They **agreed to install** a wind turbine.)
    agree   appear   bother   choose   decide   demand
    fail   hope   learn   manage   offer   plan   refuse   seem

- **verb + infinitive OR verb + somebody/something + infinitive**

    (She **asked to see** the plans. She **asked them to show** her the plans.)
    ask   choose   expect   help   intend   want

- **verb + somebody/something + infinitive**

    (They have **advised the government to invest** in renewable energy.)
    advise   allow   enable   encourage   forbid   force   invite
    order   permit   persuade   recommend   remind   teach
    tell

- **verb + –ing**

    (She **admitted breaking** the window.)
    admit   appreciate   avoid   celebrate   consider   delay
    deny   dislike   enjoy   finish   imagine   keep
    mind   miss   postpone   practise   risk   suggest

- The verb + –ing is also used after these expressions:

    spend/waste time, it's no good, it's not worth, it's no use:

    He **spends** his free **time shopping** for clothes.

- Some verbs are followed by either an infinitive or a verb + –ing with the same meaning:

    love*   begin   continue   hate*   prefer*   like*   start

    I **love playing** tennis.

    I **love to play** tennis.

    * When these verbs are used with would, they are always followed by the infinitive:

    I **wouldn't like to work** in a factory.

    I**'d prefer to buy** it online than go to a shop.

- Some verbs followed by either an infinitive or a verb + –ing with a difference in meaning:

Relative clauses and relative pronouns

There are two types of relative clause:

1 Defining relative clauses

These say which person or thing is being talked about. They give essential information:

The school **which I went to** had more than 1,000 pupils.

The relative clause says which school is being talked about.

2 Non-defining relative clauses

These give extra information, but do not say which person or thing is being talked about because we already know:

Leeds University, **which was founded in 1904**, has an excellent reputation.

We know which university is being talked about. The relative clause just adds extra information.

Differences between defining and non-defining relative clauses:

Defining relative clauses:	Non-defining relative clauses:
- do not use commas: The village where I live only has one shop. - can use *that* instead of *who* or *which*: The school that I went to had more than 1,000 pupils. - can omit *who*, *which* or *that* when they are the object of the verb: The school I went to had more than 1,000 pupils.	- use commas: Nagwa Mohamed, who spoke at the meeting, is the new head of the department. - cannot use *that* instead of *who* or *which*. - cannot omit the relative pronoun (*who* or *which*).

	verb + infinitive	verb + –ing
remember	You must **remember to write** your name at the top of the page. (an action you have to do)	I **remember going** to school for the first time. (a memory of something in the past)
stop	He **stopped to answer** the phone. (He stopped something he was doing in order to answer the phone.)	He **stopped speaking**. (He stopped the activity he was doing.)
try	She's **trying to improve** her vocabulary, so she's reading a lot. (Her objective is to improve her vocabulary.)	She **has tried learning** word lists as a way of improving her vocabulary. (Learning word lists is a method to reach her objective.)

Language reference

The following are relative pronouns:

- **Who** refers to people:
  The customers **who** come to this shop are generally young and well-off.
- **Which** refers to things:
  I prefer going to shops **which** give you individual attention.
- **Whose** refers to either people or things and adds information by mentioning something belonging to a person or thing:
  Children **whose** parents both work are often lonelier.
  I live in a city **whose** districts are separated by canals.
- **What** means 'the thing which' and is often used after a verb:
  She couldn't find **what** she wanted in the shop.
- **Where** can:
  - refer to something which happens/happened in a place:
    In my holidays, I go back to the village **where** I was born.
  - add information about a place:
    I come from Suzhou, **where** there is a big computer industry.
- **When** can be used to add information about a time:
  We came to Abu Dhabi in 2005, **when** I was 14.
- **Why** is used in the phrase *the reason why*:
  Greenhouse gases are causing global warming, and this is one of **the reasons why** we have to find forms of energy which do not pollute the atmosphere.

Unit 7

Reference devices

Reference devices are used to avoid repeating the same vocabulary too often:
Twenty-five per cent of the people in the survey said they (the people) would repeat the experience.

These are some common reference devices and their uses:

- **it/its** refers to the thing which was mentioned last:
  My country gives grants for **its** students to study abroad.
  It can also refer back to an idea or an argument:
  There has been a 20% fall in the number of tourists. **It** has led to a fall in income for hotels.
- **they/them/their** refer to people or things:
  There are now 20% more cars than ten years ago, but **they** only consume 10% more fuel.
- **this** can also be used to refer to the thing which was mentioned last:
  Larger cities need more water. **This** has meant that there is less water available for agriculture.

- **this/these/that** can be used as adjectives:
  Children from rural areas find it more difficult to go to university. Governments have tried various measures to deal with **this** problem.
- **one** refers to a singular countable noun from a group:
  There are several reasons why people are happier than in the past. **One** (or **One reason**) is that they have more free time.
- **he/him/his** refers to the boy or man who was mentioned last:
  Sergei sent **his** passport to the consulate because **he** wanted to apply for a visa.
- **she/her** refers to the girl or woman who was mentioned last.
- **that** can be used to the thing which was last mentioned and is often used when giving a reason:
  The number of tourists fell, and **that** is why hotels' income also fell.
- **another** refers to the second or third singular countable noun in a group:
  There are several reasons why people are happier than in the past. One is that they have more free time. **Another** is that they have more money.
- **ones** refers to a plural noun:
  Children from rural areas find it more difficult to go to university than children from urban **ones**.
- **other** is an adjective used before uncountable nouns or plural countable nouns:
  Some furniture is exported to Europe. **Other** furniture is produced for the home market.

Zero, first and second conditionals

Conditional sentences express a condition (*If ...*) and the consequence of the condition. To draw attention to the condition, put it at the beginning of the sentence:
If I want to discuss something important with my friends, I usually phone them and arrange to meet.
To draw attention to the consequence, put the condition after:
I'll call you tonight if I have time.
Note: in writing, if the condition comes first, a comma is used. If the consequence comes first, no comma is used.

Zero conditional

If/Unless + present tense, present tense:
*If I **don't have** a lot of homework to do, I **go** out with my friends.*

It is used to express something which is always or generally true.

First conditional

If/Unless + present tense, future tense / modal verb (*can*, *should*, *must*, etc.):
We **can go** to the park tomorrow if it **doesn't rain**.
If I **get** high enough marks in my exams, I'**ll study** biology at university.

It expresses a future condition which the speaker thinks is possible or likely.

Second conditional

If/Unless + past tense, would/could/might + infinitive:
If my parents **weren't** so busy, I'**d spend** more time with them.

It expresses an imaginary, impossible or improbable present or future condition:
If I lived in California, I'd eat ice cream every day. (imaginary – she doesn't live in California)
If they offered me fifty thousand dollars a year, I'd accept the job. (improbable that they'll offer fifty thousand dollars)

Unit 8

Time conjunctions

You can use time conjunctions (*when, after, before, until*, etc.) to join phrases which say the time something happens with the main part of the sentence:
I'm going to do a postgraduate course after I've graduated. (*after I've graduated* says when I will do a postgraduate course).

Depending on the context and the tenses of the verbs (see below), **when** can mean:

- after:
  Few people continue to dress like students when they have graduated.
- at about the same time:
  When students graduate, often the hardest thing is to find a job which meets their expectations.
- at the same time:
  Workers should be forbidden to smoke when they are working.

Until means 'up to the time that':
Many young people live with their parents until they get married.

Tenses with time conjunctions

- When talking about something which finishes before something in the main part of the sentence, use either a simple or a perfect form (underlined):
  Most people hope to find a well-paid job when they graduate from university (at about the same time as they graduate).
  Most people hope to find a well-paid job after they have graduated from university (after they graduate).

- When talking about actions which happen at the same time, use a simple tense:
  He wears very smart clothes when he goes to work/ (Not: *when he's going to work*)

- If you are talking about two actions which happen at the same time but one takes longer than the other, use a continuous tense for the action which takes longer:
  I hope to pass my driving test when I'm studying in New Zealand.
  (Not: *when I study in New Zealand*)

- When talking about the future, use a present tense with *when, after, before, until*, etc.:
  I won't travel to Canada until I pass my IELTS test.
  (Not: *until I will pass my IELTS test*)
  I'll visit Russia when I've saved enough money.
  (Not: *when I will save enough money*)

Word list

Abbreviations: n/np = noun / noun phrase; v/vp = verb / verb phrase; adj/adjp = adjective / adjective phrase; adv/advp = adverb / adverb phrase; T/I = transitive / intransitive; C/U = countable / uncountable

The numbers indicate the page in the unit on which the word of phrase first appears. RS indicates that the word or phrase appears in the recording script.

Unit 1

a'broad *adv* (8) in or to a foreign country

a'ccustomed to *adj* (11) If you are accustomed to something, you have experienced it often enough for it to seem normal to you.

ad'just *v* [I] (10) to change the way you behave or think in order to suit a new situation

con'cern *n* [C/U] (10) something that involves or affects you or is important to you

'customs *plural n* (11) things that have been done for a long time in a society and are part of that society's culture

de'fine (as) *v* [T] (10) to say exactly what something means

'evidence *n* [U] (10) something that makes you believe that something is true or exists

ex'perience *v* [T] (8) If you experience something, it happens to you or you are involved in it.

fi'nancial 'matters *plural n* (10) subjects connected with money

give rise to *vp* (10) to cause

go wrong *vp* (10) to develop problems

'immigrant *n* [C] (12) someone who comes to live in a different country

inter'nationally 'recognised qualifi'cations *plural n* (8) qualifications (=what you get when you pass exams) that are accepted in many different countries

'lifestyle *n* [C] (12) the way that you live

make sense *vp* (11) to have a meaning or reason that you can understand

'notice *v* [I/T] (11) to see something and be aware of it

point of view *n* [C] (10) an opinion

'problem-solving skills *plural n* (11) the ability to find solutions to problems

'process *n* [C] (11) a series of changes that happen and have a particular result

re'source *n* [C] (10) something that a country, person or oranisation has which they can use

seek out *vp* [T] (10) to look for something you want to have

stage *n* [C] (10) a period of development or a particular time in a process

stand out *vp* (11) to be very easy to see or notice

su'rroundings *plural n* (11) the place where someone or something is and the things that are in that place

take 'action *vp* (10) to do something to solve a problem

take 'something 'seriously *vp* (10) to believe that something is important and that you should pay attention to it

re'fer to sth/sb (as) *vp* (11) to call someone or something a particular name

'values *plural n* (10) beliefs about what is morally right and wrong and what is most important in life

work sth out *vp* (10) to understand something or decide something after thinking very carefully

Unit 2

a'pproach *n* [C] (18) a way of doing something

arti'ficial *adj* (18) not natural, but made by people

'attitudes (towards) *plural n* (24) how people think or feel about something and how this makes them behave

a'void *v* [T] (20) to choose not to use something or have something

con'ventional *adj* (27) Conventional objects or ways of doing things are the usual ones which have been used for a long time.

cre'ate *v* [T] (18) to make something happen or exist

crop yields *plural n* (19) the amount of a plant such as grain, fruit or vegetable that is grown

e'mit *v* [T] (18) to send out gas, heat, light, etc. into the air

'farming tech'niques *plural n* (19) methods used for working on farms

food stall *n* [C] (23) a small shop with an open front or a table from which food is sold

for one thing *phrase* (RS) used to give a reason for something

'frozen food *n* [U] (24) food that has been frozen (made very cold and hard) in order to store it

gain 'access to *vp* (19) to get the opportunity to have or use something

'greenhouse 'gases *plural n* (18) gases which cause the Earth to become warmer

'hygiene *n* [U] (20) the process of keeping things clean, especially to prevent disease

'influence *v* [T] (24) to affect or change how someone behaves or thinks

'likely to *phrase* (24) If something is more likely to be or do something, it will probably be or do that thing.

'locally *adv* (24) in the area that is near to where you live or near to the place you are talking about

'luxury *n* [C] (19) something expensive that you enjoy but do not need

'man-made *adj* (19) not natural, but made by people

nu'trition *n* [U] (19) the food that you eat and the way that it affects your health

point (sth) out *vp* (RS) to tell someone a fact

re'ject *v* [T] (19) to refuse to accept or agree with something

sound *v* (17) to seem to have a particular quality

trend *n* [C] (18) a general development or change in a situation

'ultimately *adv* (19) used to emphasise the most important fact in a situation

'value *n* [U] (18) how useful or important something is

'weather con'ditions *plural n* (19) the type of weather that a place has

Unit 3

a'chieve *v* [T] (31) to succeed in doing something good, usually by working hard

base sth on sth *vp* (32) to use something as the main part of something you are developing

com'pletion (of) *n* [U] (31) when something that you are doing or making is finished

'critical *adj* (31) very important for the way things will happen in the future

ex'press *v* [T] (30) to tell someone about an opinion, a feeling or an idea by speaking or writing

'figure *n* [C] (35) a number

find something 'easy *vp* (31) to have no difficulty doing something

'fluency *n* [U] (31) the ability to speak a language well

'gestures *plural n* (29) movements that you make with your hand, arm or head to express what you are thinking or feeling or what you want someone to do

get 'going *vp* (30) to start to happen

'handle *v* [T] (30) to deal with something

hy'pothesis *n* [C] (30) a suggested explanation for something which has not yet been proved to be true

i'deal *adj* (31) perfect or the best possible

'imitate *v* [I/T] (30) to copy the way someone or something looks, sounds or behaves

in'clusion (of) *n* [U] (29) when you have something as a part of something else

language acqui'sition *n* [U] (30) the process of learning to speak a language

'level (of) *n* [C] (31) the amount or standard of something

'literate *adj* (30) able to read and write

(im)ma'ture *adj* (30) (not) completely grown or developed

'matter *v* [I] (31) to be important or to affect what happens

more or less *phrase* (31) almost

'native 'speaker *n* [C] (31) someone who speaks a language as their first language

no 'longer *phrase* (31) in the past but not now

o'besity *n* (34) the state of being extremely fat

on a 'diet *phrase* (34) If someone is on a diet, they eat less food in order to become thinner.

'options *plural n* (29) the things that you can choose between in a particular situation

po'tential *adj* (31) possible, but not yet proved

raise a 'question *vp* [T] (31) to cause people to think about something

reach *v* [T] (31) to get to a particular level

re'cruitment *n* [U] (36) the process of trying to find someone to work for an organisation

the re'verse *n* (30) the opposite of what has just been said

sus'pect *v* [T] (31) to think that something is probably true

tongue *n* [C] (31) a language

(by) 'trial and 'error *phrase* (31) a way of learning the best way to do something by trying different methods

Unit 4

'accuracy *n* [U] (41) how correct or exact something is

'amateur *n* [C] (38) someone who does something as a hobby and not as their job

'amateur *adj* (RS) doing something as a hobby and not as your job

am'bitious 'project *n* [C] (38) a planned piece of work which will need a lot of effort and will be difficult to achieve

a'nonymous *adj* (38) If someone is anonymous, their name is not given.

a'ttract a'ttention *vp* (41) to cause people to notice something and be interested in it

'carry out re'search *vp* (38) to study something in order to discover information about it

collabo'ration *n* [C/U] (38) when two or more people work together to create or achieve something

disa'ppointing results *plural n* (38) results are not as good as you had hoped or expected

dis'courage sb from doing sth *vp* (43) to try to persuade someone not to do something

do re'search *vp* (43) to study something in order to discover information about it

e'volve *v* [I/T] (38) to develop or make something develop, usually gradually

ex'periment (with) *v* [I] (38) to try something new in order to see what happens and how succesful it is

'feedback *n* [U] (40) comments about something that you have done or made, given to help you improve it if necessary

in res'ponse to *phrase* (38) as a reaction to something that has happened or been done

keep in touch (with) *vp* (42) to continue to communicate with someone, for example by telephoning them or writing to them

keep up (with) *vp* (42) to be able to understand and deal with something that is happening or changing fast

lack in'centive *vp* (38) to have nothing to encourage you to do something

'latest 'fashions *plural n* (37) things that have recently become fashionable

launch *v* [T] (38) to begin an activity

law *n* [C] (38) something that is always true

po'tential *adj* (38) A potential problem, employer, partner, etc. may become one in the future, although they are not one now.

pro'posal *n* [C] (38) a suggestion for a plan

publi'cation *n* [C] (40) a book, newspaper or magazine

'publish *v* [T] (40) to prepare and print a book, newspaper, magazine, article, etc. so that people can buy it

'publish *v* [T] (40) to write something that is then printed in a book, newspaper, magazine, etc.

re'strict *v* [T] (43) to limit something

re'view *n* [C] an examination of what has been written about a particular subject

re'veal *v* [T] (47) to give someone information that was not known before

'social 'networking *n* [U] (47) using websites to communicate with friends and to meet other people

trans'form *v* [T] (38) to change something completely, usually to improve it

turn out *vp* (38) to happen in a particular way, or to have a particular result

Word list

Unit 5

ad'vance 'payment n [C] (49) a sum of money that is paid some time before you get the thing you want to buy

'calculate v [T] (50) to discover an amount or number using mathematics

'challenge n [C/U] (51) something that is difficult and that tests someone's ability or determination

'climate change n [U] (48) the way the Earth's weather is changing

de'pendence (on) n [U] (48) when you need someone or something in order to exist or continue as before

de'struction n [U] (48) when something is destroyed

'drawback n [C] (51) a problem or disadvantage

en'dangered 'species n [C] (48) a type of animal or plant that soon may not exist because there are very few now alive

'estimate the cost vp (51) to use any information that you have to guess how much something will cost

'focus on vp [T] (50) to give a lot of attention to one particular subject or thing

'fossil 'fuels plural n (48) fuels such as coal or oil that are obtained from under the ground

fresh air n [U] (54) air outside buildings that is clean and cool

'harness 'energy vp (55) to control energy so that you can use it

'infrastructure n [C] (51) the basic systems, such as transport and communication, that a country or organisation uses in order to work effectively

a 'major source of elec'tricity np (50) something that produces a lot of electricity

'natural 'habitat np [C] (48) the place where animals live or plants grow naturally

'nature re'serve np [C] (48) a place where animals and plants live and are protected

the next step np (51) the next in a series of actions

'power 'station / 'power plant np [C] (50) a large building or group of buildings where electricity is produced by machines

pro'duce 'profitably vp (51) to produce something in such a way that it makes profit

re'lease into the 'atmosphere vp (48) to allow substance to get into the air around the Earth

re'newable 'energy np [U] (48) energy from sources that continue to exist, for example wind or the sun

'rising sea 'levels plural np (48) the increased height of the level of seas and oceans

'sceptical adj (50) doubting that something is true or useful

'scenery n [U] (53) attractive, natural things that you see in the countryside

switch (to) v [I] (48) to change from using one thing to using another

'unspoilt 'countryside n [U] (66) areas of land that have not been changed or damaged by people

yield v [T] (50) to produce or provide something

'wildlife conser'vation 'programme np [C] (66) a plan whose aim is to protect wild animals and plants

'zero e'missions plural np (48) If something such as a machine or an industry has zero emissions, it does not release any harmful substances into the atmosphere.

Unit 6

a'fford *v* [T] (60) to have enough money to buy something

a'ttract pub'licity *vp* (64) to get attention in newspapers, on the TV, on the Internet, etc.

'bargain *n* [C] (60) something that is sold for less than its usual price or its real value

become 'common *vp* (64) to start to happen more often

boost sales *vp* (58) to increase the number of things that are sold

'branded 'product *n* [C] (57) a product that is made by a well-known company and has that company's name or symbol on it

e'fficient *adj* (58) working well and not wasting time or energy

end up *vp* (58) to finish by doing something because of a particular situation

'forecast *v* [T] (60) to say what you expect to happen in the future

go from shop to shop *vp* (64) to go to several different shops

'highly 'profitable *phrase* (59) making a large profit

'living 'standards *plural np* (61) how pleasant and comfortable someone's life is and how much money they have

in the 'medium term *phrase* (60) during a period of time that starts now and continues for a length of time that is not particularly short or long

out'weigh *v* [T] (64) to be greater or more important than something else

'own-label 'product *np* [C] (57) a product that a particular shop makes itself and which has the name of that shop on it

pro'motion *n* [C/U] (57) activities to advertise something

'purchase *v* [C/U] (57) to buy something

at a rate of *phrase* (58) used to show the number of times that something happens or how often something happens in a particular period of time

'reckon *v* [T] (58) to think that something is probably true

'retailer *n* [C] (58) a person, shop or business that sells goods to the public

take time *vp* (58) to need a long time

tempt *v* [T] (58) to make someone want to have something

think in terms of *vp* (60) to consider something from a particular point of view

Word list 113

Unit 7

blame (for) v [T] (72) to say or think that someone or something is responsible for something bad which has happened

'broadcast v [I/T] (71) to send out a programme on television or radio

clue n [C] (71) a sign or a piece of information that helps you to solve a problem or answer a question

con'fess v [I/T] (71) to admit that you have done something wrong

con'sistent adj (71) always happening in a similar way

deal with vp [T] (70) to do what needs to be done with a particular type of person

de'ception n [U] (71) the act of making someone believe something that is not true

de'tect v [T] (71) to discover or notice something, especially something that is difficult to see, hear, smell, etc.

dis'play v [T] (72) If a person or animal displays a particular kind of behaviour, they behave in that way.

'episode n [C] (71) a single event

globali'sation n [U] (76) the process by which businesses operate in many different countries and the culture of different countries becomes more similar

go'rilla n [C] (86) a big, black, hairy animal like a large monkey

'incident n [C] (71) an event, especially one that is bad or unusual

in'tentional adj (71) planned or intended

in the wild phrase (RS) in a natural environment

in'volve v [T] (69) If someone is involved in an activity, they are taking part in it.

in'volve v [T] (71) If an activity involves doing something, that thing is a necessary part of it.

'journal n [C] (69) a magazine containing articles about a particular subject

la'boratory n [C] (71) a room used for scientific work

lin'guistic 'skills plural np (71) the ability to use language

'liar n [C] (71) someone who tells lies

'overview n [T] (69) a short description of the most important facts about something

'practical work n [U] (RS) study that involves doing something or studying real situations rather than just reading and writing

pre'dict v [T] (69) to say what you think will happen in the future

psycho'logically adv (71) in a way that relates to the human mind and feelings

re'search 'programme n [C] (71) a plan for studying something in order to find out information about it

set up vp [T] (71) to get all the necessary equipment ready for an activity

'survey n [C] (71) an examination of people's opinions or behaviour made by asking people questions

tell the 'difference vp (71) to notice that two things are different from one another

a 'version of np (71) a form of something that is slightly different from other forms of the same thing

Unit 8

'ancient *adj* (81) from a long time ago

'casual clothes *plural np* (85) clothes that are comfortable and suitable for informal occasions

ce'lebrity *n* [C] (83) a famous person

conser'vation *n* [U] (78) the act of repairing something or protecting it from damage

con'temporary *adj* (78) existing or happening at the same time as something

'decorative *adj* (81) making something or someone look more attractive

'delicate 'structure *np* [C] (78) If something has a delicate structure, the parts it is made of are easy to damage or break.

de'signer clothes / brands *plural np* (84) clothes/products made by fashionable designers

'fabric *n* [C/U] (81) cloth

flexi'bility *n* [U] (78) the ability to bend or stretch

'fragile *adj* (78) easily broken, damaged or destroyed

'functional *adj* (87) designed to be practical or useful and not only attractive

'garment *n* [C] (87) a piece of clothing

give a sense of *vp* (78) to give someone a particular impression or feeling about something

inno'vations *plural n* (77) new ideas or methods

miss the point *vp* (77) to not understand what someone means

o'riginal *adj* (78) existing since the beginning or being the earliest form of something

'origins *plural n* (81) the place where something started to exist

per'formance *n* [C] (88) the act of acting, singing, dancing or playing music to entertain people

'pastime *n* [C] (RS) an activity that you enjoy doing when you are not working

pre'serve *v* [T] (81) to keep something the same or prevent it from being damaged or destroyed

'portrait *n* [C] (78) a painting, drawing or photograph of someone

pro'duced by hand *phrase* (RS) made by a person instead of a machine

re'pair *v* [T] (78) to fix something that is broken or damaged

re'tire *v* [I] (78) to leave your job and stop working, usually because you are old

'social 'events *plural np* (78) events such as parties that are organised for people to enjoy themselves with other people

'textile(s) *n* [C] (78) any type of cloth that is made by weaving crossing threads under and over each other

u'nique *adj* (78) different from everyone and everything else

IELTS practice test

LISTENING

SECTION 1 Questions 1–5

Complete the form below.

Write NO MORE THAN THREE WORDS AND/OR A NUMBER for each answer.

KT Furniture
Customer Order Form

Customer details

Example	*Answer*
Caller's name	Sue Brown

Company name: 1 ....

Address: 2 .... Trading Estate
210 New Hampton Road
South Down

Contact number: 3 .... (mobile)

Delivery option: 1 ☐ 2 ✓ (no 4 ....)

Method of payment: credit card   Type: 5 ....

Questions 6–10

Complete the table below.

Write NO MORE THAN TWO WORDS AND/OR A NUMBER for each answer.

item	code	colour	quantity
Office chairs	ASP 23	6	5
7	8		2
Leather sofa	DFD 44	9	1
10	TX 22	silver	1

Complete IELTS Bands 5–6.5

SECTION 2 Questions 11–17

Complete the sentences below.

Write NO MORE THAN TWO WORDS for each answer.

Marathon – tips for spectators

11 To enjoy the day, make sure you .... it first.

12 Travel .... within the city centre.

13 Wear .... on the day.

14 Check the .... the night before the marathon.

15 Let the .... give drinks to runners.

16 Stay on one side of the road to avoid ....

17 Don't arrange to meet runners near the ....

Questions 18–20

What does the speaker say about the following forms of transport?

Write the correct letter, A, B, C, D or E, next to questions 18–20.

A	will take more passengers than usual
B	will suit people who want to see the start of the race
C	waiting times will be longer than usual
D	will have fewer staff than usual
E	some work schedules will change

18 taxis   ....

19 trams   ....

20 buses   ....

Practice test

SECTION 3 Questions 21–26

*Choose the correct letter, **A**, **B** or **C**.*

21 What does Ahmed say about last week's seminar?
   A He wasn't able to get there on time.
   B He didn't know all the students.
   C He couldn't understand everything.

22 What does the tutor say about Ahmed's preparation for the seminar?
   A He was better prepared than some students.
   B He completed some useful work.
   C He read some useful articles.

23 What does Ahmed say about his participation in the seminar?
   A He tended to speak to his neighbour only.
   B He spoke when other students were talking.
   C He felt embarrassed when students looked at him.

24 What does Ahmed worry about most in seminars?
   A speaking at the right time
   B taking enough notes
   C staying focused

25 What does Ahmed say about his role in the group?
   A He hasn't thought about it.
   B He'd like to change it.
   C He feels he is acting a part.

26 At the next seminar, Ahmed's tutor suggests that he should
   A give other students more help with their work.
   B observe the behaviour of other students.
   C ask other students for their views.

Questions 27 and 28

Choose TWO letters, A–E.

Which TWO strategies does the tutor suggest for the next seminar?

A speak more frequently
B behave in a confident manner
C sit next to someone helpful
D listen to what other people say
E think of questions to ask

Questions 29 and 30

Choose TWO letters, A–E.

Which TWO suggestions does the tutor make about taking notes?

A plan them before the seminar
B note down key words that people say
C note points to say later
D include self-analysis
E rewrite them after the seminar

SECTION 4 Questions 31–40

Complete the notes below.

Write NO MORE THAN TWO WORDS for each answer.

DESERT PLANTS

Background
- Deserts found in what is known as a **31** .... (or dry area).
- Annual rainfall, if any, amounts to a **32** ....
- Soil contains a lot of salt and **33** ....

General adaptations of desert plants
- They can **34** .... and store water.
- They have features that reduce water loss.

Examples of adaptations
- *Saguaro Cactus*: stores water in its **35** ....
- *Barrel Cactus*: can **36** .... or shrink according to weather
- *Old Man Cactus*: has **37** .... that reflect the sun
- *Prickly Pear Cactus*: has **38** .... to keep away animals
- *Desert Spoon*: leaves are **39** .... to reduce water loss
- *Aloe Plant*: leaf surface acts like a **40** .... covering and keeps water inside

READING

READING PASSAGE 1

*You should spend about 20 minutes on **Questions 1–13**, which are based on Reading Passage 1 below.*

Domestic robots

Machines that look after your home are getting cleverer, but they still need care and attention if they are to perform as intended

Floor-cleaning machines capable of responding to their environment were among the first commercially available domestic products worthy of being called robots. The best known is the Roomba, made by iRobot, an American company which has sold more than three million of the disc-shaped, frisbee-sized vacuuming robots. The latest model, the fifth version of the Roomba, has more sensors and cleverer software than its predecessors. Press the 'Clean' button and the robot glides out of its docking station and sets off across the floor.

Domestic robots are supposed to free up time so that you can do other things, but watching how the Roomba deals with obstacles is strangely compelling. It is capable of sensing its surroundings, and does not simply try to adhere to a pre-planned route, so it is not upset if furniture is moved, or if it is picked up and taken to clean another room. Its infra-red sensors enable it to slow down before reaching an obstacle – such as a dozy cat – changing direction and setting off again.

It steadily works its way around the room, figuring out how to get out from under the television stand or untangle itself from a stray Game Boy recharging lead. Watch it for long enough, and you can sometimes predict its next move. The machine has a 'dirt sensor' and flashes a blue light when it finds things to clean up. Only when it detects no more dirt does it stop going over the same area and, eventually, conclude that the whole room is clean. It then trundles back to dock at its recharging station.

So the first observation of life with a domestic robot is that you will keep watching it before you trust it completely. Perhaps that is not surprising: after all, when automatic washing machines first appeared, people used to draw up a chair and sit and watch them complete their wash, rinse and spin cycles. Now they just load them, switch them on and leave them to it.

The second observation is that, despite their current level of intelligence, certain allowances must be made to get the best out of a domestic robot. The Roomba can be set up to clean at particular times, and to clean more than one room (small infra-red 'lighthouses' can be positioned in doorways, creating an invisible barrier between one room and the next that is only removed when the first room has been cleaned). A 'drop-off' sensor underneath the robot prevents it from falling down stairs. All very clever, but what the Roomba will not do is pick up toys, shoes and other items left lying around. Rooms cared for by robots must be kept tidy. To start with, children will happily put things away in order to watch the robot set off, but unfortunately the novelty soon wears off.

Similar allowances must be made for other domestic robots. Sweden's Husqvarna recently launched a new version of its Automower lawn mowing robot. Before it can be used, a wire must be placed around the perimeter of the lawn to define the part to be cut. If toys and other obstacles are not cleared from the lawn before it starts work, the robot will steer around them, leaving uncut areas. However, the latest version can top up its batteries with solar power, or send its owner a text message if it gets into trouble trying to climb a mole-hill.

But there is still only a limited range of domestic robots. Machines that mop the floor, clean a swimming pool and clear muck from guttering are made by iRobot. Several surveillance robots are also on offer. The Rovio, made by WowWee of Hong Kong, is a wi-fi-enabled webcam, mounted on an extending arm, which rides along smoothly on a nimble set of three wheels. Its movement can be remotely operated over the Internet via a laptop or mobile phone. The idea is that Rovio can patrol the home when its owner is away, either automatically or under manual control: in the latter case, two-way communication allows the operator to see and talk via the machine. So you could, for instance, shout at the cat if it is sleeping on your best sofa.

Some machines are called robots even though they cannot move around. There is an ironing robot, for instance, that resembles an inflatable dummy: put a damp shirt on it, and it puffs up to remove the creases. Similarly, there are elaborate trouser presses that aspire to be robots. But do these devices really count as robots? If so, then surely dishwashers and washing machines do, too.

Yet whatever shape or size robots come in, many will be adored. Another important observation from living with a robot is that it tends to become part of the family. 'People give them names, and if they have to be sent back for repair, they carefully add a mark to them to ensure they get the same machine back,' says Nancy Dussault Smith of iRobot.

Practice test

Questions 1–6

Do the following statements agree with the information given in Reading Passage 1?

Write

> TRUE   *if the statement agrees with the information*
> FALSE   *if the statement contradicts the information*
> NOT GIVEN   *if there is no information on this*

1 Improvements have been made to Roomba over time.
2 Obstacles have to be removed from Roomba's path.
3 Roomba keeps cleaning in one place until it thinks it is dirt free.
4 People once found washing machines as fascinating as robots.
5 Comparative studies are available on the intelligence of domestic robots.
6 Roomba tidies up a room as well as cleaning it.

Questions 7–10

Answer the questions below.

Use **NO MORE THAN THREE WORDS** *from the passage for each answer.*

7   What is used to mark out the mowing area for the Automower?
8   What form of renewable energy can some Automowers use?
9   What does the ironing robot look like?
10 What do people often put on a robot when it is going to be repaired?

Questions 11–13

Label the diagram below.

Choose **NO MORE THAN THREE WORDS** *from the passage for each answer.*

The Rovio

11 .... holding webcam

Wheel design allows easy 12 ....

Manual controls give home-owner 13 .... with robot

READING PASSAGE 2

You should spend about 20 minutes on **Questions 14–26**, which are based on Reading Passage 2 below.

Deforestation in the 21st century

When it comes to cutting down trees, satellite data reveals a shift from the patterns of the past

A   Globally, roughly 13 million hectares of forest are destroyed each year. Such deforestation has long been driven by farmers desperate to earn a living or by loggers building new roads into pristine forest. But now new data appears to show that big, block clearings that reflect industrial deforestation have come to dominate, rather than these smaller-scale efforts that leave behind long, narrow swaths of cleared land. Geographer Ruth DeFries of Columbia University and her colleagues used satellite images to analyse tree-clearing in countries ringing the tropics, representing 98 per cent of all remaining tropical forest. Instead of the usual 'fish bone' signature of deforestation from small-scale operations, large, chunky blocks of cleared land reveal a new motive for cutting down woods.

B   In fact, a statistical analysis of 41 countries showed that forest loss rates were most closely linked with urban population growth and agricultural exports in the early part of the 21st century – even overall population growth was not as strong an influence. 'In previous decades, deforestation was associated with planned colonisation, resettlement schemes in local areas and farmers clearing land to grow food for subsistence,' DeFries says. 'What we're seeing now is a shift from small-scale farmers driving deforestation to distant demands from urban growth, agricultural trade and exports being more important drivers.'

C   In other words, the increasing urbanisation of the developing world, as populations leave rural areas to concentrate in booming cities, is driving deforestation, rather than containing it. Coupled with this there is an ongoing increase in consumption in the developed world of products that have an impact on forests, whether furniture, shoe leather or chicken feed. 'One of the really striking characteristics of this century is urbanisation and rapid urban growth in the developing world,' DeFries says. 'People in cities need to eat.' 'There's no surprise there,' observes Scott Poynton, executive director of the Tropical Forest Trust, a Switzerland-based organisation that helps businesses implement and manage sustainable forestry in countries such as Brazil, Congo and Indonesia. 'It's not about people chopping down trees. It's all the people in New York, Europe and elsewhere who want cheap products, primarily food.'

D   DeFries argues that in order to help sustain this increasing urban and global demand, agricultural productivity will need to be increased on lands that have already been cleared. This means that better crop varieties or better management techniques will need to be used

Practice test

E   on the many degraded and abandoned lands in the tropics. And the Tropical Forest Trust is building management systems to keep illegally harvested wood from ending up in, for example, deck chairs, as well as expanding its efforts to look at how to reduce the 'forest footprint' of agricultural products such as palm oil. Poynton says, 'The point is to give forests value as forests, to keep them as forests and give them a use as forests. They're not going to be locked away as national parks. That's not going to happen.'

E   But it is not all bad news. Halts in tropical deforestation have resulted in forest regrowth in some areas where tropical lands were previously cleared. And forest clearing in the Amazon, the world's largest tropical forest, dropped from roughly 1.9 million hectares a year in the 1990s to 1.6 million hectares a year over the last decade, according to the Brazilian government. 'We know that deforestation has slowed down in at least the Brazilian Amazon,' DeFries says. 'Every place is different. Every country has its own particular situation, circumstances and driving forces.'

F   Regardless of this, deforestation continues, and cutting down forests is one of the largest sources of greenhouse gas emissions from human activity – a double blow that both eliminates a biological system to suck up CO_2 and creates a new source of greenhouse gases in the form of decaying plants. The United Nations Environment Programme estimates that slowing such deforestation could reduce some 50 billion metric tons of CO_2, or more than a year of global emissions. Indeed, international climate negotiations continue to attempt to set up a system to encourage this, known as the UN Development Programme's fund for reducing emissions from deforestation and forest degradation in developing countries (REDD). If policies [like REDD] are to be effective, we need to understand what the driving forces are behind deforestation, DeFries argues. This is particularly important in the light of new pressures that are on the horizon: the need to reduce our dependence on fossil fuels and find alternative power sources, particularly for private cars, is forcing governments to make products such as biofuels more readily accessible. This will only exacerbate the pressures on tropical forests.

G   But millions of hectares of pristine forest remain to protect, according to this new analysis from Columbia University. Approximately 60 percent of the remaining tropical forests are in countries or areas that currently have little agricultural trade or urban growth. The amount of forest area in places like central Africa, Guyana and Suriname, DeFries notes, is huge. 'There's a lot of forest that has not yet faced these pressures.'

Questions 14–19

Reading Passage 2 has seven paragraphs, A–G.

Which paragraph contains the following information?

You may use any letter more than once.

14   two ways that farming activity might be improved in the future

15   reference to a fall in the rate of deforestation in one area

16   the amount of forest cut down annually

17   how future transport requirements may increase deforestation levels

18   a reference to the typical shape of early deforested areas

19   key reasons why forests in some areas have not been cut down

Questions 20–21

Choose TWO letters, A–E.

Which TWO of these reasons do experts give for current patterns of deforestation?

A   to provide jobs
B   to create transport routes
C   to feed city dwellers
D   to manufacture low-budget consumer items
E   to meet government targets

Questions 22–23

Choose TWO letters, A–E.

The list below gives some of the impacts of tropical deforestation.
Which TWO of these results are mentioned by the writer of the text?

A   local food supplies fall
B   soil becomes less fertile
C   some areas have new forest growth
D   some regions become uninhabitable
E   local economies suffer

Questions 24–26

Complete the sentences below.

Choose NO MORE THAN TWO WORDS and/or A NUMBER from the passage for each answer.

24   The expression 'a ....' is used to assess the amount of wood used in certain types of production.

25   Greenhouse gases result from the .... that remain after trees have been cut down.

26   About .... of the world's tropical forests have not experienced deforestation yet.

READING PASSAGE 3

*You should spend about 20 minutes on **Questions 27–40**, which are based on Reading Passage 3 below.*

So you think humans are unique

There was a time when we thought humans were special in so many ways. Now we know better. We are not the only species that feels emotions, empathises with others or abides by a moral code. Neither are we the only ones with personalities, cultures and the ability to design and use tools. Yet we have steadfastly clung to the notion that one attribute, at least, makes us unique: we alone have the capacity for language.

Alas, it turns out we are not so special in this respect either. Key to the revolutionary reassessment of our talent for communication is the way we think about language itself. Where once it was seen as a monolith, a discrete and singular entity, today scientists find it is more productive to think of language as a suite of abilities. Viewed this way, it becomes apparent that the component parts of language are not as unique as the whole.

Take gesture, arguably the starting point for language. Until recently, it was considered uniquely human – but not any more. Mike Tomasello of the Max Planck Institute for Evolutionary Anthropology in Leipzig, Germany, and others have compiled a list of gestures observed in monkeys, gibbons, gorillas, chimpanzees, bonobos and orang-utans, which reveals that gesticulation plays a large role in their communication. Ape gestures can involve touch, vocalising or eye movement, and individuals wait until they have another ape's attention before making visual or auditory gestures. If their gestures go unacknowledged, they will often repeat them or touch the recipient.

In an experiment carried out in 2006 by Erica Cartmill and Richard Byrne from the University of St Andrews in the UK, they got a person to sit on a chair with some highly desirable food such as banana to one side of them and some bland food such as celery to the other. The orang-utans, who could see the person and the food from their enclosures, gestured at their human partners to encourage them to push the desirable food their way. If the person feigned incomprehension and offered the bland food, the animals would change their gestures – just as humans would in a similar situation. If the human seemed to understand while being somewhat confused, giving only half the preferred food, the apes would repeat and exaggerate their gestures – again in exactly the same way a human would. Such findings highlight the fact that the gestures of non-human primates are not merely innate reflexes but are learned, flexible and under voluntary control – all characteristics that are considered prerequisites for human-like communication.

As well as gesturing, pre-linguistic infants babble. At about five months, babies start to make their first speech sounds, which some researchers believe contain a random selection of all the phonemes humans can produce. But as children learn the language of their parents, they narrow their sound repertoire to fit the model to which they are exposed, producing just the sounds of their native language as well as its classic intonation patterns. Indeed, they lose their polymath talents so effectively that they are ultimately unable to produce some sounds – think about the difficulty some speakers have producing the English *th*.

Dolphin calves also pass through a babbling phase. Laurance Doyle from the SETI Institute in Mountain View, California, Brenda McCowan from the University of California at Davis and their colleagues analysed the complexity of baby dolphin sounds and found it looked remarkably like that of babbling infants, in that the young dolphins had a much wider repertoire of sound than adults. This suggests that they practise the sounds of their species, much as human babies do, before they begin to put them together in the way charactcristic of mature dolphins of their species.

Of course, language is more than mere sound – it also has meaning. While the traditional, cartoonish version of animal communication renders it unclear, unpredictable and involuntary, it has become clear that various species are able to give meaning to particular sounds by connecting them with specific ideas. Dolphins use 'signature whistles', so called because it appears that they name themselves. Each develops a unique moniker within the first year of life and uses it whenever it meets another dolphin.

One of the clearest examples of animals making connections between specific sounds and meanings was demonstrated by Klaus Zuberbühler and Katie Slocombe of the University of St Andrews in the UK. They noticed that chimps at Edinburgh Zoo appeared to make rudimentary references to objects by using distinct cries when they came across different kinds of food. Highly valued foods such as bread would elicit high-pitched grunts, less appealing ones, such as an apple, got low-pitched grunts. Zuberbühler and Slocombe showed not only that chimps could make distinctions in the way they vocalised about food, but that other chimps understood what they meant. When played recordings of grunts that were produced for a specific food, the chimps looked in the place where that food was usually found. They also searched longer if the cry had signalled a prized type of food.

Clearly animals do have greater talents for communication than we realised. Humans are still special, but it is a far more graded, qualified kind of special than it used to be.

Practice test

Questions 27–31

Choose the correct letter, A, B, C or D.

27 What point does the writer make in the first paragraph?
   A We know more about language now than we used to.
   B We recognise the importance of talking about emotions.
   C We like to believe that language is a strictly human skill.
   D We have used tools for longer than some other species.

28 According to the writer, what has changed our view of communication?
   A analysing different world languages
   B understanding that language involves a range of skills
   C studying the different purposes of language
   D realising that we can communicate without language

29 The writer quotes the Cartmill and Byrne experiment because it shows
   A the similarities in the way humans and apes use gesture.
   B the abilities of apes to use gesture in different environments.
   C how food can be used to encourage ape gestures.
   D how hard humans find it to interpret ape gestures.

30 In paragraph 7, the writer says that one type of dolphin sound is
   A used only when dolphins are in danger.
   B heard only at a particular time of day.
   C heard at a range of pitch levels.
   D used as a form of personal identification.

31 Experiments at Edinburgh Zoo showed that chimps were able to
   A use grunts to ask humans for food.
   B use pitch changes to express meaning.
   C recognise human voices on a recording.
   D tell the difference between a false grunt and a real one.

Reading

Questions 32–36

Do the following statements agree with the claims of the writer in Reading Passage 3?

Write

YES	if the statement agrees with the claims of the writer
NO	if the statement contradicts the claims of the writer
NOT GIVEN	if it is impossible to say what the writer thinks about this

32 It could be said that language begins with gesture.

33 Ape gestures always consist of head or limb movements.

34 Apes ensure that other apes are aware of their gesturing.

35 Primate and human gestures share some key features.

36 Cartoons present an amusing picture of animal communication.

Questions 37–40

Complete the summary using the list of words, A–H, below.

Babbling

It seems that humans are not the only species that babble. Before young infants speak, some experts think that they produce the **37** .... mixture of human sounds. Over time, however, they copy the language of their parents, and this affects their ability to pronounce **38** .... sounds from other languages.

A **39** .... pattern has been found among dolphins. They produce a range of individual sounds when they are babies, and then combine some of these to produce the sounds of **40** .... dolphins later on.

A	adult	B	rare
C	similar	D	full
E	restricted	F	sociable
G	different	H	random

IELTS practice test 129

Practice test

WRITING

WRITING TASK 1

You should spend about 20 minutes on this task.

The chart and table below show customer satisfaction levels in the US with airlines and aspects of air travel in 1999, 2000 and 2007.

Summarise the information by selecting and reporting the main features, and make comparisons where relevant.

Write at least 150 words.

Satisfaction with the job the nation's major airlines are doing

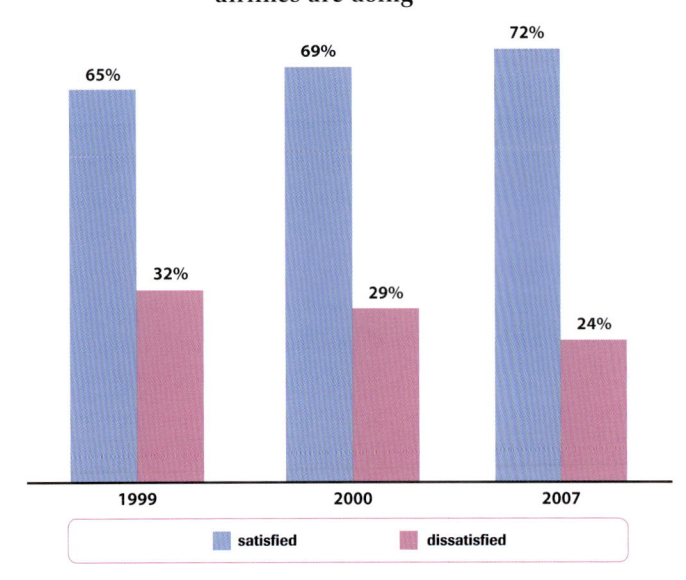

- 1999: satisfied 65%, dissatisfied 32%
- 2000: satisfied 69%, dissatisfied 29%
- 2007: satisfied 72%, dissatisfied 24%

Satisfaction with specific aspects of the flying experience, Gullup Polls

% satisfied	1999 %	2000 %	2007 %
Courtesy of flight attendants	88	90	92
Courtesy of check-in/gate agents	87	89	88
Price of tickets	45	59	65
Schedules	75	79	79
Comfort of seats	—	—	47

WRITING TASK 2

You should spend about 40 minutes on this task.

Write about the following topic.

To learn effectively, children need to eat a healthy meal at school.

How true is this statement?

Whose responsibility is it to provide food for school children?

Give reasons for your answer and include any relevant examples from your own knowledge or experience.

Write at least 250 words.

SPEAKING

PART 1

4–5 minutes

Examiner

Now, in this first part, I'd like to ask some questions about yourself. What do you do? Do you work or are you a student?

- What are you studying?
- Who do you study with?
- When did you start your course?
- Is there anything you particularly like about your studies?
- What would you like to study in the future?

- What job do you do?
- Who do you work with?
- When did you start your job?
- Is there anything you particularly like about your job?
- What other job would you like to do in the future?

Let's talk about restaurants now.

- How often do you eat in a restaurant? Why? / Why not?
- Where is your favourite restaurant?
- Do you prefer restaurant food or home-cooked food? Why?
- Have you ever complained about the food in a restaurant? Why?
- What do you think makes a restaurant successful?

I'd like to talk about the news now.

- How do you usually find out about the world news?
- When did you last listen to the news on the radio?
- Which types of news article do *not* interest you? Why?
- Do you think web-based news sites will become more popular than newspapers in the future? Why? / Why not?
- Would you like to be a journalist? Why? / Why not?

Practice test

PART 2

2–3 minutes

Examiner

Now I'm going to give you a topic and I'd like you to talk about it for one to two minutes. Before you talk, you'll have one minute to think about what you're going to say, you can make some notes if you wish. Do you understand? Here is some paper and a pencil for making notes and here is your topic. I'd like you to describe someone who you think can or could communicate well with others.

Describe someone who you think can or could communicate well with others.

You should say:

  who this person is/was

  how you know about this person

  what this person does/did

and explain why you think this person is/was a good communicator.

All right? Remember you have one to two minutes for this, so don't worry if I stop you. I will tell you when the time is up. Can you start speaking now, please?

- Do your friends think this person is/was a good communicator?
- Do you think it's easy to be a good communicator?

PART 3

4–5 minutes

Examiner

We've been talking about good communication, and I'd like to ask you some more general questions about this.

Let's consider different forms of communication.

- What forms of communication (e.g. letters, faxes) do people use these days?
- What forms of communication were popular in the past?
- How are text messages different from letters?

Let's move on to talk about communicating with people.

- Should parents or schools teach children how to communicate?
- How important are speaking and writing skills in communication?
- Do children communicate in a different way from adults?

Thank you. That is the end of the Speaking Test.

Recording script

Unit 1

CD1 Track 1

Don Hello, come in and take a seat.

Jenny Oh, thanks.

D Good ... and how can I help you?

J Well, I'd quite like to join this International Social Club and I was hoping you could help me.

D Yes, no problem. Let me just get the form up on my screen and I'll fill in your details. Let's see … yes, here we are. OK, the first thing we need is your name.

J Jenny Foo, that's F–double O.

D OK, great, and can you tell me how old you are, Jenny?

J I'm 21.

D Great, and how long have you been here in Australia, by the way?

J I arrived just last month, two weeks before the start of the academic year, just to sort things out and settle in a bit.

D Good idea. Where are you from originally?

J I'm from Kuala Lumpur – that's where I was born and brought up.

D So, you're Malaysian, are you?

J That's right, though I lived in the United States for a couple of years when I was a teenager – we went there for my father's job.

D Right. And can you tell me your current address, please?

J Sure. Just at the moment I'm lodging with a family at 13 Anglesea Road in Bondi.

D OK, let me just type that in. Er, how do you spell Anglesea, by the way?

J It's spelled A-N-G-L-E-S-E-A.

D Thanks. That's quite a long way from the city centre, isn't it? Is it a problem getting into the city centre?

J Not really, because the buses are good, and it's a nice, quiet area to live in.

D Mm, that's true. So I guess you must have a cell-phone number you can give me so we can keep you informed of events and so on.

J Yes. Let me just have a look – it's a new one, so I haven't learned the number yet. Ah, here it is. It's 040 422 9160.

D ... 9160. OK, good. And you like the family you're living with?

J Sure. They've got a little boy, who is quite noisy, but he's really no trouble.

D Fine. Now, let's see, what's next? Er, yep. Can you tell me what you do – I mean, are you working or studying?

J Well, at the moment, I'm doing a temporary job with a company here in Sydney – I'm an economist, in fact.

D OK – and how long do you think you'll be here in Sydney?

J At least a year. I may look for work here afterwards.

D Great. Now, you want to join the International Social Club, and it would be good to know a bit about your free-time interests as well. What do you like doing?

J Well, I'm quite musical and I really enjoy singing.

D Mm-hm.

J Back home, I sang with a band – just, you know, for fun. But for me, what I like best is dancing. You know, the modern sort? I really love it.

CD1 Track 2

Don So how are you getting on here? I mean, your level of English is better than most people who come from overseas to work and you've got a really nice American accent, so I don't suppose you have any communication problems in the office, though you might find some of our Australian slang more difficult to understand.

Jenny Well, a bit, but I haven't met that many Australians yet – outside of work, I mean.

D Right.

J But could you tell me a bit about the International Club, now I've joined?

D Sure. We've got – er, let's see – currently about 50 members, but people join all the time, so I should think that figure will go up. Last year, we had 30 members and the year before just 18, so we're growing and getting better known. I reckon that at this rate, next year we'll have about 80.

J And does the club hold regular meetings?

D Yes, every second Thursday evening in fact, so a couple of times a month, though of course when you start making friends, you'll be getting together with them more often than that, I guess. The next meeting will be next Thursday if I'm not mistaken. Er, yes, that's right.

J And what happens when the club meets – I mean, what sort of things are organised?

D The usual thing is for one of the members to give a little presentation about where they're from, their customs and so on, but from time to time they do other things – outings to places around Sydney, or meeting up to eat together in a restaurant or go to a concert together or something like that.

J OK, that sounds fun … and the members aren't just people from other countries, non-Australians, are they?

D No, not at all. The main point of the club is to give people like you the the chance to mix in more with people from this country, people of all ages – you'll find us very friendly! I think the contact has a positive effect on visitors to this country – and in fact, it affects us locals positively as well. You know, it's a sort of intercultural experience for everybody. And of course you should get the chance to do all sorts of activities with other members of the club if you want to – it's not just for talking. And hopefully you'll make friends with people who have similar interests.

J It sounds great. I'm really looking forward to the first meeting.

CD1 Track 3

a Well, I think the people here are very friendly and I've made a lot of new friends. And the course I'm doing is great. I think I'm learning a lot.

b Well, I'm not too keen on flying because you spend too long at airports, but I like train journeys a lot because you see the country as you travel through it. It's quite relaxing.

c I find it hard being away from my family and not seeing my friends. You know, I miss them, but apart from that it's fine.

d I've been here since I came to university, so for about two years.

CD1 Track 4

1 Well, I think the people here are very friendly and I've made a lot of new friends.

2 Well, I'm not too keen on flying because you spend too long at airports.

3 I find it hard being away from my family and not seeing my friends.

4 I've been here since I came to university, so for about two years.

Unit 2

CD1 Track 5

Debbie Good afternoon. My name's Debbie Green and I'm going to give you a short but hopefully interesting introduction to working at this hospital. I'll start with some guidelines about nutrition and fitness … er, because a hospital environment can be stressful, and so we always encourage our staff to stay fit and have a healthy lifestyle. So … just a few tips first. As you know, the key to good health is eating what we call 'a balanced diet'; many people don't do this, however. For one thing, they don't eat enough fruit and vegetables or home-prepared food. When you feel hungry, it's often too easy to grab something quick, because you're tired or busy. Cooking a healthy meal takes longer, and this is often why people live on sandwiches and fast food instead. Please – don't fall into this unhealthy trap.

Of course, you have to do a little exercise and keep fit as well. I know you'll have a lot of work and may not have time to join a gym … but consider how often you take the lift, rather than the stairs, or how often you drive rather than walk. Health wise, it may just be a question of doing things differently, rather than starting a very active sport.

In fact, being generally active is much healthier than doing lots of exercise just occasionally. As you know, this can be as risky for your heart as being inactive! As long as you do at least an hour's exercise a day – and some of you will do more than that at work – you'll find that you don't lie awake at night worrying about the next day – and that's the main advantage of exercise. Remember – this is a hospital, and you are supposed to be the healthiest people here!

Moving on to health and safety, I want to point out that it's quite OK to take a break any time that you're not busy. We know that when there's an emergency you may have to miss that cup of tea or coffee in the canteen or wherever you go, but generally you shouldn't work for more than three hours without a break, otherwise your attention levels will drop and you could then make a careless mistake.

Another important issue is hygiene. You're all trained to clean your hands at work, but remember that germs can live for a long time, so please make sure that you don't leave even a small amount of rubbish around … there are brooms in the cupboards, so use them. We do have cleaners, but they aren't always here when you need them, I'm afraid, and a little dirt can soon build up.

CD1 Track 6

Debbie Now, as you're all new, I'm just going to show you a map of the hospital and point out a few key places. Let's start with the recreation centre. At the moment, we're in the main building, that's here … and if you go out of the main entrance and just along the main road to the east … you'll find the staff recreation centre. It's this T-shaped building … and there's a range of things that you can do here to help you relax.

If you get ill, we do have a health centre for all registered employees, and this is directly behind the main hospital building. So, if you go out of the back exit, it's just in front of you, and there's a small pharmacy next to it. I'm based here and I have a few leaflets on things if you want to come and see me.

Many of you will be doing shift work, so you might like to go to the 24-hour swimming pool and sauna. They're very close by, and it doesn't cost much money to get in. If you walk out of the front of the main building, there's a road straight ahead of you … go down that and turn left into Tye Road – you'll see the pool entrance at the end of that road, just beyond the line of trees.

We've talked about eating healthily, and there's a very useful store nearby that sells a large range of organic products and health-food supplements. This is also in front of the main building, but this time you need to go beyond the turning for Tye Road and you'll see it on the right-hand corner, directly opposite another building.

Finally, if you want a healthy meal and you have very little time to get it, of course there's always the canteen inside the main building. But I would recommend a place called Jenny's Restaurant. Leave the front of the main building and head for the roundabout. When you're there, take the second turning on the left … it's just along that road before the trees. You can get a number of excellent dishes here at a reasonable price.

Well, I think that's all that's…

CD1 Track 7

Examiner Now I'm going to give you a topic and I'd like you to talk about it for one to two minutes. Before you talk, you'll have one minute to think about what you're going to say. You can make some notes if you wish. Do you understand?

Eva Ah-hah.

Ex Here's a paper and pencil for making notes and here's your topic. I'd like you to talk about somewhere you go to shop for food.

Ev Well, I'm going to talk about where I shop for food. Um, like most people, I have to go shopping for food quite frequently. Um, I live with a couple of other women and we're students, so we can't afford to eat in restaurants very often. We're all healthy eaters, but, um, I really like going to the local market because I like organic food and everything you get there is fantastic, it's so fresh. So let me tell you where it is … um, it's in this street near my home … it's a pedestrian street … you know, there are no cars. It's right in the middle of a busy district, um, it's opposite the station, so it's very convenient. Yeah – and what's it like? Well … um, it's usually pretty crowded … it's quite a popular place. There's a large number of stalls that sell food – and some shops too.

I've been going there for quite a while, so I know where the healthiest food is. I usually buy things like fruit and vegetables … also meat and cheese and fish. I've got a favourite stall, it's run by a little old lady and any of the fruit she sells is great. Er, she weighs everything very quickly … and you can't bargain with her … but the price is always reasonable.

As I've mentioned, I like it because the food tastes good, but also it's a very sociable place. People do stop and talk to each other – in fact, it's very noisy. Yeah – all in all, I like it because it's a great place to go … it's a colourful experience.

CD1 Track 8

Er, she weighs everything very quickly … and you can't bargain with her … but the price is always reasonable.

CD1 Track 9

1 … we're students, so we can't afford to eat in restaurants very often.
2 I really like going to the local market …
3 … everything you get there's fantastic – it's so fresh.
4 … it's a pedestrian street … you know, there are no cars.
5 There's a large number of stalls that sell food – and some shops, too.
6 I've got a favourite stall, it's run by a little old lady …
7 As I've mentioned, I like it because the food tastes good, but also it's a very sociable place.
8 All in all, I like it because it's a great place to go … it's a colourful experience.

Unit 3

CD1 Track 10

Tutor Come in …

Amanda Hi.

T Oh hi, Amanda … You've come to discuss your mid-term assignment, haven't you?

A Yes, that's right.

T So, what have you decided to do?

A Well, I thought I could base my study on pronunciation and get students to do some self-assessment of their own pronunciation skills.

T That's interesting. You mean get them to record themselves …

A That's right … then listen back and see where their weaknesses lie.

T Good idea. You could also do some peer evaluation.

A Oh yes … see whether their assessment of themselves matches what their classmates think.

T Ah-hah. So, how are you planning to do the assignment?

A Well, I'm going to select a short extract from somewhere and ask them to read it aloud. Maybe something from one of the textbooks we're reading.

T Why don't you look up one of my lectures on the website and find a suitable extract there? That way, you'll be using authentic spoken language, rather than written text, and it will be a model for students to listen to.

A Oh yes, that's a much better idea. I'll still have to write it out, though, won't I?

T Yes – I don't think you can expect them to remember it. Even a sentence is hard to recall.

A No, and it isn't a memory test … So when I choose the extract, what features do I need to think about?

T Um, first I'd say pick something … well, something that's about a paragraph long but that makes sense out of the context of the lecture.

A Right – a clear, well-structured passage …

T Yes, because to read something well, you've got to be able to understand it, haven't you?

A Yes, that might mean taking a while to make the selection … I guess it shouldn't consist entirely of short words!

T No – that's an obvious one. You need to think about what features of pronunciation you're going to focus on. Then make sure that your extract has examples of these.

A So some multi-syllable words … Things like *probably* and *approximately*.

T Yes – some challenges! And then there's sentence length.

A Mmm – I should include some complex sentences so that the students have to show they know where to pause.

T Exactly. I wouldn't worry about how many sentences there are – but what you do need are some obvious main points.

A So that they can stress things?

T Yes, particular words or phrases should stand out as significant. You know, we've already covered this in our classes over the weeks …

CD1 Track 11

Tutor Now, let me see. Is there a lecture that I could recommend for you?

Amanda What about the one you did at the start of term on, on the history of English?

T Yes, you could go for that – it had a lot of information which was clearly sequenced and presented, so you might find a nice chunk you can use. The topic's a bit dull, though.

A Uh-huh. I guess it's good to use something enjoyable.

T Yes, you might as well. You have a choice, so … um … the lecture on gestures and signs certainly went down well.

A Oh, I really liked that one, but I'm not sure that the content is related to what I'm doing.

T Mmm. Does that matter? … OK – there's the one on intonation patterns – I didn't take long to put that together, though … it might be a bit …

A … the topic's certainly more closely linked to the whole area of pronunciation.

T OK, so could be good … just watch out in case there are too many examples or models.

A The assignment after that lecture was fun.

T What about language and rhythm? That was one of my mini-lectures …

A Oh right, so I wouldn't have to spend too much time going through the content to find something.

T No, whereas the one on intonation patterns was a lot longer. Well, you've got a few to choose from there …

A So whatever I choose, I'll need to type it out and give them a copy each and then get them to record themselves reading the paragraph aloud.

T Yes – give them about ten minutes to prepare. You can record in next Tuesday's class if you like.

A Oh thanks. Do we have the equipment?

T That's also important – yes! They could use mobile phones, couldn't they? Though the sound quality may not be good on all of them.

A Technology can be unreliable at times … but OK.

T Well, we can also bring in some of the department's digital recorders. You just need to book those in advance.

A OK, thanks.

T Well, good luck, and let me know if you need any more help. It will certainly be interesting to look at your findings afterwards.

A Thanks, Dr White.

CD1 Track 12

Abi A couple of years ago, I went on holiday with a friend to Windsor. Um, the reason why we chose Windsor is that I've got an aunt who lives there. She's been living there for 20 years now. And, well, I've always enjoyed travelling … I've always wanted to go to the UK. At the time, my friend and I had just finished our exams at school and we were waiting to go to university. It was the summer break, and she invited us to visit her, so we decided to go.

Before we went, we hired a car, which we picked up when we reached the airport. I remember it was a bright green Mini. We drove it straight to my aunt's house in Windsor and left it outside for a day or two. This was because she lived in the centre of town and most places,

like Windsor Castle, were easy to reach on foot. However, one morning we took a trip to a gallery. There was an art exhibition that I wanted to see. So we set off, but after half an hour, 'bang' – we had a flat tyre. Now, unfortunately, neither of us knew how to change a tyre. So the next thing we did was to call the emergency services and explain the situation. Well, I speak fairly good English, but I didn't know how to say *tyre* and I was on the phone, so that made it worse … I just had to keep saying 'We've got a problem with the wheel.' And during all this, my friend was making hand signals at me and eventually I just said 'Flat'. Well, it was amazing … as soon as I said that word, she went 'Oh right, I understand'. Twenty minutes later, a recovery van arrived and fixed our flat tyre, with no charge. So – what have I learned from this experience? It was a difficult situation, but ever since then, I've known that *a flat* in English means 'a flat tyre'!

CD1 Track 13

sheep	jeep
climb	crime
vent	went

CD1 Track 14

Abi A couple of years ago, I went on holiday with a friend to Windsor. Um, the reason why we chose Windsor is that I've got an aunt who lives there. She's been living there for 20 years now. And, well, I've always enjoyed travelling … I've always wanted to go to the UK. At the time, my friend and I had just finished our exams at school and we were waiting to go to university. It was the summer break, and she invited us to visit her, so we decided to go.

Unit 4

CD1 Track 15

Lecturer Today, I'm going to be talking about amateur journalism; in other words, journalism practised by ordinary people, not professional journalists. For people like you, who want to get some real writing experience, this can be a good way to get started, and later I'll be offering you some practical tips to help you.

Amateur journalists are providing more and more news. I think the main cause of this change has been the Internet. Nowadays, anyone close to an important event can write a report and email it to a newspaper, or they can take a photo with a digital camera or use their mobile phone to make a video film of what's happening.

Also, amateur journalism isn't just for people who are in the right place at the right time. People can now write reports and articles about things which a big organisation might not be interested in and post their ideas on their website or blog. This means that all sorts of people can express their views.

Also, in the past, if you wanted to make your opinions known, one of the few ways of doing this was to send a letter to a newspaper, but normally newspapers only print a few of the thousands of letters they receive each day. Now, people can write about the things which are really important to them and the people around them and they put it in a blog. As a result, amateur journalists often write about something which is a local issue, and by 'local issue', I mean something happening in the school in their area or the traffic in their town, but not something necessarily of national or international interest.

Amateur journalism is a growing phenonemon. There are now major online newspapers. *Ohmynews* in South Korea, for example, has a large number of readers, and for this reason, they can attract advertising and get income from this. And, as a result, it's become a profitable business.

CD1 Track 16

Lecturer But how can you get involved? How can you begin to write articles which will be published on sites like these?

Well, first you must have something interesting to say, something you want to communicate with readers. Assuming you have this, it's important in an article to attract people's attention and gain their interest, so put the main facts first, answering these questions: Who? Why? When? How? and Where?

Get those basic facts down to start with and get people interested. Then fill in the details in the rest of the article: the best model is really shaped like a pyramid. You put the most important facts at the top of the article and lots of smaller details down below.

Remember, you want people to keep reading, so you need to hold your readers' interest. A really good technique for doing that is to put in quotations from people who are part of the story – what they really said. You know the sort of thing, um, 'Tanya, mother of two, said: "It all happened so quickly that we didn't have time to react."' Quotations bring the article alive.

Once you've written your article, go over it again to make sure that any figures you quote are correct. Make sure that Tanya really has two children and not one or three. Then, after that, once you've got your ideas down, rewrite your article, making sure that your paragraphs don't contain more than three sentences – people like them to be brief and to the point, and this will help to hold their attention.

And another thing to bear in mind: if they're reading online, people will soon stop reading your piece and start reading something else, so keep the whole article brief. Don't put in a conclusion – just let your article end without it.

Another good piece of advice is to remember that old cliché which we've all heard – that a picture is worth a thousand words. It's true, so if you can, include a picture. It'll attract more attention and illustrate what you've been saying.

Finally, you need to write a headline – something eye-catching which will get people to just skim the article to start with, and then, if it's well written, they'll read it more carefully afterwards.

CD1 Track 17

Elena Well, I think it helps people in quite a lot of ways, for instance to get information or to book air tickets. It helps people to study and to do research for their homework and their studies or even to get advice about how to study.

CD1 Track 18

Elena Mm, well, I'm not sure. Some people do perhaps, for example young people who should be studying instead, but a lot of people use the Internet for their jobs or for other things. Maybe too much time chatting to friends, not enough time doing other things. Mm, too much time sitting down. But many people leave the Internet connected all day because they use it instead of a telephone for messages or instead of going to the library, so I think it depends. For some things, it saves time.

Unit 5

CD1 Track 19

Igor Morning.

Travel agent Good morning. Er, just a moment and I'll be with you. Um, now, how can I help you?

I Yes, I phoned you earlier about an eco-holiday – you know, one of those holidays where you don't damage the environment at all and you get close to nature.

T Yes, I remember. Mr Petrov, isn't it?

I Yes, Igor Petrov. You said you were going to look up what was available at rather short notice.

T I did, and I've got a few things here. Just before I show them to you, though, let me get down a few details.

I OK.

T Right. Now, how long are you hoping to go for – a week, a month?

I I originally planned to go for three weeks, but I think actually two would be better.

T Fine, I'll just note that down. Mm, I think it's a good length for a holiday. You don't want to go for too long or it's difficult to get back to work again afterwards, I always think. And what's the limit on how much you're prepared to pay?

I Yes, I don't really want to go above £1,750 if I can help it.

T Mm … Fine, but when you come to look at the brochures, I should just point out that each of them has a discount if you pay in advance.

I Oh! That's good. How much is it?

T It depends on the holiday you choose, but it's worth bearing in mind. Do you have any special requirements which I should note down, by the way?

I Er, yes, one thing I'm keen on is having travel insurance while I'm away, so can you give me a quote?

T Well, I can't actually at the moment because our internet connection is down just now, but as soon as we have it up and running again and we know what holiday you've chosen, I'll give you a call. Is there anything else?

I Yes, there is, actually. I'm not a meat eater, so you'll need to specify to the airline that I need to eat vegetarian meals when I fly.

T OK … vegetarian meals. By the way, what nationality are you, Mr Petrov?

I I'm Russian. From St Petersburg originally.

T I just ask because I may need to see if you'll need a visa for some of the places you might visit. I'm just pointing that out because you want to go fairly soon and it can sometimes be quite a lengthy process.

CD1 Track 20

Igor So, what options are still available?

Travel agent OK. There are these three possibilities which I managed to print out earlier. I thought they looked good.

I OK, let's have a look.

T Um, the first is called the Dumbarton Tablelands. It looks pretty good to me. It's in Western Australia. The holiday really involves being close to and watching animals – almost living with them, in fact, because you get to stay in a quite luxurious house or cabin built high up in a tree and surrounded by lovely countryside. And, you know, there are birds and lizards and things if you like that sort of thing, so you're very sort of …

I Close to nature.

T Close to nature, that's right.

I Sounds interesting. I guess I could enjoy that. Er, what else have you got?

T Well, there's this one in the Bago Nature Reserve, where you go and stay with a local family in their house in a small mountain village away from other tourists and the usual tourist spots, so you discover lots about the way they live and you sort of live in the family, share their meals, help them with their work, that sort of thing.

I Mm. Not so much of a holiday, then.

T Well, it depends on you. It's very different, and they say a change is as good as a rest. And then there's San Luis Island.

I Mm. What happens at San Luis?

T Well, it's a small island, just a few miles from the coast of Central America, but I'm not sure if it's really up your street. You might like it because international tourism hasn't spoilt it yet, but I'd say it's more a holiday for young people. You go and live in a hostel and, you know, you help paint the local school and you get to meet the kids and sort of try your hand at teaching.

I Teaching what?

T Oh, English or maths, whatever you're good at. What makes the island interesting, though, is their emissions policy. There are no cars – you have to walk or use a bicycle to get about, and you get there by sailing boat.

I Sounds wonderful.

CD1 Track 21

Jamila OK, well, I'm going to talk about Tennyson Down, which is a … a large steep hill not very far from where I live in the south of England. You have to walk up it, you walk quite a long way up, about a mile or two miles, until you get to the top, where there's, there are these fantastic views across the sea in all directions, you can see all around the island. At the top of the hill, there's this wonderful stone column – it's a memorial to a famous British poet.

I've been there, I, perhaps, I think perhaps the last time was a few years ago, I went with my family – my parents and my sister. We walked up there. It was a lovely sunny day and there weren't too many people around. The weather was quite warm. We could see for perhaps 20 miles and then once you're up at the top, actually we, you, we sat down and I think we had a picnic, ate some sandwiches and then continued the walk. You walk down another two or three miles, until you reach The Needles, which are some spectacular rocks standing out in the sea, very spectacular, and then we walked down to a, a place called Alum Bay, where there's a car park and bus stops, and took a bus back home.

Why is the place so beautiful? I think it's particularly beautiful because it's such an unspoilt area, it's protected. It's all very green and although it's quite steep, it's easy to walk on, and all in all, it's a wonderful day out, good exercise, fresh air, fantastic views and very, very relaxing.

Examiner Thank you. Do you think you'll ever go there again?

J I think so, yes, probably. I'd like to.

E And have any of your friends visited this place?

J Mm, I'm not sure. Possibly, but not with me!

CD1 Track 22

Jamila Well, I think in general people like to go to places which are well-known tourist destinations because, you know, generally people like to feel safe when they're on holiday, especially when they travel to a foreign country. I think usually people choose places where there are plenty of hotels, so they can get good accommodation, and plenty of things to do, so they don't get bored. Also people tend to choose places where they think the weather will be good, especially if they want to do things outdoors.

CD1 Track 23

1 … there are these fantastic views across the sea in all directions …

2 At the top of the hill, there's this wonderful stone column …

3 It was a lovely sunny day and there weren't too many people around.

4 … until you reach The Needles, which are some spectacular rocks standing out in the sea, very spectacular …

5 Why is the place so beautiful? I think it's particularly beautiful because it's such an unspoilt area, it's protected.

6 … it's a wonderful day out, good exercise, fresh air, fantastic views and very, very relaxing.

Unit 6

CD2 Track 1

So I thought that I'd first say a few words to help orientate you round the banking system. As new arrivals, one of the first things you'll want to do is open a bank account. This will allow you to receive your money transfers, pay your bills by direct debit and all sorts of other things that will make your life easier.

One mistake I think a lot of people make is to just wander into the first bank they see, thinking that all banks are much the same, and ask to open an account. In actual fact, they all offer something slightly different, and some of the differences can affect you quite seriously. For example, for those of you who are studying at the university here, you may have noticed that there are two or three banks with branches near the university – Great Western and Moneysafe, for example – but only one – Finley's – actually has an office inside one of the university buildings. For the others, you'd have a bit more of a walk.

Some banks give away free gifts: Evergreen offers a laptop to people who keep a balance of more than £5,000 for nine months; with International Union, you'll get a phone when you open your first account; and one or two others, like Moneysafe and Northern Star, offer mountain bikes or vacuum cleaners if you put money on deposit. That sort of thing.

More seriously, you should look at the sort of interest rates the bank will offer you, both if you need an overdraft or loan, or if you're hoping to get some interest on your savings. At the moment, Northern Star offers the highest rate of interest to savers, but Great Western will lend money at a lower percentage than normal to people registered on higher education courses. So you can see it really is worth looking around.

Another thing it's a good idea to enquire about are bank charges. Again, they're not all the same. Some charge the same across the board, such as Evergreen, Finley's and Northern Star, but Moneysafe actually say that if you're in credit, your account won't cost a thing – though, just like the others, as soon as you go into the red, their prices become pretty steep.

CD2 Track 2

Of course, one of the things you'll want as soon as you open your account is a debit card, so I thought I'd give you a little tour of these essential little pieces of plastic. If you look at the slide, you'll see that on the front at the top they tend to have either the name of the bank or the company which has issued the card. Then a bit more than halfway down on the right, you'll see this hologram with a picture which appears to move as you move the card around in front of you. This sort of detail makes cards very hard to forge, although, like with anything else, there are people out there who'll try. Then, on the back, there's another of those sophisticated high-tech details, and that's the magnetic strip, which is this black thing going from one side to the other, which contains certain coded details. While we're on the back, you'll see another lighter strip with three numbers at the end. That's your security number, which they always ask for when you use the card for an internet purchase or over the phone, and it also has a space where you, as the card holder, should put your signature so that shop assistants can compare it when you sign a payment slip.

Going back to the front, in the bottom right-hand corner, you'll usually find the bank logo and just to the left of it, there's your own name in raised print.

One thing you always need for telephone and internet sales is the expiry date, and on the card in front of you, that's just above the cardholder's name. Finally, in most places, you have to insert your card into a machine and key in your PIN. Just above the card number on the left, you can see a chip, and that chip is there to verify that the PIN you have entered is correct.

CD2 Track 3

Irina Well, actually, I don't usually find advertisements very persuasive, so I remember this one quite well, because it was for an energy drink – you know, one of those really colourful drinks which you're supposed to drink to help you have more strength or be more active when you do a sporting activity … or anything else you enjoy, like dance. In fact, I saw it on television one night, which is also strange because I don't generally watch much television … I don't usually have time and even if I do, when they're advertising something, I usually go off and do something else – make a telephone call or do the washing-up or something. Anyway, this one showed one of those Olympic athletes – I can't remember her name – winning the hundred metres and then showing the product, with all, you know, one hundred percent natural ingredients. I mean, the advert in itself wasn't anything special, it was just like most other adverts, except that it had this person who, at the time, was pretty famous and successful. At the time, I was studying hard for my university entrance exams and I was also in my school volleyball team, so I thought why not, I'll try it and I did. The drink was quite nice – I mean, it didn't have a strong taste, but the flavour was fine. It was quite expensive, so I don't buy it often, but it's, you know, it's an energy drink, and I like it and think it does make me feel a bit more energetic!

CD2 Track 4

Examiner Now, we've been talking about advertising, and I'd like to ask you some more general questions related to this. Let's consider first of all company advertising. How important do *you* think it is for companies to advertise their products?

Irina Well, I think it's very important, because if companies don't … I mean, unless companies advertise a new product, we won't know that it exists and we can't buy it. In other words, companies give us – how do you say – information about their products so that we can choose the one we want. I think also it's important because companies – what's the word – compete with each other and they have to try to win, mm, I mean attract customers. For example, you know, if they want people to buy some clothes in the latest fashion, or for instance, er, a special new drink for people doing sports.

CD2 Track 5

Irina Well, actually, I don't usually find advertisements very persuasive, so I remember this one quite well, because it was for an energy drink.

CD2 Track 6

Irina Well, actually, I don't usually find advertisements very persuasive, so I remember this one quite well, because it was for an energy drink – you know, one of those really colourful drinks which you're supposed to drink to help you have more strength or be more active when you do a sporting activity … or anything else you enjoy, like dance. In fact, I saw it on television one night, which is also strange, because I don't generally watch much television … I don't usually have time and even if I do, when they're advertising something, I usually go off and do something else – make a telephone call or do the washing-up or something. Anyway, this one showed one of those Olympic athletes – I can't remember her name – winning the hundred metres and then showing the product, with all, you know, one hundred percent natural ingredients. I mean, the advert in itself wasn't anything special, it was just like most other adverts, except that it had this person who, at the time, was pretty famous and successful. At the time, I was studying hard for my university entrance exams and I was also in my school volleyball team, so I thought why not, I'll try it and I did. The drink was quite nice – I mean, it didn't have a strong taste, but the flavour was fine. It was quite expensive, so I don't buy it often, but it's, you know, it's an energy drink, and I like it and think it does make me feel a bit more energetic!

Unit 7

CD2 Track 7

Victor Hi, Fumiko, how is the psychology course going?

Fumiko Oh hi, Victor, I'm really enjoying it, but I've got a project this term that is … you know, part of my assessment, and the topic's really hard.

V Oh – is it ideas that you need?

F Oh thanks … but I think I've got plenty … that's the trouble – I don't really know where to start. My tutor's given me such a huge area to cover that I can't seem to narrow it down to something I can manage.

V So what's the topic, then? Maybe I can help.

F Well, it's … er, oh, 'The mystery of human relationships'.

V Your tutor's Mr Dresden, I bet!

F How do you know?

V Well, he gives very … shall we say 'broad' project titles. I mean, when I had him, one of my topics was 'Happiness is dot, dot, dot'!

F He makes you think, doesn't he?

V Yeah. The thing about Mr Dresden is that he likes to find out what you really enjoy working on.

F That's a good idea in theory. If I had more time, it would be fine.

V So what reading have you done so far?

F Well, he's done one lecture on my topic – that was a few weeks ago – and then he gave us a couple of articles from a journal.

V Have you still got them?

F I put them away somewhere without looking at them – I'll find them eventually. But I've just got these books from the library. I might find something useful in these.

V Have you been on the Internet?

F I have, and there are some fascinating reports … but they made me realise just how much has been written!

V Well, what exactly have you got to do for the project? I guess you have to present it, so, er, there will be charts and things?

F Well, actually, Mr Dresden didn't ask for data – he said that the important thing was to read about the topic and definitely include a list of all our sources.

V I told you, didn't I? He's just getting you to find stuff out.

F Mmm. I could do a survey and interview some people of different ages.

V OK – well, maybe I can help you a bit.

F Could you?

V I've got an English Lit seminar in ten minutes and I have to go in the library and find a couple of handouts for it.

F Oh, OK. It'll be getting late after that.

V Look, tell you what, I'll text you in half an hour. If the seminar doesn't last too long, we could have a coffee in the canteen afterwards.

F Oh, I hope so – that would be great.

(*Pause*)

V Right, so let's design a plan. What ideas have you got so far?

F Well, I wondered about doing something about relationships in the wild first – you know, maybe starting with animals.

V That's quite a good idea … but I think the very first thing you need to do is give a definition of what you mean by your key terms.

F Oh, so I need to say what terms like 'relationship' mean?

V Yeah. Um, you could just do a diagram – you know, like you do when you brainstorm something.

F Oh yes – OK, I'll do that first.

V Right. After that, you could do a bit of background on the animal world … yes, a quick look at relationships among ape groups would work.

F Yeah – interesting – just to show that relationships are part of life … So that's the definition and background – what next?

V Well, then you have to move on to people. Are you going to target a particular age group? Or something else?

F Well, I thought that first I would look at different … well, there are so many places, aren't there, where we form relationships? In the office …

V Yeah … within the family. Even toddlers aged 18 months or under have relationships.

F Yeah … so I'll present those …

V You mean the 'contexts' for relationships.

F Yes, that's the word.

V You do have to find a way to limit the scope of the study.

F Yeah. I could examine the 21-to-30 age group.

V Or the next thing might be to select one type of relationship and go with that.

F Good idea! Um, I'll pick friendship and look at what makes that type of relationship work and …

V Well, why don't you go through the stages in a friendship? But I would keep it simple – just select six.

F Six, OK. I guess I could fit my practical work in here.

V Yes, it's the sort of area that you can canvas people's opinions on. Ah, it might be good to get some opinions from people over the age of 60.

F And – as a contrast – why don't I end by looking into the future? Maybe the future changes in …

V Yeah, or better still, the influences – you know, with all the social networking that goes on now.

F OK, influences … oh, that's been such a help, Victor. Thanks so much.

V No problem … I'd better go and get some work done myself …

CD2 Track 8

Victor Right, so let's design a plan. What ideas have you got so far?

Fumiko Well, I wondered about doing something about relationships in the wild first – you know, maybe starting with animals.

V That's quite a good idea ... but I think the very first thing you need to do is give a definition of what you mean by your key terms.

F Oh, so I need to say what terms like 'relationship' mean?

V Yeah. Um, you could just do a diagram – you know, like you do when you brainstorm something.

F Oh yes – OK, I'll do that first.

V Right. After that, you could do a bit of background on the animal world ... yes, a quick look at relationships among ape groups would work.

F Yeah – interesting – just to show that relationships are part of life ... So that's the definition and background – what next?

V Well, then you have to move on to people. Are you going to target a particular age group? Or something else?

F Well, I thought that first I would look at different ... well, there are so many places, aren't there, where we form relationships? In the office ...

V Yeah ... within the family. Even toddlers aged 18 months or under have relationships.

F Yeah ... so I'll present those ...

V You mean the 'contexts' for relationships.

F Yes, that's the word.

V You do have to find a way to limit the scope of the study.

F Yeah. I could examine the 21-to-30 age group.

V Or the next thing might be to select one type of relationship and go with that.

F Good idea! Um, I'll pick friendship and look at what makes that type of relationship work and ...

V Well, why don't you go through the stages in a friendship? But I would keep it simple – just select six.

F Six, OK. I guess I could fit my practical work in here.

V Yes, it's the sort of area that you can canvas people's opinions on. Ah, it might be good to get some opinions from people over the age of 60.

F And – as a contrast – why don't I end by looking into the future? Maybe the future changes in ...

V Yeah, or better still, the influences – you know, with all the social networking that goes on now.

F OK, influences ... oh, that's been such a help, Victor. Thanks so much.

V No problem ... I'd better go and get some work done myself ...

CD2 Track 9

Examiner Do you find it easy to make new friends?

Speaker 1 Umm, 'make new friends', um, maybe ... new friends ... I think so, but it isn't easy. I think other people have to decide that!

Speaker 2 Mmm, I'm not sure, I've never thought about that, but I, er, think I probably do. I've met plenty of new people in Paris and I'm quite good friends with some of them.

CD2 Track 10

Examiner I'd like to talk about your family now. Do you come from a large or small family?

Dominic Oh, um, my family's pretty big – I've got three brothers ... one's older than me, and the other two are younger – they're ten and 13. And then I've got two sisters as well. They're both older than me. Karen's, um, 25 this year, and Corrine's 28. She's just qualified to become a doctor.

E When did you last visit relatives?

D Relatives ... Er, let me see ... it's hard to remember. Um, most of my relatives live near us in the, um ... what's the word, um, they live in a busy area around the city – you know, not in the centre where we are. And so we meet up in the city if there's a birthday or something. I guess I visited my aunt about a year ago when she invited us to see her new apartment.

E What don't you like about visiting relatives?

D Well, that's an interesting question. Um, if I were really honest, I'd say that when I was younger, I hated going to see them – yeah, I thought it was so boring. But, well, my gran lives with us now, and we often chat and, you know, we care about each other. If I don't go out this evening, for example, I'll eat dinner and chat with her.

E Who in your family has been most successful?

D Um, I think it depends on what you mean by 'successful'. If you mean making money, then it's my dad for sure, because he has this, um – I've forgotten, um, well, he has many of the same type of shop ... you know, he started his business and now he's got ten stores. But I think my sister's been successful, too – as I said, she's just become a doctor.

E Do you think you're similar to your sister?

D I'm sorry, could you repeat the question?

E Do you think you're like your sister?

D Er, yes and no. Er, we look alike, but my sister is very hard-working. She knows what she wants, whereas I'm still trying to make some decisions about that. I think I'd do well if I worked harder, so ...

CD2 Track 11

1 The one I like best is, um, well, it's quite big and it has different speeds so that you can go faster or slower, you know, and it's great, 'cause there's also a TV screen on each machine so you can watch and listen to some programme at the same time. It makes it much easier!

Complete IELTS Bands 5–6.5

2 I've got two brothers. The youngest one is still at school, he's got two more years there. And my oldest brother is a … um, I don't know the word in English – he's a doctor who looks after animals.

3 I've got quite a few hobbies, I guess. I like playing the guitar and singing – though I'm not very good at either. Um, I also like drawing, but I don't draw typical things – you know, like the scenery or people … my pictures are … well, they're not things you recognise from real life!

4 I often go to visit the park in my city because it's very beautiful and, er … let me see … er, it makes me feel, er – what's the word? Well, like I don't have any problems, which is good for my health!

CD2 Track 12

1 When I was younger, I hated going to see them – yeah – I thought it was so boring.

2 My sister's very hard-working. She knows what she wants, whereas I'm still trying to make some decisions about that.

CD2 Track 13

1 Being an only child has its advantages – I mean, I get all my parents' attention.

2 Before I left home and came here to study, I used to visit my grandparents about twice a week, but now it's much more difficult.

3 My gran, who lives on her own, is always so pleased to see me.

4 Both my parents are architects, but my mum gets more work than my dad!

Unit 8

CD2 Track 14

Good morning, everyone … as you know, we're continuing with the part of the textile course where we look at some different types of stitching – or stitching techniques – and today we're looking at one that comes from Japan. It's called *sashiko*.

Now, what does that word mean? Well, it translates as 'little stitches' and in its modern form, um, you can see from these pictures, it produces a very, er, very beautiful, decorative design on things like cushions, curtains and quilted covers – all produced by hand, of course – and many sold in shops these days. But *sashiko* began long ago, and its Japanese origins were much more functional than this.

It started among farming communities, in mountain villages, in the north of Japan's main island. Centuries ago, transport was difficult in these places, and the bitter climate made it hard to grow fibre plants for spinning and weaving into warm cloth. Also, there were no sheep in Japan at this time, so, er, no wool either, and this meant that people were left with a locally produced material, called *asa*, that was hard-wearing but not very warm. So, what they did was to dye this local fabric blue – because the dye was thought to strengthen the fibres – and they solved the problem of warmth by stitching together many layers of this cloth. In this way, they produced clothes that were warm but not too bulky. It was done, er, with a white, heavy thread, um, so there were many shades of blue cloth – light and dark – and white stitching, and so a typical 'look' or image was created … like this. They used designs based on traditional Japanese patterns that had their own names, such as 'sea wave' … perhaps to reflect the wavy effect of the design. Here's another example.

Now, each garment that was made at this time was planned for a specific purpose. So, for example, waistcoats were heavily stitched on the back and shoulders if they were going to be worn while carrying heavy baskets. And it wasn't only country people who relied on *sashiko* clothing. In Japanese towns, firemen dressed for duty in *sashiko*-stitched garments – jackets, trousers, hoods and gloves – which were soaked with water to protect them.

So the point here is that *sashiko* clothing was essential for survival at one time. And even though making things in this way took up many hours for people who also had to work, do household tasks and so on, it was a vital skill. The wife of someone like a farmer, for instance, had to spend time making clothes, and she would do the stitching without a frame or structural support. And the garments, once you put them on, were flexible and moulded themselves to the wearer. If you look at a genuine *sashiko* garment today, then you can see the evidence of wear and get a feel for the shape of the wearer's body, which is fascinating.

Then, in 1895, traditional life changed, and *sashiko* was no longer necessary because rail travel reached northern Japan, and warm textiles could then be imported. However, since the 1970s, *sashiko* has been revived in Japan and has also been taken up by quilters and embroiderers in the USA and the UK. Nowadays, the designs are a little different. There are vertical and horizontal stripes, for example, or the stitches can be arranged to produce a diamond effect … here we are. Similar fabrics to those used traditionally can be found in modern furnishing or dressmaking departments or from suppliers so that the traditional appearance of a *sashiko* item has been maintained.

Now, there are exhibitions of ancient *sashiko* items, but the disappointing thing is this. While old pots and ceramics are considered to be treasures and preserved, even with cracks, ancient garments made by poor village women have not been given such a high value … and, sadly, many of them have been thrown away, rather than getting the attention of collectors. This is a pity because they say a great deal about how people once lived and about their technical skill … and it's no coincidence that *sashiko* has now become a pastime on an international level.

CD2 Track 15

Examiner We've been talking about a museum that you enjoyed visiting, and I'd like to discuss with you one or two more general questions related to this. Let's consider first of all museums and young people. What benefits can schoolchildren gain from visiting museums?

David Oh, OK. Um, well, they can learn about the culture of their country or other countries … you know … about customs and the way people lived – what they wore, what they did and all that kind of thing. Museums are sometimes a bit expensive, but if the school pays, it's OK, and there's such a lot to see. The displays can be really good.

Examiner What benefits can schoolchildren gain from visiting museums?

Lin I think the benefits are huge! First of all, they can experience things directly … you know, they're not in the classroom any more, they're in a different environment, and the exhibits seem much more real … they see the actual objects, not just pictures of them. Another benefit is that, um, museums often have activities for children to participate in, so that they can learn about things like history, science, the world and so on.

CD2 Track 16

Examiner How do you think most children feel about visiting a museum?

David I think they find them boring. I don't think they really understand what museums are for … they don't find them fun. Like me – I used to prefer to play football. If we had to go to a museum, I wasn't happy about that.

Examiner How do you think most children feel about visiting a museum?

Lin Well, I think some children enjoy looking at all the displays and exhibits … because when you get inside a museum, it's like going into another world. But I think there are also children who are too, um, restless to look at things. And they see this big, old building and think that it can't be interesting or have anything that would entertain them.

CD2 Track 17

Examiner Are museums more educational now than they were when your parents were young?

David Well, in the past, there was nothing to do there. Because years ago, museums were in very old buildings and they were quiet and people weren't able to touch things.

Examiner Are museums more educational now than they were when your parents were young?

Lin I don't think there's any doubt that museums are much better at educating children now because that's what they are designed to do. In the past, I think museums had a different function, um, they were just places to keep ancient objects, like coins or pots, but now they're … well, there are many interactive displays.

CD2 Track 18

Museums are sometimes a bit expensive, but if the school pays, it's OK, and there's such a lot to see.

CD2 Track 19

1 First of all, / they can experience things directly, / … you know, / they're not in the classroom any more, / they're in a different environment.

3 I don't think there's any doubt / that museums are much better at educating children now … / In the past, I think museums had a different function, / um, they were just places to keep ancient objects, / like coins or pots, but now they're, / … well, / there are many interactive displays.

Practice test

CD2 Track 20

Man Good afternoon, KT Furniture, can I help you?

Woman Oh, hello, yes, um, I'm setting up a new office and I don't have internet access yet, but I'd like to place an order for some furniture.

M That's fine. You can do it over the phone, and I can fill in the form for you this end.

W Oh great, thanks.

M I just need to take a few customer details first, if that's OK?

W Yes, fine.

M What name is it?

W My name?

M Yes.

W Oh, it's Sue Brown

M Sue Brown – thanks.

(Pause)

M Good afternoon, KT Furniture, can I help you?

W Oh, hello, yes, um, I'm setting up a new office and I don't have internet access yet, but I'd like to place an order for some furniture.

M That's fine. You can do it over the phone, and I can fill in the form for you this end.

W Oh great, thanks.

M I just need to take a few customer details first, if that's OK?

W Yes, fine.

M What name is it?

W My name?

M Yes.

W Oh, it's Sue Brown .

M Sue Brown – thanks. And what's the name of your company, Ms Brown?

Complete IELTS Bands 5–6.5

W It's a clothing company, er, it's called 'Dress your best'.
M OK, I'll just note that down … 'Dress – for – best'.
W No – 'your best'.
M Oh right, got it. So you make smart clothes?
W Yes, formal dress for weddings and special occasions. We also repair and alter clothes.
M I see. And where are you located – what's your postal address?
W Right – well, we're on Kirby Trading Estate.
M Kirby – how do you spell that?
W It's K-I-R-B-Y.
M Oh, I know that area. It's New Hampton Road, isn't it?
W Yes, that's right, number 210 – in South Down.
M OK, and can I have a contact number for our delivery man?
W Sure – it's probably best if I give you my mobile number.
M OK.
W The number's 09356 788 545.
M OK … double 7 8 …
W No – 7 double 8, 5-4-5.
M Ah … OK, that's great. Now, just a couple more questions before I take your order …
W Fine.
M We have two delivery dates this month, and you should be able to have either.
W When are they?
M Well, there's one on the 16th of the month, but there's a charge of 40 dollars for that one.
W Oh, that's a lot!
M Mmm. Or there's option 2, which is the end of the month … I'll have to confirm the date later … and that's a free delivery.
W I'll take option 2, thanks, I don't want to pay a charge.
M OK – I'll note down 'no charge'.
W We haven't organised the office yet, so there should be plenty of time.
M Mm-hm. And lastly, you don't have an account with us … so how would you like to pay?
W Oh – I'll pay by credit card.
M OK – will that be Visa?
W Is American Express OK?
M Absolutely fine.

(*Pause*)

M So – what would you like to order?
W Well, I've been looking in your catalogue, and you have some office chairs that look very comfortable for our type of work.
M Is there an item code?
W Yes, it's ASP 23.
M OK – those chairs come in pink, white and black.
W Yes, the pink looks nice, but I think the darker colour's better for us – you can see light materials on it more easily.
M That's true.
W We'll have five of those, I think.
M OK. I've got that. Anything else?
W Do you have any striped mats?
M I'm sorry, not at the moment – they're out of stock. We should have some in next month.
W Never mind. Um … Well, um, I'd also like two of your glass desks.
M They're lovely, aren't they?
W Yes – you seem to have two sizes.
M Basically large or small … I think the code for the small ones is …
W I think we'll have the large ones – the code here is TG 586.
M OK, so that's two glass desks. Any lamps for those?
W No – we have to get special lamps for our work.
M Oh, I see. Do you have another supplier for those?
W Yes … um, we do need some furniture for our customers, though.
M OK – for a waiting area or something?
W Well, we have to discuss the work with them, so we need a nice sofa …
M Something soft and …
W I thought leather …
M Ah yes, a good choice.
W There's a three-seater here – DFD 44. That seems to be in red, cream or chocolate brown.
M Yes. It does come in yellow as well.
W Yellow … Mmm. I'd thought of red … but … that sounds lively – yes, I'll have that colour. I think brown's a bit too dull, and cream shows the dirt too much.
M Yeah, you're right. Anything else? A coffee table, perhaps?
W Yes, I think so. Maybe TX 22, the silver one.
M A very good choice.
W Well, that's it, I think.
M OK … I'll just add that up for you and then take your credit-card details …

CD2 Track 21

Announcer Now, we're grateful to Fred McKinnon for coming in to the studio today to give everyone a few tips about the city marathon that's taking place next Saturday …

Fred Thanks, Shweta. Yes, we're all very excited about the big event. Let me just remind listeners that a marathon is a 26-mile, or 42-kilometre, race, and this year we have 12,000 runners taking part. So, if you're thinking of going out to support the runners – and I know that many of you are – here are some tips to help make your day more enjoyable.

First of all, be certain to plan your day. Don't leave everything to the last minute. Many roads are going to be closed – we don't have exact times for these closures yet, but my big advice to you is don't rely on your car to get you anywhere. In fact, the best way to get around the town will be on foot. You may choose to cycle, but you still won't be able to go on roads near the runners' route.

Now, we did a broadcast last week in which we told all our runners to wear the right kind of shoes … and I'm going to tell you to put on sensible clothes. A lot of visitors will be coming to the city, you may be hunting for someone in the race that you want to support, the weather may be hot or it may be wet … Which leads me on to another thing – make sure you look at the forecast on Friday night. If it's going to rain, take an umbrella; and if it's going to be hot, take some drinks. However, please don't try to pass these to the runners. We already have hundreds of volunteers, who'll be standing on the roadside, so let them give out the drinks.

When you get into the town, find yourself a spot to stand in … you may well want to walk up and down the route, but please don't cross the road. There could be thousands of people running towards you, some very tired and not able to focus clearly. We don't want any accidents, and runners don't want obstacles like you in their path. What they do need is your support – particularly when their energies are low – so cheer them on, and for once, don't worry about noise! The louder, the better.

Lastly, if you have friends or relatives who're taking part in the run, please don't say that you'll see them at the finish line. If everyone does that, the whole area will be terribly congested, and you won't be able to find anyone. Well, that's most of the advice …

(*Pause*)

Now, I mentioned transport earlier and I've just got a few more bits of information about travel on the day.

As I said before, roads in the town centre will be closed, but if you need to be picked up at your home, then you could take a taxi some of the way. Unlike the trams and trains, however, they'll be held up on the roads, so passengers shouldn't expect them to be as punctual as they normally are. Don't be put off by this, though – there'll be extra drivers working that day, and you'll get one eventually.

Um, if you're meeting up with friends and want to be around when the runners set off (that's 9 a.m., by the way), whatever end of the city you're coming from, I'd say use the trams. They still have routes that cross roads, and this will inevitably lead to some problems, but they're likely to have more reliable timetables than buses at this time of day and, as you know, unlike taxis, they can carry plenty of passengers.

Lastly, the buses. Quite a number of bus routes will be altered slightly, and it's already been decided that some will be closed. There won't be fewer drivers, but they will be operating on different routes and some will have longer breaks than they normally do. We'll be including a full list of all the bus routes and numbers and where they'll be going in this week's local paper, so, er, look out for that. Well, um, that's it from me. Back to you, Shweta.

Announcer Thanks very much, Fred.

CD2 Track 22

Tutor Come in!

Ahmed Hi.

T Oh, hello, Ahmed … how are you?

A Fine, thanks.

T Have a seat. So … how do you think the seminar went last week?

A Oh, well … I enjoyed it, yes, though I'm not sure I really followed parts of the discussion that took place – you know, about the theory and all that …

T Well, we can talk about that later … but were you comfortable in a group?

A Oh, it's better, I think, than working on your own – though you're comparing yourself all the time with the other students there.

T OK, well, let's talk about how you did and look at some strategies to help you in the future.

A That would be great.

T Now, one of the things that students often overlook when they go to seminars is that you do need to prepare for them. You can't rely on other people.

A I know, and I did look at the results of the experiments we did in class and write them up beforehand … as you said.

T Yes … and that was good, it made it easier to analyse them. But you have to do some background reading as well. Did you get the list of articles I sent round?

A Mmm – I've started to read them …

T OK, well, you'll know that for next time.

A Yes, yes, sure.

T So let's move on to your participation in the seminar.

A Right.

T Perhaps you can tell me how you think that went?

Complete IELTS Bands 5–6.5

A Yeah, well, I'm not used to talking to more than a couple of people – it's very different from the way we learn in my home country.

T Yes, I appreciate that.

A So I think I, um … well, I know I should have included everyone, but I think I kept turning to the person next to me.

T Is that because you were avoiding eye contact?

A I don't think so – I'm not shy – it's just habit, I think.

T Well, that will improve as we do more seminars.

A Uh-huh.

T Um, another difficulty is knowing when to speak.

A Like when it's your turn?

T Yes.

A I felt I did wait for a pause …

T Yes, you handled that quite well.

A The thing I'm really concerned about is keeping up with the discussion.

T Ah, does your mind wander off?

A Sometimes. I jot down a lot of information, but I still find myself thinking about something else when lots of other students are talking.

T Mmm. If there's an assignment to do at the end of a group, that usually helps!

A I'm sure it does.

T OK. Now, the last thing I want to look at is the role that you play in the seminar.

A What do you mean?

T Well, when students work in groups, they don't all behave the same way. Some students are quiet, some look for support, some ask a lot of questions ….

A Oh … that's a new idea to me. I don't know what I'm like …

T That's probably because you're thinking about your own performance all the time.

A I guess so. I mean, should I be different in some way?

T What I would say is that when we do the next seminar, you should look more at the people around you … you know, look outside yourself.

A Like, ask myself how they feel?

T Yes, or what they're looking for from the group.

A OK.

T It doesn't take much, but it's important to watch what other students are doing.

A OK, I'll do that.

T Fine. Now, …

(*Pause*)

T Now, I'm going to suggest a couple of strategies for next week's seminar.

A OK – that's great. I need to participate more.

T Well, it's not a question of saying more – but we need everyone to feel comfortable about giving their views.

A Then the discussion is better.

T Yes. So … you're a confident person …

A Should I make sure I'm near someone who's quiet?

T You can do, but it's more about how well you pay attention to other students.

A OK – so I need to be attentive.

T Yes, and then encourage someone else to say more by saying: 'What did you mean when you said …?' or 'What do you think about the idea that …?'

A That way I'm talking …

T Yes, but you'll find that other people will talk, too. You'll all start to get really involved.

A Right – they're good suggestions.

T The other thing that can really help is the way you take notes.

A Yeah, I know I write down everything, but I should be stricter with myself.

T Well, you actually need to think a few days ahead.

A Really?

T Yes – 'What's the topic?' and 'What's the best way of making notes?'

A I see. So I have a strategy when I walk in the room.

T Exactly. Then, when you read through them later, they'll make sense and you won't have to write them out again.

A I always have to do that!

T The other thing I would say is that you should include a small column in your notes where you can jot down things you want to go back to before the seminar ends.

A Like a reminder.

T Yes. Notes aren't just for later – you can use them as a prompt when there's a pause in the discussion.

A That's been really helpful.

T OK – see you in class tomorrow.

A Thanks.

CD2 Track 23

In today's lecture, I'm going to continue our work on plants and talk about plants that live in the desert. Now, just a bit of background information first. As you know, about a third of the world is covered in desert, and the sort of area they're found in is important. Deserts are usually created because the area of land where they lie is located in something that's called a 'rain shadow'. Now, this is a region that's beneath a mountain range, and what happens is that the wind blows over the mountains towards the area, but as it does so, the air loses its moisture and becomes very dry.

Because of this 'downwind' location, rainfall often totals just a few inches a year or, in some regions, there's absolutely none. And you can imagine the effect of this … It means that whatever rain does fall evaporates quickly from the ground, and that makes the soil salty … and also leaves behind a whole range of other minerals as well.

Now, despite this, deserts are home to many living things. In fact, they're second only to tropical rainforests in the variety of plant and animal species that live there.

So, how do plants grow in a place that's so dry? Well, they're specially adapted to do this. In fact, many of the fascinating features of desert plants are adaptations – these are traits that help the plant survive in its harsh environment. And desert plants have two main adaptations: the first is that they have an ability to collect water and to store it. Some have large root systems and amazing internal water-storage systems. The second adaptation is that they have features that can actually reduce water loss … and these are often very special leaf designs or additions to the plant structure.

So let's have a look at some examples. Desert plants often look very different from any other plants …

OK. This first one is the Saguaro Cactus, which grows in North America. It looks a bit like an open hand with long fingers. This plant has a large network of roots that extend far, far away from its trunk, and these roots collect water after rain, then the water's taken here to the green stem. This is where all its water is kept, and it keeps the whole plant alive until the next rain comes. It's a pretty, woody plant – in fact, um, its skeleton is actually used in building materials, so it's quite strong.

This next plant is called the Barrel Cactus – named because it does look rather like a barrel. It can grow up to a metre in height, which is pretty big, and it has long, yellow spines. Now, this plant has an interesting adaptation because its shape allows it to expand when it rains – hence the barrel – and store water in its spongy tissue. But then it shrinks in size during dry times as it uses the stored water. So that's a clever design.

This third cactus – often just one plant reaching upwards – has these white hairs all over its surface. It's called the Old Man Cactus because of the white hairs, and these help the plant reflect the hot desert sun. So this adaptation is a water conservation aid if you like.

Another adaptation not directly connected with water but with survival is found on something like the Prickly Pear Cactus. There are hundreds of these in the Mexican desert. I'm sure you've seen them on films and adverts … Um, yes, so because desert plants store water in their spongy tissue, animals will eat them. So the plant has sharp thorns specially designed to prevent the predator from being able to – well, get near it at all.

Our next plant is called the Desert Spoon. This plant has long leaves that fan out, and they're very succulent because they can also store water inside. However, they're also usually very tough, and this helps keep the water inside and also makes them less tasty.

Finally, we come to the Aloe Plant. This is one that many people keep in their homes. It's an attractive plant which has leaves that look and feel rather waxy. This surface behaves in a similar way to a plastic wrapper and helps the plant to hold the water in. It's a wonder plant, this one. Its juice has been used as a medicine for centuries, and even today, you can find it in products on the pharmacists' shelves or in creams and lotions.

OK … well, we're going to take a closer look …

Acknowledgements

Author acknowledgements

We would like to give our warmest thanks to the editors and production staff for all their support, feedback and hard work during this project: Dilys Silva, Catriona Watson-Brown, Andrew Reid, Diane Jones, Sophie Clarke and Sarah Salter; also to John Green (audio producer), Tim Woolf (audio editor), Elizabeth Walter (wordlists) and Kevin Doherty (proof reader). Thanks also to the team at Wild Apple: Tracey Cox, Steve Crabtree and Rebecca Crabtree. Our special thanks to Clare Rose for her help and advice on *sashiko* and to Anna Stravrakis Gurkina for her contribution to the Speaking materials in the book.

The authors and publishers are grateful to the following for reviewing the material:

Phil Biggerton, Taiwan; Michelle Czajkowski, China; John Langille, UAE; Simon Feros, South Korea; Shida Lee, Hong Kong; Nick Moore, New Zealand; Wayne Rimmer, Russia; James Terrett, UK.

Guy Brook-Hart dedicates his part in this book to his son, Esteban, with love.

Development of this publication has made use of the Cambridge International Corpus (CIC). The CIC is a computerised database of contemporary spoken and written English which currently stands at over one billion words. It includes British English, American English and other varieties of English. It also includes the Cambridge Learner Corpus, developed in collaboration with the University of Cambridge ESOL Examinations. Cambridge University Press has built up the CIC to provide evidence about language use that helps to produce better language-teaching materials.

Text and photo acknowledgements

The authors and publishers acknowledge the following sources of copyright material and are grateful for the permissions granted. While every effort has been made, it has not always been possible to identify the sources of all the material used, or to trace all copyright holders. If any omissions are brought to our notice, we will be happy to include the appropriate acknowledgements on reprinting.

The publisher has used its best endeavours to ensure that the URLs for external websites referred to in this book are correct and active at the time of going to press. However, the publisher has no responsibility for the websites and can make no guarantee that a site will remain live or that the content is or will remain appropriate.

Text

pp. 10–11: Courtesy of Anna Jones and Xuan Quach, The University of Melbourne; p. 14 (A–D): diagram courtesy of California Energy Commission; p. 14 (BR): Based on information from HSBC Bank; pp. 18–19: Spiked-online.com; pp. 30–31: Copyyright 2009 Scientific American, a division of Nature America, Inc. All rights reserved; p. 36: By permission of Professionally Speaking & the Ontario College of Teachers; p. 38: © The Economist Newspaper Limited, London 12/03/2009; pp. 50–51: Time Magazine; p. 54 (T): Diagram courtesy of California Energy Commission; p. 58: © The Economist Newspaper Limited, London 18/12/2008; p. 71: MacMillan Publishers; p. 78: *Beetle Mania* by Angela Wintle, adapted from Sussex Life Magazine, pp. 101–104; pp. 120–121: © The Economist Newspaper Limited, London 04/06/2009; pp. 123–124: Reproduced with permission. Copyright 2010. Scientific American, a division of Nature America, Inc. All rights reserved; pp. 126–127: © New Scientist Magazine; p. 130: The Gallup Organization Ltd.

Photos

p. 8 (photo 1): Thinkstock; p 8 (photo 2): © Fancy/Alamy; p. 8 (photo 3): Demotix/www.photolibrary.com; p. 8 (photo 4): © MIXA/Alamy; p. 8 (BL): © Serge Kozak/Corbis; p. 9: © Fotosearch/SuperStock; p. 10 (T): © cultura/Corbis; p. 10 (B): © Inspirestock/Corbis; p. 13 (TL): Thinkstock; p. 13 (BL): © Image Source/Alamy; p. 13 (TR): Shutterstock/Monkey Business Images; p. 13 (BR): Thinkstock/Stockbyte; p. 17 (photo 1): Inga Spence/FLPA; p. 17 (photo 2): © Robin Townsend/AgStock Images/Corbis; p. 17 (photo 3): © ICP/Alamy; p. 17 (photo 4): Photolibrary Group/The Garden Picture Library/Gary K. Smith;p. 17 (photo 5): Getty Images/John W. Banagan; p. 17 (photo 6): © Chris Sattlberger/cultura/Corbis; p. 18 (L) & 18–19 (B/G): Thinkstock; p. 20 (CL): Shutterstock/Dusan Zidar; p. 20 (CR): Shutterstock/Tyler Olson; p. 20 (BL): Shutterstock/Romanchuck Dimitry; p. 20 (BR): © age fotostock/SuperStock; p. 22 (T): © TTL Images/Alamy; p. 22 (UC): © Francesco Carucci (editorial)/Alamy; p. 22 (BC): Shutterstock/Steve Lovegrove; p. 22 (B): © Michael Hawkridge/Alamy; p. 23: Thinkstock/ Jupiterimages; p. 28 (photo A): © Purestock/SuperStock/Corbis; p. 28 (photo B): © Janine Wiedel Photolibrary/Alamy; p. 28 (photo C): © Art Directors & TRIP/Alamy; p. 28 (photo D): © vario images GmbH & Co.KG/Alamy; p. 30: iStock photo/ © Serhiy Kobyakov; p. 37 (T): © ICP-UK/Alamy; p. 37 (TR): © PhotoStock-Israel/Alamy; p. 37 (C): Shutterstock/withGod; p. 37 (CL): Thinkstock; p. 37 (CR): © Art Directors & TRIP/Alamy; p 37 (BR): Photolibrary Group/Franck Dunouau; p. 38 (inset): Sipa Press/Rex Features; p. 38 (main): CERN/Science Photo Library; p. 40 (R): Shutterstock/arindambanerjee; p. 40 (L): Cartoonstock/Marty Bucella; p. 42: © Jim Craigmyle/Corbis; p. 45: © Paul Buck/epa/Corbis; p. 48 (photo 1): Photolibrary Group/Radius Images; p. 48 (photo 2): © Marco Simoni/Robert Harding World Imagery/Corbis; p. 48 (photo 3): Dr Morley Read/Science Photo Library; p. 48 (photo 4): Thinkstock; p. 48 (photo 5): Getty Images/Gerry Ellis; p. 49 (TR):Suzanne Long/Alamy; p. 49 (BR): Ian Woodcock/Alamy; p. 50 & 50–51 (B/G): © Roine Magnusson/Johnér Images/Corbis; p. 51: Paul Wootton/ Science Photo Library; p. 52: David Nunuk/Science Photo Library; p. 53: Shutterstock/DavidYoung; p. 57 (TR): Thinkstock/Stockbyte; p. 57 (CL): © British Retail Photography/Alamy; p. 57 (C): © Alex Segre/Alamy; p. 57 (CR): © imagebroker.net/SuperStock; p. 58 (L&R): Thinkstock; p. 60: © H. Mark Weidman Photography/Alamy; p. 62 (TR): © DreamPictures/Shannon Faulk/Purestock/SuperStock; p. 62 (CR): Getty Images; p. 62 (BR): Bloomberg via Getty Images; p. 62 (CL): © NetPics/Alamy; p. 62 (BL): Rex Features; p. 64: Thinkstock; p. 66:© Dan Walden; p. 68 (photo 1): Photolibrary Group/Imagebroker.net/Stefan Obermeier; p. 68 (photo 2): Shutterstock/Arieliona; p. 68 (photo 3): Thinkstock/Christopher Robbins; p. 68 (photo 4): Getty Images/Ghislain & Marie David de Lossy; p. 71: Radar Pictures/The Kobal Collection; p. 77 (photo 1): Shutterstock/elwynn; p. 77 (photo 2): Getty Images/Ryan McVay; p. 77 (photo 3): © Richard T. Nowitz/Corbis; p. 77 (photo 4): © David Ball/Corbis; p. 77 (photo 5): Getty Images/IPL via Getty Images; p. 77 (photo 6): © Kai Chiang/Golden Pixels LLC/Corbis; p. 77 (photo 7): © Ocean/Corbis; p. 78 (TL): akg/De Agostini Picture.Library; p. 78 (BR): © Jamie Wilson/Dreamstime.com; p. 81 (T & C): Courtesy of Clare Rose; p. 81 (B): Courtesy of Susan Briscoe; p. 83 (BL): Getty Images/Shannon Fagan; p. 83 (BR): Thinkstock/Bananastock; p. 83 (BC): Shutterstock/Edyta Pawlowska; p. 85: Shutterstock/Monkey Business Images; p. 120: © Mantis Mix/Alamy; p. 122 (BL): © Hugh Threlfall/Alamy; p. 123: © All Canada Photos/SuperStock; p. 126: © Ocean/Corbis.

Illustrations:

Kveta pp. 59, 61, 122

Peter Marriage pp. 14, 16, 26, 35, 36, 46, 74, 76, 86, 92, 93, 94(t), 130

Andrew Painter p. 94(b)

Martin Saunders pp. 21, 54, 56

David Whamond p. 73

Cover photos by rfimages (top); Fotalia/Monkey Business (upper centre);
© Corbis (lower centre); and Photos to Go/Photolibrary Group (below).